Muslims and Crusaders

Muslims and Crusaders supplements and counterbalances the numerous books that tell the story of the crusading period from the European point of view, enabling readers to achieve a broader and more complete perspective on the period. It presents the Crusades from the perspective of those against whom they were waged, the Muslim peoples of the Levant. The book introduces the reader to the most significant issues that affected their responses to the European crusaders and their descendants who would go on to live in the Latin Christian states that were created in the region.

This book combines chronological narrative, discussion of important areas of scholarly enquiry and evidence from primary sources to give a well-rounded survey of the period. It considers not only the military meetings between Muslims and crusaders, but also the personal, political, diplomatic and trade interactions that took place between Muslims and Franks away from the battlefield. Through the use of a wide range of translated primary source documents, including chronicles, dynastic histories, religious and legal texts and poetry, the people of the time are able to speak to us in their own voices.

Niall Christie received his PhD in Islamic History from the University of St Andrews, Scotland, in 2000. He teaches the history of Europe and the Middle East at Langara College in Vancouver, Canada. He is the author of numerous articles and *The Book of the* Jihad *of 'Ali ibn Tahir al-Sulami (d. 1106): Text, Translation and Commentary* (in press).

Introduction to the series

History is the narrative constructed by historians from traces left by the past. Historical enquiry is often driven by contemporary issues and, in consequence, historical narratives are constantly reconsidered, reconstructed and reshaped. The fact that different historians have different perspectives on issues means that there is often controversy and no universally agreed version of past events. Seminar Studies was designed to bridge the gap between current research and debate, and the broad, popular general surveys that often date rapidly.

The volumes in the series are written by historians who are not only familiar with the latest research and current debates concerning their topic, but who have themselves contributed to our understanding of the subject. The books are intended to provide the reader with a clear introduction to a major topic in history. They provide both a narrative of events and a critical analysis of contemporary interpretations. They include the kinds of tools generally omitted from specialist monographs: a chronology of events, a glossary of terms and brief biographies of 'who's who'. They also include bibliographical essays in order to guide students to the literature on various aspects of the subject. Students and teachers alike will find that the selection of documents will stimulate the discussion and offer insight into the raw materials used by historians in their attempt to understand the past.

Clive Emsley and Gordon Martel
Series Editors

Muslims and Crusaders

Christianity's Wars in the Middle East, 1095–1382, from the Islamic Sources

Niall Christie

Routledge
Taylor & Francis Group

LONDON AND NEW YORK

First published 2014
by Routledge
2 Park Square, Milton Park, Abingdon, Oxon OX14 4RN

and by Routledge
711 Third Avenue, New York, NY 10017

Routledge is an imprint of the Taylor & Francis Group, an informa business

British Library Cataloguing in Publication Data
A catalogue record for this book is available from the British Library

Library of Congress Cataloging in Publication Data
Christie, Niall.
  Muslims and Crusaders : Christianity's Wars in the Middle East, 1095–1382,
from the Islamic Sources / Niall Christie.
    pages cm. – (Seminar Studies in History)
  Summary: "Muslims and Crusaders presents the Crusades from the perspective of those
against whom they were waged, the Muslim peoples of the Levant"– Provided by publisher.
  Includes bibliographical references and index.
  1. Crusades.   2. Islam–Relations–Christianity–History–To 1500.
3. Christianity and other religions–Islam–History–To 1500.   4. Muslims–
Middle East–History–To 1500.   I. Title.
  D157.C474 2014
  909.07–dc23

                                                                          2013047621

ISBN: 978-1-138-02273-7 (hbk)
ISBN: 978-1-138-02274-4 (pbk)
ISBN: 978-1-315-77389-6 (ebk)

Typeset in 10/13.5pt ITC Berkeley
by Graphicraft Limited, Hong Kong

For Mum, Dad, Katie, Morag and Iona – my first teachers,
For my students, past and present – educators all,
And as always, for Steph – my constant guide.

Contents

DOCUMENTS   121

Chronology

610	The Prophet Muhammad begins to receive the revelation of the *Qur'an* at Mecca.
622	Emigration of the Muslims from Mecca to Medina.
630	Muslim conquest of Mecca.
630–2	Islam spreads across Arabia.
656–61	Caliphate of 'Ali ibn Abi Talib.
661–750	Umayyad Caliphate rules from Damascus. Muslim world expands to stretch from Transoxania and India in east to France and Spain in west.
750–1258	First reign of the 'Abbasid Caliphate, from Baghdad (mostly) from 762.
910	'Abd Allah (or 'Ubayd Allah) al-Mahdi establishes Fatimid Caliphate at Qayrawan.
945–1055	Buyid domination of 'Abbasid caliphs.
969	Fatimids take Egypt, reign from Cairo from 973.
1055	Seljuks take Baghdad and establish Great Seljuk Sultanate.
1071	Alp-Arslan defeats Romanus Diogenes at Manzikert (Malasjird). The establishment of the Seljuk Sultanate of *Rum* follows.
1090	Hasan-i Sabbah takes Alamut, establishes Isma'ili Assassins. From 1097 the Assassins claim to have the true Isma'ili *imam* resident among them.
1092	Deaths of Seljuk vizier Nizam al-Mulk and sultan Malik-Shah. Fragmentation of the Great Seljuk Sultanate.
1096 (Sep)	People's Crusade annihilated by Seljuks of *Rum*.
1097 (19 Jun)	Crusaders take Nicaea.
1097 (1 Jul)	Crusaders defeat Seljuks of *Rum* at Dorylaeum (Eskişehir).
1097 (c. 10 Sep)	Crusaders defeat Seljuks of *Rum* at Heraclea (Ereğli).
1098–1111	Periodic protests in Baghdad calling for Seljuk response to the First Crusade.

1098 (10 Mar)	Baldwin of Boulogne takes control of Edessa (Urfa).
1098 (29 Jun)	Crusaders take Antioch.
1098 (Jul)	Fatimids take Jerusalem from Seljuks.
1098 (11–12 Dec)	Crusaders take Ma'arrat al-Nu'man.
1099 (15 Jun)	Crusaders take Jerusalem.
1099 (12 Aug)	Crusaders defeat Fatimid forces at Ascalon.
1105	Al-Sulami publicly composes *Kitab al-Jihad* at Damascus.
1109 (12 Jul)	Crusaders take Tripoli.
1110–15	Great Seljuk sultan seeks to aid Muslims of Levant against Franks.
1115 (Sep)	Great Seljuk sultan's forces defeated by Franks of Antioch at Danith.
1119 (28 Jun)	Ilghazi of Mardin defeats and kills Roger of Antioch at Battle of Balat/ *Ager Sanguinis*.
1127	Succession of 'Imad al-Din Zangi at Mosul.
1128 (Jan)	Succession of Zangi at Aleppo.
1144 (24 Dec)	Zangi takes Edessa.
1146 (14 Sep)	Death of Zangi. Sayf al-Din succeeds at Mosul and Nur al-Din succeeds at Aleppo.
1146 (Oct–Nov)	Nur al-Din foils a Frankish attempt to retake and hold Edessa.
1147	Diplomatic agreement between Nur al-Din and Mu'in al-Din Unur.
1148 (24 Jun)	Crusaders decide to attack Damascus.
1148 (23–28 Jul)	Crusader attack on Damascus fails.
1149 (29 Jun)	Nur al-Din and Mu'in al-Din defeat and kill Raymond of Antioch at Inab.
1153 (22 Aug)	Franks take Ascalon from the Fatimids.
1154 (Apr)	Nur al-Din takes Damascus.
1163 (Sep)	Ousted Fatimid vizier Shawar seeks support of Nur al-Din.
1164 (Apr–Oct)	Shirkuh's first expedition to Egypt restores Shawar to vizierate.
1167 (Feb–Aug)	Shirkuh's second expedition to Egypt, including the Battle of al-Babayn (19 March 1167).
1168 (Nov)	Amalric takes Bilbays in Egypt. The Fatimid caliph al-'Adid appeals to Nur al-Din for help.
1168 (Dec)	Shirkuh sets out for Egypt.
1169 (Jan)	Franks withdraw from Egypt. Shirkuh enters Egypt. Shawar is executed and Shirkuh is made Fatimid vizier.
1169 (23 Mar)	Death of Shirkuh. Saladin becomes Fatimid vizier.
1171 (Jun)	Nur al-Din orders Saladin to abolish the Fatimid caliphate.

1171 (Sep)	Saladin abolishes Fatimid caliphate.
1171 (Oct–Nov)	Saladin makes abortive attack on Shawbak (Crac de Montréal).
1173 (Jun)	Saladin conducts campaign against Kerak.
1174 (15 May)	Death of Nur al-Din.
1174 (Jul–Aug)	Saladin repels Sicilian attack on Alexandria.
1174 (28 Oct)	Saladin takes Damascus.
1175 (Jan)	Nizari Assassins attack Saladin.
1175 (13 Apr)	Saladin defeats Zangids at the Horns of Hamah.
1176 (22 Apr)	Saladin defeats Zangids at Tall al-Sultan.
1176 (May)	Nizari Assassins attack Saladin again.
1176 (29 Jul)	Peace treaty between Saladin and the Zangids.
1176 (Aug)	Saladin besieges Masyaf, comes to agreement with Assassins.
1177 (25 Nov)	Franks defeat Saladin at Montgisard.
1179 (Apr)	Saladin defeats Franks in the Jawlan (Golan).
1179 (Jun)	Saladin defeats Franks at Marj 'Uyun.
1179 (29 Aug)	Saladin destroys Frankish castle of Bayt al-Ahzan, raids Frankish territory.
1181 (4 Dec)	Death of al-Salih Isma'il. Saladin claims succession to Aleppo.
1182 (May–Jul)	Saladin raids Kingdom of Jerusalem.
1183	Reynald of Châtillon's Red Sea expedition is defeated.
1183 (11 Jun)	Saladin takes Aleppo.
1183 (Oct–Dec)	Saladin attacks Kerak.
1184 (Aug)	Saladin attacks Kerak again.
1185 (Apr)	Saladin makes a truce with the Franks.
1186 (4 Mar)	Peace treaty with Mosul recognizes Saladin's authority.
1187 (Jan)	Reynald of Châtillon plunders a Muslim caravan.
1187 (2 Jul)	Saladin takes Tiberias.
1187 (4 Jul)	Saladin destroys the Frankish field army at Hattin and subsequently conquers much Frankish territory.
1187 (2 Oct)	Saladin takes Jerusalem.
1189 (29 Aug)	Franks under Guy of Lusignan besiege Acre.
1191 (20 Apr)	Philip II Augustus arrives at Acre.
1191 (8 Jun)	Richard I the Lionheart arrives at Acre.
1191 (12 Jul)	Acre surrenders to the Franks.
1191 (7 Sep)	Richard defeats Saladin at Arsuf. Richard subsequently takes Jaffa, while Saladin demolishes Ascalon.

1191 (Oct)	Richard attempts, unsuccessfully, to march on Jerusalem.
1192 (23 May)	Richard takes Darum.
1192 (24 Jun)	Richard seizes a Muslim caravan, subsequently attempts to march on Jerusalem again.
1192 (5 Jul)	Richard forced to turn back from Jerusalem.
1192 (30 Jul)	Saladin almost retakes Jaffa.
1192 (1–3 Sep)	Peace treaty between Saladin and Richard.
1193 (4 Mar)	Death of Saladin at Damascus. Succeeded by sons and relatives.
1196 (Jun)	Al-'Adil Muhammad takes Damascus from al-Afdal 'Ali.
1197	Crusaders take Beirut and Sidon.
1200 (Feb)	Al-'Adil Muhammad takes Cairo and becomes head of the Ayyubid confederation.
1202	Authority of al-'Adil Muhammad recognized by al-Zahir Ghazi of Aleppo.
1206	Temujin/Chingiz Khan launches campaign of world conquest.
1218 (May–Aug)	Crusaders attack Damietta and storm part of its defences.
1218 (31 Aug)	Death of al-'Adil Muhammad. Territories divided among his three eldest sons.
1219 (19 Mar)	Demolition of the fortifications of Jerusalem begins.
1219 (5 Nov)	Crusaders take Damietta.
1221 (Aug)	Muslims defeat crusaders and negotiate their evacuation from Egypt.
1226	Al-Kamil Muhammad offers Jerusalem to Frederick II.
1229 (Feb)	Peace agreement between al-Kamil Muhammad and Frederick II returns most of Jerusalem to the Franks.
1229 (18 Mar)	Frederick II crowns himself King of Jerusalem at the Holy Sepulchre.
1236–41	Mongols invade Russia and eastern Europe.
1239 (7 Dec)	Al-Nasir Dawud takes Jerusalem, but returns it to the Franks the following year as part of an alliance agreement.
1243	Mongols subdue Seljuk Sultanate of *Rum*.
1244 (23 Aug)	Khwarazmians take Jerusalem.
1244 (17 Oct)	Khwarazmian–Egyptian coalition defeats Frankish–Syrian coalition at Harbiyya (La Forbie).
1245 (2 Oct)	Al-Salih Ayyub takes Damascus.
1246 (Mar)	Khwarazmians besiege Damascus.
1246 (18 May)	Khwarazmians are defeated and wiped out by troops from Homs and Aleppo.

1249 (6 Jun)	Crusaders under Louis IX take Damietta.
1249 (21 Nov)	Al-Salih Ayyub dies. Shajar al-Durr and collaborators conceal his death.
1250–1382	Bahri/Turkish Mamluk Sultanate.
1250 (9 Feb)	Mamluks defeat crusaders at al-Mansura. Louis is subsequently captured.
1250 (2 May)	Mamluks kill Turan-Shah and take control of Egypt, appointing Shajar al-Durr as *sultana*.
1250 (May)	Crusaders evacuate Egypt.
1250 (July)	Shajar al-Durr abdicates. Aybak al-Turkumani becomes sultan, then *atabeg* for an Ayyubid prince.
1254	Aybak deposes Ayyubid charge and re-assumes position of sultan, bringing Ayyubid Sultanate of Egypt to definite end.
1255	Hülegü launches campaign into Persia and Iraq.
1256	Hülegü destroys Alamut and Persian Nizari Assassins.
1258	Hülegü takes Baghdad and executes 'Abbasid caliph.
1260 (25 Jan)	Hülegü takes Aleppo.
1260 (2 Mar)	Mongol forces take Damascus. Hülegü returns east at about the same time.
1260 (3 Sep)	Mamluks defeat Mongols at 'Ayn Jalut. Mamluks complete conquest of Syria soon after.
1260 (24 Oct)	Murder of Qutuz. Baybars becomes Mamluk sultan.
1261 (13 Jun)	Baybars resurrects 'Abbasid caliphate at Cairo.
1261–1517	Second reign of the 'Abbasid caliphate.
1265–73	Baybars suppresses Nizari Assassins of Syria.
1268 (18 May)	Baybars takes Antioch.
1277 (20 Jun)	Death of Baybars.
1279 (Nov)	Qalawun takes power.
1281 (29 Oct)	Qalawun defeats Mongols at Hims.
1289 (27 Apr)	Qalawun takes Tripoli.
1290 (10 Nov)	Death of Qalawun.
1291 (18 May)	Al-Ashraf Khalil takes Acre.
1365 (Oct)	Peter of Cyprus briefly occupies Alexandria.
1382	Sultanate usurped by the Circassian *mamluk* Barquq.
1382–1517	Burji/Circassian Mamluk Sultanate.
1396 (25 Sep)	Crusaders defeated by Ottomans at Nikopolis (Nikopol).
1517	Ottoman conquest of Egypt.
1898	Kaiser Wilhelm II visits tomb of Saladin.

1899   Sayyid 'Ali al-Hariri describes European colonialism as a crusade in his history of the crusading period.

1906–66   Life of Sayyid Qutb, an influential figure in the development of modern Muslim extremism.

1987   Foundation of Hamas.

1988 (approx.)   Usama ibn Ladin (Osama bin Laden) founds al-Qa'ida.

1990–1   US-led coalition forces eject Iraqi forces from Kuwait and briefly occupy Iraq.

2001 (11 Sep)   Al-Qa'ida makes co-ordinated terrorist attacks on US targets including the World Trade Center and the Pentagon.

2001 (16 Sep)   US President George W. Bush declares 'crusade [. . .] on terrorism'.

2006   Hamas wins Palestinian Authority elections.

Who's who

Al-'Adil Muhammad (btw. 1143 and 1145–1218): Al-Malik al-'Adil Muhammad ibn Ayyub was Saladin's brother and one of his closest supporters. He was entrusted with major responsibilities, including governing Egypt from 1174 to 1183 while Saladin was conquering Syria, and acting as Saladin's principal ambassador to Richard the Lionheart. After Saladin's death he inherited territories in the northern and eastern frontier regions of the Ayyubid state but soon outmanoeuvred Saladin's sons to take control of the family confederation. He died on 31 August 1218 while *en route* to fight against the forces of the Fifth Crusade at Damietta.

Al-Afdal Shahanshah (1066–1121): Al-Afdal was the son and successor of the Fatimid vizier Badr al-Jamali (d. 1094), reigning as vizier from 1094 until his death. He initially sought to establish an alliance with the forces of the First Crusade against the Seljuks, but when this failed he attempted to oppose them, only to be defeated in battle at Ascalon on 12 August 1099. He subsequently sought to reform the army, but was himself assassinated on the orders of the Fatimid caliph al-Amir (r. 1101–30) in December 1121.

Alp-Arslan (*c.* 1030–73): Alp-Arslan became the Great Seljuk sultan in 1063. While he actually spent more time fighting against members of his own family or pursuing his own territorial ambitions in Armenia and Georgia, he is probably best known for defeating the Byzantine emperor Romanus Diogenes (r. 1068–71) at the Battle at Manzikert (Malasjird) in 1071, an event that opened Asia Minor to Turkmen invaders and spurred Byzantine appeals for aid to the powers of western Europe.

Al-Ashraf Khalil (*c.* 1262–93): Al-Malik al-Ashraf Khalil ibn Qalawun was the Mamluk sultan of Egypt and Syria from 1290 to 1293. Al-Ashraf only became the heir apparent in 1288, when his older, more popular brother 'Ali died, and apparently Qalawun himself had been reluctant to appoint his younger son to succeed him. However, he ascended smoothly to the throne, and one of his first major acts as sultan was to conduct the conquest of Acre that his father had been planning, taking the city by storm on 18 May 1291, something that gave him great prestige. However, by 1293 he had alienated a number of important emirs, including his deputy, and he was killed by a group of conspirators on 14 December while out hunting.

Aybak (d. 1257): 'Izz al-Din Aybak al-Turkumani was a *mamluk* emir who became sultan of Egypt after the abdication of Shajar al-Durr in July 1250, whom he then married. Forced by other *mamluk* emirs to abdicate in favour of a puppet Ayyubid child prince five days later, he became strong enough to depose the Ayyubid sultan and take power into his own hands again in 1254, ruling for three years. However, his jealous wife Shajar al-Durr, hearing that he planned to marry another woman who would replace her as his chief wife, had him murdered by slaves while he was in a bath-house in April 1257.

Baha' al-Din ibn Shaddad (1145–1234): Baha' al-Din Yusuf ibn Shaddad was born and educated in Mosul. He spent time as a teacher in Baghdad and then back in Mosul, and also served the Zangid rulers of the latter as an ambassador. In 1188 he performed the *hajj*, and on the way home he was recruited into the retinue of Saladin, who made him the *qadi* of his army. Thereafter the two men were close friends. After Saladin's death Baha' al-Din served a number of the sultan's descendants before retiring. He wrote a number of works, of which the best known is his important biography of Saladin, *al-Nawadir al-Sultaniyya wa-l-Mahasin al-Yusufiyya* (The Rare Qualities of the Sultan and the Merits of Yusuf).

Baldwin of Boulogne (btw. 1061 and 1070–1118): Baldwin took part in the First Crusade, including founding the County of Edessa in March 1098. After the death of his brother Godfrey de Bouillon in 1100 he became the first Frankish King of Jerusalem, reigning until his own death. In the years that followed he secured and expanded the holdings of the Kingdom of Jerusalem. He died while on campaign in Egypt on 2 April 1118.

Baybars al-Bunduqdari (1220s–1277): Al-Malik al-Zahir Baybars al-Bunduqdari was the Mamluk sultan of Egypt and Syria from 1260 to 1277. A member of the Bahri Mamluk regiment, he was chosen to rule after the assassination of his predecessor Qutuz (r. 1259–60) in the wake of the Battle of 'Ayn Jalut. Baybars spent much of his reign fighting multiple enemies; he subdued the Syrian Assassins, fended off the Mongols and waged yearly campaigns against the Franks that included the conquest of Antioch in May 1268. He is also credited with putting many of the political, military and religious structures of the Mamluk state in place.

Chingiz Khan (d. 1227): Temujin, better known by his title Chingiz Khan (or Genghis Khan ['Universal King']), was a Mongol chieftain who in 1206 forged a confederation of tribes on the steppes of eastern Asia. He entertained visions of world conquest, launching campaigns into northern China (1211), Central Asia (1215) and the empire of the Khwarazm-Shahs (in present-day Iran and Turkmenistan [1218]). By his death he ruled an empire stretching from the east coast of China to Rey, Nishapur and Georgia in the west. His empire would be further expanded by his successors over the course of the thirteenth century.

Conrad III (1093–1152): Conrad III was the King of Germany from 1138 until his death, and was a leader of the Second Crusade. Conrad initially sought to take his armies overland to the east, but Turkish attacks and short-ages of supplies depleted his forces, and he eventually travelled with his remaining troops from Constantinople to Acre by sea. In June 1148 he, Louis VII of France (r. 1137–80) and Baldwin III of Jerusalem (r. 1143–63) decided to mount an attack on Damascus, which failed in the face of both the inhabitants' resistance and the approach of Muslim reinforcements (July 1148). Conrad left for Germany the following September.

Frederick I Barbarossa (1122–90): King of Germany from 1152 and Holy Roman Emperor from 1155, Frederick Barbarossa ('red-beard') went on both the Second (as a deputy for his uncle Conrad III) and Third Crusades. Despite his attempts to prepare the way ahead of his departure on the Third Crusade, Frederick's journey to the east was difficult, with his forces coming into conflict with both the Byzantines and the Seljuks of *Rum*, as well as suffering from food shortages and problems crossing difficult terrain. Frederick himself drowned in the River Saleph (Silifke) in Cilicia (Southern Turkey) on 10 June 1190, and his army subsequently broke up after reaching Antioch.

Frederick II (1194–1250): Frederick II was King of Germany from 1211, and Holy Roman Emperor from 1220, until his death. Frederick took the cross in 1215, but problems in his own lands forced him to postpone his departure for the Holy Land, and in September 1227 he was excommuni-cated by the pope for delaying. Frederick went east nonetheless, and there he negotiated with al-Kamil Muhammad the return of Jerusalem to Christian hands but with the Temple Mount and some nearby territories remaining under Muslim control, an agreement that angered both Christians and Muslims alike (February 1229). Even after returning home in May, Frederick remained involved in the crusading movement, providing support in particular in the form of diplomatic activity.

Genghis Khan See *Chingiz Khan*.

Guy of Lusignan (c. 1150–94): The son of a southern French nobleman, Guy of Lusignan became the King of Jerusalem, after the death of King Baldwin V (r. 1185–6), by virtue of his being married to the king's mother Sibyl, who seized the throne after the death of her son. In July 1187 Guy led the army of the Kingdom of Jerusalem to its defeat at the hands of Saladin, himself being captured. Released in 1188, he gathered his forces and besieged Acre the following year, the arrival of the forces of the Third Crusade providing reinforcements. By the time that the city fell to the crusaders Sibyl had died, and Guy's claim to the throne with her, but Guy was able to buy Cyprus from Richard I of England, establishing a dynasty there that would rule until 1489.

Hülegü (c. 1217–65): Hülegü was the brother of the Mongol Great Khan Möngke (r. 1251–9). In 1253 his brother sent him to lead the ongoing Mongol campaigns in Persia and Iraq. Hülegü destroyed Alamut in 1256, effectively ending the Persian branch of the Assassins, and then took Baghdad on 12 February 1258, killing the caliph and temporarily ending the 'Abbasid caliphate. He went on to conquer northern Syria, but returned home in the spring of 1260 to take part in the selection of the next Great Khan after Möngke's death. The small army that he left in Syria was defeated by the Mongols at 'Ayn Jalut in September 1260, and the Mongol advance stalled. In the meantime, the Mongol Empire broke up, and Hülegü established a largely independent state in Iraq and Persia known as the Ilkhanate.

Husayn, Saddam (1937 or 1939–2006): Saddam Husayn was the President of Iraq from 1979 to 2003. Originally of peasant origins, Husayn rose through the ranks of the socialist Ba'th Party, which took a firm grip on power in Iraq in 1968. In 1979 he took over the presidency and engaged in a programme of political repression and military action within the country to secure his position and remove his opponents. He also engaged in foreign conflicts, including a war with Iran in 1980–8 and an invasion of Kuwait in 1990 that was driven back by a UN coalition force. Further conflict with the UN, and especially the USA, resulted in a US-led invasion of Iraq in 2003, in the course of which Husayn was captured. He was convicted of crimes against humanity by an Iraqi court in November 2006 and executed on 30 December.

Ibn 'Asakir (1105–76): 'Ali ibn al-Hasan ibn 'Asakir was born into a family of Shafi'i scholars and began his study of religious texts at the age of 6. In 1126 he began to travel for the sake of learning, studying with religious scholars in major centres across the Muslim world, including Baghdad, Mecca, Medina, Kufa, Merv, Nishapur and Herat, before settling back in Damascus. After Nur al-Din took the city in 1154 Ibn 'Asakir became a propagandist for the sultan, preaching the *jihad* on his patron's behalf. Ibn 'Asakir wrote several works, including his immense and famous biographical dictionary of the notables of Damascus, entitled *Ta'rikh Madinat Dimashq* (The History of the City of Damascus), and a collection of *hadiths* on the *jihad*, entitled *al-Arba'in Hadithan fi'l-Hathth 'ala al-Jihad* (The Forty *Hadiths* for Inciting *Jihad*).

Ibn al-Athir (1160–1233): 'Izz al-Din Abu'l-Hasan 'Ali, known by his family name of Ibn al-Athir, was an Iraqi scholar and historian. While he spent most of his life in Mosul, he also travelled repeatedly to Baghdad and also in Syria, including serving for a time in the army of Saladin. He wrote a number of works but is best known for his *Ta'rikh al-Bahir fi'l-Dawla al-Atabakiyya* (The Dazzling History of the Atabeg State), which is a rather partisan history of the Zangids of Mosul; and especially his *Kamil fi'l-Ta'rikh* (The Complete History), a chronicle of the world from the Creation to his own time. Ibn al-Athir's works are based on a mixture of other historical chronicles, some archival documents and eyewitness accounts, including those of family members who served the Zangid regime in various capacities.

Ibn al-Qalanisi (1073–1160): Abu Ya'la Hamza ibn Asad al-Tamimi, better known by his family name of Ibn al-Qalanisi ('the son of the hatter') was the author of *Dhayl Ta'rikh Dimashq* (The Continuation of the History of Damascus), a chronicle of the city that is one of the earliest Muslim sources for the crusading period. Ibn al-Qalanisi himself was both an educated scholar and an important figure in the city's administration; among other posts, he was twice head of the urban militia. In writing his history, Ibn al-Qalanisi made use of a wide range of sources including earlier histories, official documents and correspondence, eyewitness accounts and his own personal experiences of the dramatic events that unfolded in and around Damascus during his lifetime. His own work then became a major source for other historians such as Ibn al-Athir and Sibt ibn al-Jawzi.

Ibn Shaddad See *Baha' al-Din ibn Shaddad*.

Ibn Taymiyya (1263–1328): Taqi al-Din Ahmad ibn Taymiyya was a Hanbali religious scholar. He was born in Harran, and in 1268–9 his family fled before the Mongol advance to Damascus. There his father became the head of a *madrasa*, and in 1284 Ibn Taymiyya succeeded him in this position. In 1293 he became involved in a political conflict, which led to the first of a number of spells in prison, yet at other times he served the Mamluk sultans preaching the *jihad*, especially against the Mongols. He was a staunch advocate of the *jihad* in all its forms, whose ideas were highly influential in his own time and continue to be today.

Ilghazi (*c.* 1062–1122): Najm al-Din Ilghazi ibn Artuk was a Turkmen chieftain. He initially served the Great Seljuks, but in 1108 or 1109 he took control of Mardin in what is now Turkey, establishing himself as effectively independent. In 1118 he expanded his influence over Aleppo, after its citizens appealed to him for protection from Roger of Salerno, the regent of Antioch (r. 1113–19). The following year he destroyed Roger's army at the Battle of Balat/*Ager Sanguinis*, the regent himself being among the slain. Ilghazi did not then follow up his victory with the conquest of Antioch itself, something that chroniclers of the time blamed on drunkenness, but which was more likely a result of strategic concerns.

'Imad al-Din al-Isfahani (1125–1201): 'Imad al-Din Muhammad ibn Muhammad al-Isfahani was born in Persia but educated at Baghdad. He initially worked for the vizier of the 'Abbasid caliph, then Nur al-Din, before passing into Saladin's service in 1175. He soon became Saladin's personal secretary and almost constant companion until the latter's death in 1193, after which he retired to Damascus and devoted himself to literary activity. Both a historian and a literary enthusiast, he has left us, in addition to an anthology of twelfth-century Arabic poetry, an autobiographical account of the campaigns of Saladin entitled *al-Barq al-Shami* (the Syrian Lightning), and an account of the years 1187 to 1193 entitled *al-Fath al-Qussi fi'l-Fath al-Qudsi* (Qussian Eloquence on the Conquest of Jerusalem).

Kalavun See *Qalawun*.

Al-Kamil Muhammad (btw. 1177 and 1180–1238): The son of the Ayyubid sultan al-'Adil Muhammad, al-Malik al-Kamil Muhammad ibn Muhammad (r. 1218–38) succeeded his father in Egypt while the forces of the Fifth Crusade were besieging Damietta. In the wake of the fall of the city al-Kamil Muhammad, with the acquiescence of his brother al-Mu'azzam 'Isa of Damascus (r. 1218–27), offered to return the old Kingdom of Jerusalem to the crusaders in exchange for their evacuation from Egypt, but the offer was refused. The crusader advance on Cairo was unsuccessful, however, and eventually they were forced to negotiate a safe withdrawal. Al-Kamil Muhammad did later negotiate the return of Jerusalem to Frederick II in 1229, though retaining the Temple Mount and other surrounding territories, a move that proved immensely unpopular among Christians and Muslims alike.

Louis IX (1214–70): Louis IX was King of France from 1226 until his death. He was a pious man from an early age, and in 1244 he took his first vow to go on crusade. After seeking to set his affairs in order at home he set out in 1248, but despite initial success in capturing Damietta his crusade against Egypt was a failure, with Louis himself being captured by the Mamluks in 1250. Louis was released in exchange for Damietta and the evacuation of the crusaders from Egypt, and after four years spent improving the defences of the Kingdom of Jerusalem he returned home. He sought to promote further piety and justice in both his own personal behaviour and the administration of his realm, then in 1267 resolved to go on crusade again, this time in North Africa. He landed at Tunis in July 1270 but fell ill soon after, dying on 25 August. He was canonized in 1297.

Malik-Shah (1055–92): Malik-Shah was a son of Alp-Arslan, who appointed him as his heir to the Great Seljuk Sultanate in 1066. While he had to face some initial rebellions from other members of his family when his father died in 1073, by 1084 he had secured his position and was able to embark on campaigns of expansion to both the east and the west; in the west, he mounted expeditions against the Fatimids, Georgia and the Byzantine Empire, which included the successful conquest of northern Syria. Malik-Shah died in murky circumstances during a hunting expedition in November 1092, a month after the killing of his vizier Nizam al-Mulk by the Nizari Assassins, and the Great Seljuk Sultanate fragmented as various claimants fought over his legacy.

Al-Mas'udi (before 893–956): Abu'l-Hasan 'Ali ibn al-Husayn al-Mas'udi was a Muslim scholar, traveller and geographer. He journeyed throughout and beyond the Muslim world, including in China, India, Africa, the Byzantine Empire and eastern and central Europe. He has left us two geographical works, *Muruj al-Dhahab wa-Ma'adin al-Jawhar* (Meadows of Gold and Mines of Gemstone) and the shorter *Kitab al-Tanbih wa-l-Ishraf* (The Book of Instruction and Supervision), which contain important accounts of Europeans dating from before the Crusades.

Muhammad (*c.* 570–632): The Prophet Muhammad was born in the Arabian city of Mecca. Orphaned at an early age, he was brought up in the house of his uncle and pursued a successful career as a merchant. According to Muslim belief, in 610 Muhammad started receiving revelations from God, which would eventually be compiled, after his death, into the Muslim scripture known as the *Qur'an*. Muhammad gathered a group of followers but was forced to emigrate from Mecca in 622, after his teachings encountered opposition from the pagan authorities there. He settled at Medina, from which he fought an eight-year war with Mecca, finally taking the city in 630 and demonstrating that the Ka'ba, its holiest site, was meant to be devoted to worship of the one true God. Muhammad died two years later, on 8 June 632, but the Muslim world expanded dramatically over the decades that followed his death.

Mu'in al-Din (d. 1149): Mu'in al-Din Unur was a Turkmen *mamluk* of Tughtigin, who took power in Damascus through a military coup in April 1138, although without deposing its leaders. Instead, Mu'in al-Din ruled as *atabeg* and commander of the army, thus wielding effective power while maintaining the Burid dynasty in place. He thereafter maintained Damascus' independence through a mixture of warfare and alliances with the Franks and the Zangids, including defending the city successfully against the Second Crusade. He died of dysentery on 28 August 1149.

Al-Nasir Dawud (1207–58): Al-Nasir Dawud was the son of the Ayyubid sultan of Damascus, al-Mu'azzam 'Isa (r. 1218–27). Al-Nasir Dawud succeeded to his father's throne in 1228 but was driven out the following year by other members of his family. He received lands in Palestine and Transjordan as compensation, and made his capital at Kerak. As a result of family politics he lost further territories, even being forced to hand back Jerusalem after he took it from the Franks in 1239. Forced out of Kerak in 1249, he spent the following years unsuccessfully trying to find a new state to rule, and eventually died in May 1258 after a failed attempt to assist Baghdad against the Mongols.

Nur al-Din (1118–74): Nur al-Din Mahmud ibn Zangi inherited the western half of his father's territories, including Aleppo and Edessa, when the latter died in 1146. From there he pursued a policy of expansion into Muslim Syria while simultaneously fighting against the Franks, including advancing on Damascus with a relief force when the Second Crusade attacked it in 1148. Thereafter he himself made several attempts to take the city, citing the need for Muslim unity against the Franks, and finally achieving its handover to him in April 1154. In the 1160s he sent forces to intervene in Egypt, which resulted in it coming under the control of his deputies Shirkuh and then Saladin. When the latter proved unco-operative Nur al-Din prepared an army with which to take direct control of Egypt, but became ill and died before the expedition could be launched.

Osama bin Laden See *Usama ibn Ladin*.

Al-Qadi al-Fadil (1135–1200): 'Abd al-Rahman ibn 'Ali al-'Asqalani al-Qadi al-Fadil was the director of the Fatimid chancery when he came to Saladin's attention. Saladin, at the time the Fatimid vizier, took him into his service in 1171, and the two men soon became close friends and collaborators. Saladin appointed al-Fadil to run the administration of Egypt, which included providing the greater portion of the finances that enabled the sultan to conquer Syria. Al-Fadil, despite poor health, outlived Saladin, serving two of the latter's sons before his own death in 1200. The official documents and letters that al-Fadil composed are a major source for the life and career of the sultan.

Qalawun (1222–90): Al-Malik al-Mansur Qalawun al-Alfi ('of the thousand [*dinars*]') was the Mamluk sultan of Egypt from 1279 to 1290. Qalawun was a Kipchak Turkish *mamluk* who became an emir in the Bahriyya under Baybars. He seized control of the sultanate during the extended struggle for power that followed Baybars' death, and then once he had consolidated his position he directed his attention to external threats, turning back a second Mongol attempt to invade Syria at the Battle of Hims in 1281, and also conquering a number of Frankish strongholds, including Tripoli in 1289. He was preparing to take the last Latin capital, Acre, when he died on 10 November 1290.

Qutb, Sayyid (1906–66): An Egyptian member of the Muslim Brotherhood, Qutb has been seen by some as the most influential figure in the birth of modern Islamist extremist movements. Early in his life he was attracted to western ways, but he reportedly became disillusioned after the foundation of Israel and a visit to America in 1949–51 during which he came to see western society as decadent, materialist and anti-Arab. He sought to encourage his contemporaries to return to a pure form of Islam as laid out in *Qur'an* and Islamic law, rejecting modernization and materialism as forces drawing humans away from God. Anything contrary to Islam was evil and should be opposed, with force if necessary. Qutb was executed by the Egyptian government for treason on 29 Aug 1966, but his ideas were highly influential in the development of later organizations such as Hamas and al-Qa'ida.

Qutuz (d. 1260): The *mamluk* al-Muzaffar Qutuz usurped the throne of the Mamluk Sultanate in 1259, deposing the young sultan al-Mansur 'Ali (r. 1257–9). Qutuz justified his action on the grounds that a more experienced sultan was needed to defend the sultanate against the Mongol advance. He may also have claimed to be a descendant of the eastern Khwarazm-Shah dynasty that had been destroyed by the Mongols in the course of their campaigns, now seeking legitimate revenge. In any case, Qutuz led his army from Egypt into Syria, where it defeated the Mongol forces at the Battle of 'Ayn Jalut in 1260. However, Qutuz himself was assassinated en route back to Egypt by a group of Mamluks, one of whom was Baybars, who became the new Mamluk sultan.

Raymond III of Tripoli (1140–87): Raymond III became Count of Tripoli in 1152 while still a minor, actually taking government into his own hands three years later. He spent ten years, from 1164 to 1174, as a captive of Nur al-Din, during which time he probably gained a greater familiarity with Islam and Muslims than did his contemporaries. He twice served as regent of the Kingdom of Jerusalem (1174–6 and 1185–6). Raymond opposed Guy of Lusignan's appointment as King of Jerusalem in 1186, but was forced to accept him by his own vassals. During the Battle of Hattin in July 1187 Raymond attempted to break the cordon that the Muslims had cast around the Frankish army, but while he and his followers escaped, his effort did not save his co-religionists. He escaped to Tripoli, where he died in September, probably of pleurisy.

Reynald of Châtillon (*c.* 1125–87): A knight from central France, Reynald of Châtillon became Prince of Antioch in 1153, holding the principality for ten years. However, in 1160 or 1161 he was captured by Nur al-Din and imprisoned for over 15 years, and like Raymond of Tripoli this probably gave him a better knowledge of Islam and its followers than that of his contemporaries. By the time that Reynald was released his lands had passed into the hands of his stepson, but in 1176–7 he received Hebron and Transjordan. He took part in a number of military actions against the Muslims, including his notorious Red Sea expedition of 1183 that threatened Mecca and Medina, and in early 1187 captured a Muslim caravan during a period of truce, an act that Saladin used as a pretext to launch the campaign that culminated in the Battle of Hattin. At the battle Reynald was captured and personally executed by Saladin.

Richard I (1157–99): Richard the Lionheart was King of England from 1189 to 1199. Richard took a vow to go on crusade soon after the fall of Jerusalem to Saladin in 1187, but political concerns at home and a desire to set his realm in order before his departure prevented him from leaving until mid-1190. En route to the Holy Land, he took Cyprus from its Byzantine ruler (May–June 1191), an act that would provide Europeans with a foothold in the eastern Mediterranean for centuries. He finally arrived at Acre on 8 June 1191, and after its fall (12 July) began his efforts to take Jerusalem from Saladin. However, after over a year of inconclusive campaigning the two men, who apparently admired each other greatly, were forced to recognize a stalemate, and peace was made between them on 2 September 1192.

Saladin (1138–93) Salah al-Din Yusuf ibn Ayyub was born in Tikrit in Iraq. After reaching adulthood he served in the army of Nur al-Din. He accompanied his uncle Shirkuh on his three expeditions to Egypt in the 1160s, and after his uncle's death on 26 March 1169 became vizier to the Fatimid caliph. In September 1171 he abolished the Fatimid caliphate and in the years following extended his territories into the rest of *Bilad al-Sham*, mostly at the expense of his Muslim neighbours. He also directed periodic attacks against the Franks, and on 4 July 1187 scored a major victory against them at the Battle of Hattin, which enabled him subsequently to take much of their territory, including Jerusalem. The last years of his life were spent fighting the forces of the Third Crusade to a stalemate (1189–92). He died in Damascus on 4 March 1193.

Al-Salih Ayyub (1206 or 1207–49): Al-Salih Ayyub was the eldest son of the Ayyubid sultan al-Kamil Muhammad (r. 1218–38). Even though he had been removed from the succession, in 1240 he managed to seize control of Egypt. In summer of 1244 Khwarazmian Turkish warriors in his employ sacked Jerusalem, then allied with him to defeat other members of his family at the Battle of Harbiyya (La Forbie) the following October, a victory that assisted him in taking Damascus from his uncle in 1245. He thereafter ruled two major Ayyubid centres until his death, which took place on 21 November 1249 while he was defending Egypt from the forces of St Louis' crusade. By now he had built up large contingents of *mamluk* troops in his armies, and it was left to them to save Egypt after his death.

Shajar al-Durr (d. 1257): Shajar (or Shajarat) al-Durr was a Turkish slave and concubine of the Ayyubid sultan al-Salih Ayyub. When she gave him a son, al-Salih Ayyub freed and married her, even though her son died while young. When al-Salih Ayyub died in 1249, while the crusaders were active in the Nile Delta, Shajar al-Durr was able, in collaboration with a senior *mamluk* emir, to ensure that resistance continued by concealing the sultan's death. After the crusaders were defeated the sultanate was taken up by al-Salih Ayyub's son Turan-Shah (r. 1250), but the new sultan alienated his father's *mamluks* and was eventually murdered by them. Shajar al-Durr was then elected *sultana*, ruling for about 80 days before being replaced by the *mamluk* emir Aybak, whom she married. Threatened by her husband's plans to take a second wife, she had him murdered, but was herself killed soon after, apparently by his vengeful concubines.

Shirkuh (d. 1169): Asad al-Din Shirkuh ibn Shadhi was a Kurd from Dvin, near Tiflis (Tbilisi, Georgia). In about 1138, after Shirkuh killed a man in an argument, he was expelled – along with his brother Ayyub (d. 1173) – from Tikrit, where Ayyub had been serving as castellan. The brothers passed into the service of Zangi and later Nur al-Din, and Shirkuh led the three expeditions that Nur al-Din sent to intervene in Egypt in the 1160s. In 1169 he was appointed as vizier by the Fatimid caliph, but died of unclear causes on 23 March. He was succeeded in his post by Saladin, his nephew and the son of Ayyub.

Sibt ibn al-Jawzi (1185 or 1186–1257): Shams al-Din Yusuf ibn Qizughli, known as Sibt ibn al-Jawzi ('the grandson of Ibn al-Jawzi', meaning the famous historian and jurisprudent 'Abd al-Rahman ibn al-Jawzi, c. 1116–1201), was a well-known religious scholar and preacher. He was initially brought up by his illustrious grandfather, and then after the latter died he moved to Damascus, where he spent most of his time teaching, writing and preaching. He also went on preaching tours in the Jazira and Syria, and is said to have moved his audiences to tears with his eloquence. He wrote a number of works, including a universal history entitled *Mir'at al-Zaman fi Ta'rikh al-A'yan* (The Mirror of Time concerning the History of Important People).

Al-Sulami (1039 or 1040–1106): 'Ali ibn Tahir al-Sulami was a Damascene religious scholar and grammarian, a member of a family of scholars who followed the Shafi'i school of law. He taught Arabic grammar in the Umayyad Great Mosque in Damascus. Over the course of 1105 al-Sulami publicly composed a treatise on jihad, Kitab al-Jihad (the Book of the Jihad) at the Mosque of Bayt Lihya in the agricultural suburbs of Damascus, aiming thereby to call on his fellow Muslims to oppose the crusaders. His call seems to have been mostly ignored by the political authorities of the day, but his ideas probably influenced later, more successful calls to the jihad against the Frankish invaders.

Tughtigin (d. 1128): Zahir al-Din Tughtigin began his career as a Turkish emir in the service of the Seljuk rulers Alp-Arslan and Tutush (r. 1078–95). The latter appointed him as atabeg of Damascus in 1093, and by 1105 he had established himself as an effectively independent ruler there. Tughtigin thereafter devoted most of his attention to securing and expanding his own territory, fighting or allying with other Muslim and Frankish powers as circumstances dictated. In 1115 he managed to be recognized by the Great Seljuk sultan Muhammad (r. 1105–18) as the emir of Damascus, with his family, the Burids, having right of inheritance of the title. He died in 1128 after a two-year illness, and was succeeded by his son Buri (r. 1128–32).

Turan-Shah (d. 1250): Al-Mu'azzam Turan-Shah ibn Ayyub was one of the last Ayyubid sultans of Egypt (r. 1249–50). Turan-Shah was governing Ayyubid territories in the northern Jazira when the first crusade of St Louis attacked Egypt, so when his father al-Salih Ayyub died in November 1249, his father's wife Shajar al-Durr, in collaboration with a senior mamluk emir, concealed the sultan's death, and resistance continued, with the crusaders being defeated in battle in February 1250. Turan-Shah arrived on 24 February, in time to take part in the last stages of the defeat of the crusade, but he soon alienated his father's mamluks by promoting his own ahead of them. On 2 May, before St Louis had even left Egypt, Turan-Shah was murdered by a group of Bahri mamluks, who installed Shajar al-Durr as the new sultana.

Usama ibn Ladin (Osama bin Laden, 1957–2011): Usama ibn Ladin was born on 10 March, 1957 in Riyadh, Saudi Arabia, and was the son of a rich businessman. At university he earned a degree in civil engineering, but he also developed a radical belief that Muslim nations needed to be liberated from interference by foreign powers. He became involved in the Afghan jihad against the Soviet occupation of Afghanistan, using his wealth to support the resistance. Then in 1988 he founded al-Qa'ida (al-Qaeda, 'the Base'), which would in time become a world-spanning terrorist network. Ibn Ladin was outspoken in his criticism of the Saudi monarchy's invitation of American forces onto Saudi soil in 1990, and was eventually banished. Soon after he began organizing operations against American targets, of which the most notorious was the attacks of 11 September 2001. He was eventually tracked down and killed by American special forces on 2 May 2011.

Usama ibn Munqidh (1095–1188): Usama ibn Murshid ibn 'Ali, better known as Usama ibn Munqidh (his family name), was a Bedouin emir and man of letters. Born at his clan stronghold of Shayzar, he enjoyed a chequered career that included political entanglements and frequent journeys, as well as fighting in armies against the crusaders. He ended his days as a dependent of Saladin at the remarkable age of 93. Usama was famous in his own day as a poet, but he also wrote a number of other works, of which the best known to modern readers is his *Kitab al-I'tibar* (Book of Contemplation), an account of his experiences that includes his lively observations on the Franks.

Zangi (*c*. 1084–1146): 'Imad al-Din Zangi ibn Aq Sunqur was the son of a Turkish emir who served the Great Seljuk sultan Malik-Shah. He was appointed to the governorship of Mosul in 1127 and immediately began enlarging his territory, including negotiating the handover of Aleppo in 1128. He continued to expand his holdings to the west and east at the expense of Franks and Muslims alike, including repeated attempts to take Damascus. On 24 December 1144 he scored his most famous victory, taking Edessa and thus bringing the first Frankish capital under Muslim control, an act for which he was lauded as a *mujahid* by his contemporaries, despite the fact that he was unquestionably ruthless and primarily driven by political ambition. He died on 14 September 1146, allegedly stabbed by a Frankish slave after having drunk himself into unconsciousness.

Glossary

'Abbasids: The dynasty of Sunni caliphs reigning at the time of the Crusades. The 'Abbasids deposed and took power from the previous reigning dynasty, the Umayyads, in 750. Soon after they established their capital at Baghdad, from which they reigned until the Mongol conquest of 1258 (with the exception of a portion of the ninth century, when they made Samarra their capital). Baybars re-established the caliphate in Cairo in 1261, from which they reigned until the Ottoman conquest of the Mamluk state in 1516–17.

Allah: The Arabic word for God, meaning the god worshipped by followers of all the major monotheistic faiths.

Al-Andalus: The Arabic term used to refer to the Iberian Peninsula and the Muslim states therein. The modern Spanish word 'Andalucia' derives from this.

Assassins: See *Nizaris*.

Atabeg: Turkish: 'father-lord'. *Atabegs* were military regents, ruling on the behalf of a (usually underage) Seljuk prince. They were normally originally *mamluks*. Needless to say, in a significant number of cases *atabegs* usurped power from their charges.

Awlad al-Nas: Arabic: 'the sons of the people'. The term used to refer to the descendants of *mamluks* in the Mamluk Sultanate. Although they might be wealthy and privileged, they were usually limited in how far they could ascend the military–political hierarchy.

Ayyubids: Term used to refer to the family of Ayyub ibn Shadhi (d. 1173), the father of Saladin (r. 1169–93). After Saladin's death, other Ayyubids took over his territories, ruling them until the mid-thirteenth century.

Bahri (Turkish) Mamluk Sultanate: The first period of *mamluk* rule in Egypt and Syria (1250–1382), named after the Bahriyya and characterized by the fact that most of the sultans were Kipchak Turks.

Bahriyya: An important *mamluk* regiment. The Bahriyya was created by the Ayyubid sultan al-Salih Ayyub (r. 1240–9). The name derives from the fact that their original barracks was on Rawda island on the River (Arabic: *bahr*) Nile.

Bilad al-Sham: Arabic: 'the country of Syria'. The term used in the Arabic sources to refer to, approximately, modern Syria, Lebanon, Jordan, Israel, the Palestinian autonomous areas and the edge of south-eastern Turkey. Sometimes the region is simply referred to as *al-Sham*.

Burji (Circassian) Mamluk Sultanate: The second period of *mamluk* rule in Egypt and Syria (1382–1517), during which most of the sultans were Circassians.

Burjiyya: Another important *mamluk* regiment. The creation of the Burjiyya is usually ascribed to the Mamluk sultan Qalawun (r. 1279–90). Their name derives from the fact that they were originally quartered in a tower (Arabic: *burj*) of the Citadel in Cairo.

Buyids: Also known as the Buwayhids. Members of the Persian Shi'ite Buyid dynasty took control of Baghdad and the 'Abbasid caliphs in 945. Rather than ending the Sunni 'Abbasid line of caliphs, they had themselves appointed as their 'deputies', wielding effective power but maintaining the caliphs as figureheads. Buyid rule in Baghdad was continuous until 1055, when they were displaced by the Seljuks.

Caliph: Anglicization of the Arabic term *khalifa*. After the death of the Prophet Muhammad in 632 his followers elected a new leader for their community. The title given to this leader was *khalifa* (deputy, successor), a term that indicated leadership without suggesting that he was another prophet. The subsequent early caliphs were chosen by (approximate) consensus, but the caliph Mu'awiya ibn Abi Sufyan (r. 661–80) established a dynastic succession (the Umayyad caliphate), and the dynastic principle continued to be followed by other families who claimed the caliphate.

Dar al-'Adl: Arabic: 'the house of justice'. A building where the ruler or his deputy would appear regularly to hear and address the grievances of his subjects. Probably the best known example is that of Nur al-Din (r. 1146–74) established in Damascus after his takeover of the city in 1154.

Dar al-'Ahd: See *Dar al-Sulh*.

Dar al-Harb: Arabic: 'the abode of war'. In Islamic law, *dar al-harb* is non-Muslim territory, against the inhabitants of which Muslims were expected to fight.

Dar al-Islam: Arabic: 'the abode of Islam'. Territory where Islam is the dominant religion, and in particular the religion of the rulers.

Dar al-Sulh: Arabic: 'the abode of peace'. Also known as *dar al-'ahd* (the abode of the treaty), *dar al-sulh* is non-Muslim territory, the inhabitants of which are allowed to retain their autonomy, provided that they pay tribute and recognize Muslim authority.

Fada'il: Arabic: 'merits'. Texts praising the merits of their subjects. Muslim writers wrote *fada'il* works on a range of topics, including places (e.g. Damascus, Jerusalem) and activities (e.g. *jihad*).

Fatimids: Isma'ili Shi'ite dynasty of caliphs. The Fatimids established themselves as rulers in Qayrawan (in modern Tunisia) in 910, with their leader, 'Abd Allah (or 'Ubayd Allah), being regarded by his supporters as the rightful *imam* and caliph (ruling with the title al-Mahdi [r. 910–34]). In 969 they took control of Egypt. They founded Cairo and made it the seat of their caliphate for the next two centuries, at times enjoying significant influence in Arabia, the Holy Land and Syria. However, their power declined in the eleventh century, passing into the hands of their viziers, the last of whom was Saladin, who abolished the caliphate in 1171.

Funduq: The Arabic word for a trade hostelry where merchants could stay and store goods, derived from the Greek *pandokheion* (inn). *Funduq* is used in modern times to refer to a hotel.

Hadith: Arabic: 'report'. Accounts of the sayings and actions of the Prophet Muhammad and his Companions. The *hadith* are used alongside the *Qur'an* to assist in understanding the holy book's teachings. From a very early stage Muslim scholars began collecting and writing commentaries on the *hadith*, including establishing a number of practices for judging their authenticity.

Hajj: Arabic: 'greater pilgrimage to Mecca'. A 'pillar of Islam'; every Muslim is expected to undertake the *hajj* at least once during their lifetime, if they are able. Taking place on the 1st–10th of the Muslim month of Dhu'l-Hijja, it involves a number of ritual practices and ends with the 'Id al-Adha (feast of sacrifice), a commemoration of Abraham's near-sacrifice of his son Ishmael that is celebrated across the Muslim world.

Halqa: Arabic: 'circle'. Term used to refer to (a) a circle of students gathered around a scholar, and (b) a regiment in the armies of the Mamluk Sultanate made up of (mostly) free-born troops of various origins.

Hamas (*Harakat al-Muqawama al-Islamiyya* [Islamic Resistance Movement]): Created in 1987 by members of the Muslim Brotherhood, the charter of Hamas dedicates the organization to the destruction of Israel. Militant action is combined with the promotion of social welfare and Muslim piety, which has helped to improve the movement's popularity, and it won Palestinian

Authority elections in 2006. The following year, after conflict with militants from the rival Fatah faction of government, Hamas became the ruling power in the Gaza Strip. Currently its membership is split between hard-liners who continue to advocate violence against Israel and moderates who favour negotiation.

Hanafis: Followers of the Sunni legal school named after Abu Hanifa (d. 767). Well-known Hanafis from the crusading period include Sibt ibn al-Jawzi (d. 1257) and the Zangid sultan Nur al-Din (r. 1146–74).

Hanbalis: Followers of the Sunni legal school of Ahmad ibn Hanbal (d. 855). Probably the most famous Hanbali scholar of the crusading period is Ibn Taymiyya (d. 1328).

Ifranj: Arabic: 'Franks'. The term used by the Muslim sources to refer to the Europeans. The term was originally used by Muslim writers to refer to the inhabitants of the Frankish empire of Charlemagne (r. 768–814), whence its derivation, but with the onset of the Crusades it became a term used for Europeans in general, including both those who came to the Levant and their descendants who were born in the Latin states.

Imam: At the basic level, the Arabic term for a prayer-leader. It is also the term used to refer to the spiritual leader of the Muslim community, especially in Shi'ite Islam, where the identities and precise attributes of the *imams* are often defining features of each different strand of Shi'ism.

Iqta': Arabic: 'assignment'. An *iqta'* was a grant to an emir of the right to collect taxes from a particular area of land, given in return for a promise of military service, in a way similar to a classic European feudal fief. An *iqta'* was usually temporary, which did not encourage the holder to see it as anything other than a source of revenue to be taxed as much as possible before it was re-assigned.

Isma'ili Shi'ism: In the wake of the death of the *imam* Ja'far al-Sadiq in 765 a split occurred within Shi'ite Islam, provoked by the fact that the next *imam*-designate, Ja'far's son Isma'il, had predeceased his father. While the Shi'ites who would become the Twelvers turned to another son of Ja'far, others maintained that Isma'il's son Muhammad was the rightful *imam*, even though he also had apparently died before Ja'far. They maintained that Muhammad had not in fact died, but had instead become hidden and would eventually return as the *mahdi*. The Isma'ilis became a hierarchical, secretive movement that nevertheless actively sought to proselytize, attracting many followers.

Ithna 'Ashari Shi'ism: See *Twelver Shi'ism*.

Al-Jazira: Arabic: 'the Peninsula'. The region roughly covering modern south-eastern Turkey, north-eastern Syria and north-western Iraq. It is mostly bracketed by the Tigris and Euphrates rivers.

Jihad: Arabic: 'striving'. A struggle undertaken on the behalf of the religion. This can include *al-jihad al-akbar* (the greater *jihad*), which involves both an internal struggle against one's own inner sinfulness and an external struggle in writing or speaking to defend one's faith; and *al-jihad al-asghar* (the lesser *jihad*), military action on behalf of Islam, undertaken within strict regulations including prohibitions on killing non-combatants, destroying property or deliberately killing oneself on the battlefield.

Jizya: The poll tax paid by non-Muslims living in Muslim territory, for which they receive rights of protection by their Muslim rulers. Non-Muslims were also expected to abide by certain restrictions, including wearing distinctive dress, not building places of worship or seeking to convert Muslims, and not riding horses or bearing arms. The extent to which these restrictions were actually enforced was highly variable.

Ka'ba: The shrine of the Black Stone at Mecca. The Ka'ba is believed to have been built by Abraham and Ishmael, and is the holiest site of Islam.

Khalifa: See *Caliph*.

Koran: See *Qur'an*.

Kuffar: Arabic: 'blasphemers' or 'infidels'. A term applied by the Muslim sources to the Franks, whose claims that Jesus was the son of God were seen by the Muslims as blasphemous. The term is used frequently in the *Qur'an* to refer to pagans who refuse to accept the message of Islam, thus enabling Muslim writers to equate the Franks with them.

Madrasa: *Madrasas* were colleges where various subjects were taught, but especially Islamic religion, theology and law. Under the Seljuks Sunni *madrasas* proliferated and became the standard institutions where prospective state officials and religious scholars received their education. *Madrasas* continued to be founded by the Zangids, Ayyubids and Mamluks throughout the crusading period.

Mahdi: In both Sunni and Shi'ite Islam, a messianic figure who will return to restore truth and justice. Belief in the *mahdi* is particularly prominent in Twelver Shi'ism, where he is identified as the Twelfth *imam* Muhammad al-Muntazar, who is regarded as currently being in 'greater concealment'.

Malikis: Followers of the legal school of Malik ibn Anas (d. 795). While there were a significant number of Maliki scholars in the Levant in the crusading period, the school was much more prominent in Spain and North Africa.

Mamluk: Arabic: 'owned'. A slave. The term is used in particular for slave-soldiers. Such slaves were normally bought while young on the fringes of the Muslim world, educated in both Islam and the arts of war, and then released upon attaining adulthood. They then formed contingents of troops serving their former masters, and constituted the backbone of the Muslim armies of the crusading period. Most *mamluks* were Turks or Circassians, but they also included slaves of other ethnicities. When capitalized, the term Mamluk usually refers to the Mamluk Sultanate, the sequence of rulers who controlled Egypt and Syria from 1250 to 1517, who were mostly of *mamluk* origin.

Mihrab: A prayer niche in a mosque, oriented towards Mecca and hence indicating the direction of prayer.

Minbar: A pulpit in a mosque, from which speeches and prayers are given, including the *khutba* (sermon) at the Friday noon prayer.

Mirrors for Princes: A genre of Muslim literature that takes the form of books of guidance for rulers on good conduct and wise and just governance.

Mujahid: One who strives in the *jihad*. The term is used in particular for fighters in the military *jihad*. A number of rulers included it among their titles as a way of asserting (genuinely or not) their devotion to the *jihad* against the Franks.

Mushrikun: Arabic: 'polytheists'. A term used by the Muslim sources of the Franks as a way of denigrating them. The Franks, as Christians, could be accused of being polytheistic in that they could be presented as worshipping three gods (the Holy Trinity), in contrast to the Islamic insistence on God's oneness. Since the term is also used in the *Qur'an* of the pagans who opposed the Prophet Muhammad, Muslim writers were thus able to associate the Franks with earlier enemies of Islam.

Nizaris: The Nizari Isma'ili Shi'ites split from the Fatimids in 1094 when the Fatimid vizier al-Afdal Shahanshah (d. 1121) set aside the heir apparent, Nizar (d. 1097), in favour of the latter's younger brother. Nizar was killed soon after, but some of his supporters maintained that his son had been brought to Alamut in Persia, and the line of *imams* continued there. The followers of this line, the Nizaris, engaged in a programme of political assassination over the next two centuries before being neutralized and driven underground by the Mongols and Mamluks. It is as a result of this programme that they are also sometimes referred to as the Assassins, and various lurid stories were recorded by the sources about their activities and practices, including tales of them using hashish (from which the word 'assassin' ultimately derives) as part of their activities. The Nizaris reappeared in central Persia in the fifteenth century and now form the largest Isma'ili community in the world, acknowledging the leadership of a living *imam*, the Aga Khan IV (b. 1936).

Pillars of Islam: Five major ritual practices that characterize the religious observances of a Muslim: (1) *shahada* (profession of faith); (2) *salat* (ritual prayer); (3) *zakat* (almsgiving); (4) *sawm* (fasting); and (5) *hajj* (greater pilgrimage). The precise manner in which these are observed varies depending on local customs and the particular form of Islam followed by the Muslim in question.

Qadi: A judge or magistrate, versed in Islamic law. *Qadis* were primarily expected to apply the existing body of legal rulings to cases that needed to be considered, rather than to develop new rulings through delivering legal opinions. The latter was the function of legal experts known as *muftis*.

Al-Qa'ida (al-Qaeda): Arabic: 'the base'. A multinational terrorist network that conducts operations against targets across the world. Al-Qa'ida was founded by Usama ibn Ladin (Osama bin Laden, d. 2011) in about 1988 with the purpose of supporting Afghan resistance to the Soviet occupation of Afghanistan. It has since grown to become a worldwide network with various allies and affiliates, that has the primary aim of ridding the Muslim world of western influence and establishing its own vision of a unified Muslim state. However, in recent years it has also become highly decentralized, which prevents it from acting as a unified body and limits its capabilities.

Qur'an (Koran): The Muslim holy book, believed to record the actual words of God revealed to Muhammad starting in 610 and ending shortly before the Prophet's death in 632. According to Muslim tradition the Prophet was illiterate, so the revelations were preserved by his Companions and then compiled during the following decades. Muslims believe that the *Qur'an* clarifies the earlier revelations made to the Jews, Christians and others, correcting their errors and misunderstandings, and it is indeed striking that in many parts it reads like a commentary on the Bible and requires a familiarity with the earlier scripture to understand it.

Ramadan: The ninth month of the Muslim year, and the month during which the revelation of the *Qur'an* to Muhammad began. Muslims observe the *sawm* (fast) during Ramadan in commemoration of this.

Rum: The Arabic word for the Byzantines. The word derives from the Greek *Rhomaioi* (Romans), the term that the Byzantines, seeing themselves as the inheritors of the Roman Empire, used to refer to themselves. The Arabic word was also used to refer to eastern Christians, especially followers of Greek Orthodox Christianity; and to Asia Minor, where many of the conflicts between the Muslims and the Byzantines took place.

Salat Ritual prayer. A 'pillar of Islam'. Most Muslims perform the *salat* five times a day, at dawn, noon, mid-afternoon, dusk and in the evening. Before praying, Muslims conduct ritual ablutions to purify themselves. The prayer consists of changes in bodily posture, from standing, to kneeling, to self-prostration, accompanied by ritual recitations and invocations, including passages from the *Qur'an*. *Salat* should be conducted facing Mecca, if possible.

Saljuqs See *Seljuks*.

Sawm: Fasting, especially fasting during Ramadan, which is a 'pillar of Islam'. Muslims, except for those for whom dispensations are made due to age or illness, fast from dawn until sunset during the Muslim month of Ramadan. This commemorates the first revelation of the *Qur'an* and ends with the 'Id al-Fitr (feast of the breaking of the fast).

Seljuks: A clan of Central Asian Turks who entered the Muslim world in the late tenth century as part of the wider immigration of Turks into the region. They converted to Islam and led their forces in a campaign of conquest that included the taking of Baghdad and the installation of one of their number as the caliph's deputy in 1055; this deputy became known as the sultan (the Great Seljuk sultan) and wielded effective power in the state. Seljuk expansion continued west, and in the wake of the Battle of Manzikert in 1071 a second Seljuk sultanate, the Seljuk Sultanate of *Rum*, was established in Asia Minor. The Great Seljuk Sultanate fragmented at the end of the eleventh century, and by the time that the crusaders arrived in the Levant many of the rulers there paid only nominal allegiance to the Great Seljuk sultan.

Shafi'is: Followers of the legal school of Muhammad ibn Idris al-Shafi'i (d. 820). The most famous Shafi'i of the crusading period is Saladin (r. 1169–93).

Shahada: Profession of faith. A 'pillar of Islam'. The two-part declaration of faith, 'There is no god except God, and Muhammad is the Messenger of God', is spoken regularly by Muslims as part of their ritual observances.

Al-Sham: See *Bilad al-Sham*.

Shaykh: A term used to refer to (1) a highly regarded scholar or teacher and (2) the master of a Sufi order.

Shi'ites: Followers of a variety of forms of Islam who trace their spiritual origins to early Muslims who advocated that a member of the family of the Prophet's cousin and son-in-law 'Ali ibn Abi Talib (r. 656–61) should lead the Muslim community. The term derives from the Arabic *shi'at 'Ali* (the party of 'Ali). The various strands of Shi'ism have since developed their own distinctive theologies and practices. Shi'ites constitute about 10–15 per cent of the Muslim population of the world.

Sufi: A Muslim mystic. Sufis seek to gain a direct, higher-state experience of God through a variety of means, including asceticism and group rituals involving prayer, chanting, music or dance. The name derives from the garments of *suf* (wool) that they traditionally wore. During the crusading period many Sufis, sometimes with the encouragement of rulers, formed *tariqas* (orders) gathered in convents and at Muslim saints' tombs.

Sultan: Arabic: 'power'. Originally used by the Seljuk 'deputies' of the 'Abbasid caliph, the term 'sultan' came to be used as an honorific mark of political power by a number of Muslim rulers, with or without caliphal approval.

Sunnis: Followers of the majority form of Islam, currently constituting about 85–90 per cent of the total Muslim population of the world. The name derives from the Sunna, a word used to refer to the sayings and actions of the Prophet and his Companions, which act as a guide to Muslim conduct and are preserved in the *hadith*.

Turcomans: See *Turkmen*.

Turkmen: Free nomadic Turks who served in the armies of the Seljuks and later dynasties. They generally travelled with their families and flocks, at least initially, though many then settled in the new lands taken by the Seljuks. They were esteemed for their abilities as highly mobile horse-archers, though they were also often seen as undisciplined.

Twelver Shi'ism: When the *imam* Ja'far al-Sadiq died in 765, the Shi'ite community faced a crisis, as the next *imam*-designate, Ja'far's son Isma'il, had died before his father. Many Shi'ites eventually accepted that the next *imam* was another son of Ja'far, Musa al-Kazim (d. 799), while others developed contrasting views that led to the birth of Isma'ili Shi'ism. Meanwhile the followers of Musa continued to trace a line of *imams* through his descendants until the tenth century when, according to their beliefs, the twelfth *imam*, Muhammad al-Muntazar, went into 'greater concealment', from which he will return as the *mahdi* at the end of time. The Twelvers, as they became known, form the majority of Shi'ites in the world today.

'Ulama' (Ulema): The class of Muslim scholars educated in religion, theology and law. Muslim rulers would often patronize the *'ulama'* as a means to prove their devotion to Islam.

Umayyads: The first dynasty of caliphs to establish a hereditary succession. The first caliph of the Umayyad dynasty, Mu'awiya ibn Abi Sufyan (r. 661–80), took control of the Muslim state after fighting a civil war against the caliph

'Ali ibn Abi Talib (r. 656–61). Later he designated his son Yazid (r. 680–3) to succeed him. Members of the Umayyad family continued to rule, making their capital at Damascus, until 750, when they were ousted by the 'Abbasids.

Vizier: The deputy of a ruler, and often a powerful figure in the state. The word derives from the Arabic *wazir*, which is used in the modern day to refer to a government minister.

Zakat: Almsgiving. A 'pillar of Islam'. Muslims are required to donate a portion of their wealth to suitable charitable causes each year. The money is used, for example, to support the poor and travellers, and to ransom prisoners.

Zangids: The family of 'Imad al-Din Zangi (r. 1127–46). After Zangi's death his lands passed to various members of his family, including most prominently his sons Nur al-Din (r. 1146–74) at Aleppo and Sayf al-Din (r. 1146–49) at Mosul. Nur al-Din also secured the handover of Damascus in 1154. While Damascus and Aleppo were lost to Saladin in 1174 and 1183 respectively, Zangi's descendants continued to rule territories in Iraq and the Jazira until the mid-thirteenth century.

Guide to Muslim names

Muslim names consist of a number of components:

1 *Ism* (given name): This is the name given to a child at birth, which usually takes one of the following forms: (1) the Arabic form of a Biblical name, as found in the *Qur'an*, for example Ibrahim (Abraham) or Maryam (Mary); (2) an originally Arabic name, for example Muhammad or Fatima; (3) a compound of the word 'Abd (servant of) and an epithet of God, for example 'Abd Allah (Servant of God) or 'Abd al-Malik (Servant of the King); or (4) a non-Arabic name, for example Tughtigin.

2 *Nasab* (lineage): This follows the *ism* and normally refers to the individual's father, though some historical figures were known by *nasabs* indicating an ancestor instead. For males, the Arabic *nasab* consists of *ibn* ('son of', sometimes shortened to *bin* or simply *b.*) followed by the father's name (usually their *ism*). For females, it consists of *bint* ('daughter of', sometimes shortened to *bt.*) followed by the father's name; for example, the Prophet's daughter was called Fatima bint Muhammad. In Persian, the equivalent of *ibn* is *i* suffixed to the *ism*, for example Hasan-i Sabbah.

3 *Kunya* (parental honorific): This often precedes the *ism* and is a name taken by a parent after the birth of their first child, consisting of *Abu* ('father of') or *Umm* ('mother of') followed by the child's name. In the period covered by this book an honorific epithet was often used instead of a child's name.

4 *Laqab* (honorific): *Laqabs* are titles, and in medieval times one individual might be granted several by their political superiors. They often come before the other elements of the name. Common forms for *laqabs* include compounds ending in *al-Din* ('of the faith'), *al-Mulk* ('of the kingdom') or *al-Dawla* ('of the state'); or compounds beginning with *al-Malik* ('the king'), although others exist. Examples include Sayf al-Din ('Sword of the Faith'), Nizam al-Mulk ('Good Order of the Kingdom'), Taj al-Dawla ('Crown of the State') and al-Malik al-'Adil ('the Just King'). When referring

to historical figures using their 'Malik' *laqab*, scholars often omit the first part; thus the last example cited would usually be referred to simply as 'al-'Adil'.

5 *Nisba* (ascription): This is a wide category encompassing a range of descriptors including geographical origin, profession, ethnicity, preferred school of law or simply a distinctive attribute, and an individual again might have several *nisbas*. *Nisbas* usually come last, begin with the definite article *al-* and end with a long *i* (if male) or with *iyya* (if female).

To take an example: probably the most famous Muslim from the crusading period is Saladin (r. 1169–93), whose name in Arabic can be given as:

Al-Malik al-Nasir Salah al-Din Abu'l-Muzaffar Yusuf ibn Ayyub al-Tikriti al-Kurdi.

This can be translated as 'The King who Aids (*laqab*), Righteousness of the Faith (*laqab*), Father of the Victorious (*kunya*, honorific in this case), Joseph (*ism*, Qur'anic form of Biblical name), son of Job (*nasab*, again with Qur'anic form of Biblical name), of Tikrit (*nisba*), the Kurd (*nisba*)'.

Note that 'Saladin' is a Latin corruption of the sultan's *laqab* 'Salah al-Din'. Not all the components of Muslim names are used in the sources when referring to a particular individual, nor is there a standard practice for deciding which elements to include or omit, or which order to place them in, so an individual might be referred to using different names at different times or by different authors, and the various components of their names might also come in different orders depending on the choice of the writer in question.

For further details, see P.M. Holt, *The Age of the Crusades* (1986), pp. xi-xii, and Jere L. Bachrach, *A Middle East Studies Handbook* (1984), p. 4, on which the above discussion draws heavily.

List of plates

Acknowledgements

Writing the acknowledgements in a book is always both a difficult and an enjoyable task: difficult, because one is sure to miss somebody who deserves mention, and enjoyable, because one is reminded of the support and encouragement of friends and colleagues that have led to its successful completion. I have many people to thank. Mari Shullaw first asked me to write this book, and remained a source of advice and wisdom throughout much of the writing process. Lutz Richter-Bernburg read my first draft and gave me a meticulous and expert commentary thereon. Barrie Brill, Deborah Gerish, Jessica Hemming, David Nicolle and Warren Schultz also read the manuscript and gave me vital feedback. Paul Cobb continued to provide invaluable mentoring and support. Reuven Amitai, Karen Cooper, Karen Ewing, Daniel Gagnon, Jen Knapp, and Angus Stewart all provided additional helpful advice and suggestions. My friends and colleagues at Langara College, Corpus Christi College and the University of British Columbia also provided ongoing encouragement. I would also like to thank Laura Mothersole, Catherine Aitken, Ruth Berry, Nicky Connor and the publishing team at Routledge for their hard work on bringing this book to publication. Finally, I am immensely grateful to my parents and sisters, who first gave me a love of books and history; to my students, who have continued to educate and challenge me with their responses to the historical materials that I have shared with them; and last, but by no means least, to my wife, Steph, whose unfailing love and support were constant and necessary contributions to the completion of this book.

PUBLISHER'S ACKNOWLEDGEMENTS

The documents have been reproduced with kind permission (some have been shortened and edited) from Ashgate, Penguin and IFP Orient. Whilst every effort has been made to trace copyright holders, this has not been possible in all cases. Any omissions brought to our attention will be remedied in future editions.

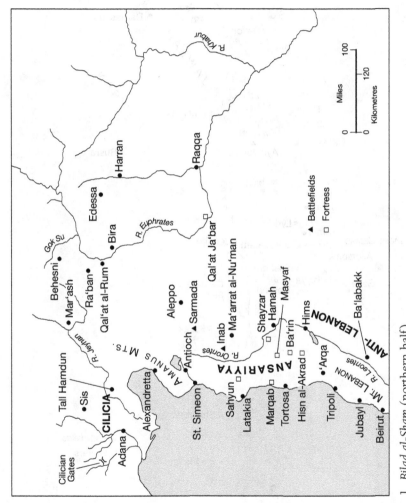

1 *Bilad al-Sham* (northern half)

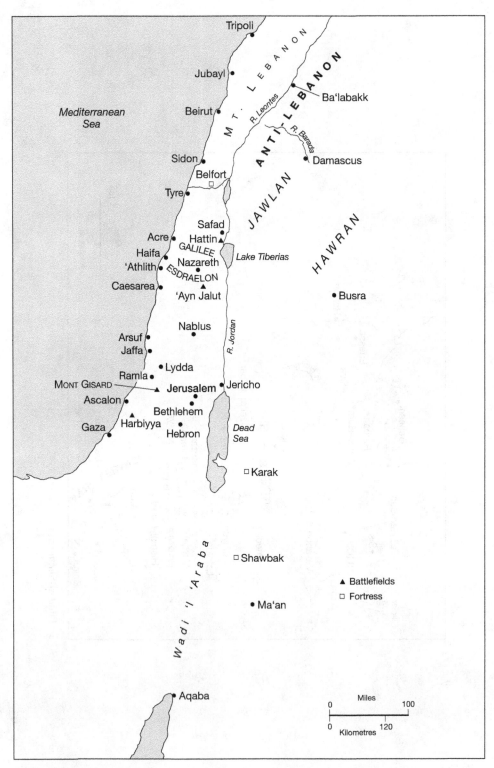

Tripoli

Jubayl

MT. LEBANON

R. Leontes

ANTI-LEBANON

Ba'labakk

Beirut

R. Barada

Mediterranean
Sea

Sidon

Damascus

Belfort

JAWLAN

Tyre

Safad

HAWRAN

Acre

Hattin

Haifa

GALILEE

Lake Tiberias

'Athlith

Nazareth

Caesarea

ESDRAELON

'Ayn Jalut

Busra

Nablus

R. Jordan

Arsuf

Jaffa

Lydda

Ramla

MONT GISARD

Jerusalem

Jericho

Ascalon

Bethlehem

Gaza

Harbiyya

Hebron

Dead
Sea

Karak

Shawbak

W a d i   ' l   ' A r a b a

Battlefields

Fortress

Ma'an

Aqaba

Miles

0   100

0   120

Kilometres

2 *Bilad al-Sham* (southern half)

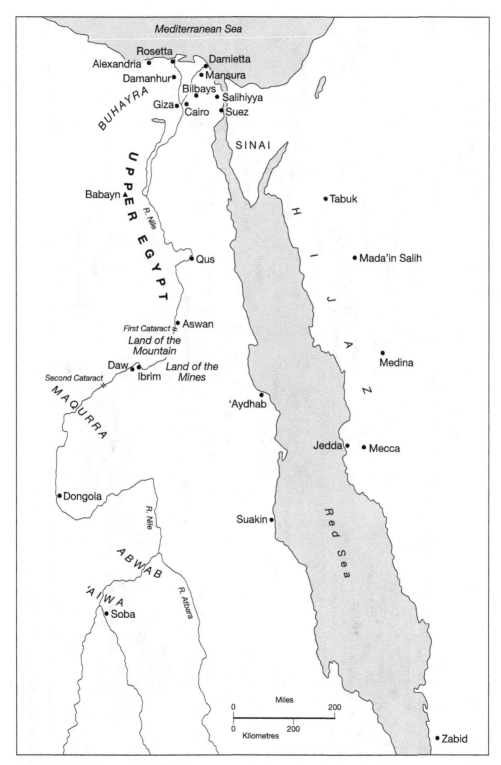

3 The Nile Valley and the Red Sea

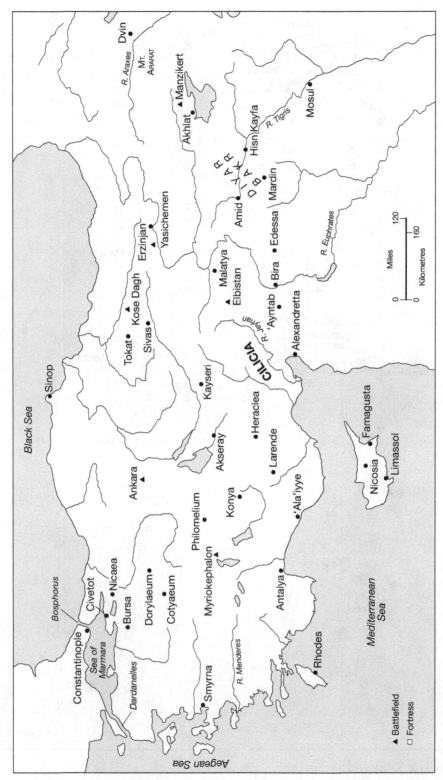

4 Asia Minor and the northern *Bilad al-Sham* and Jazira

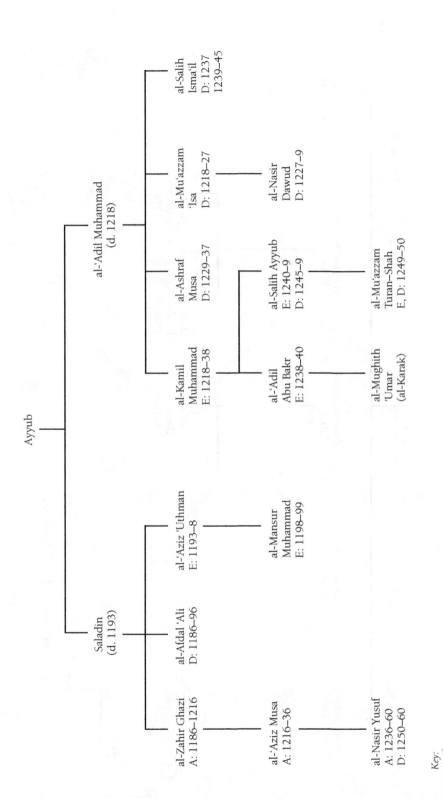

Ayyub

Saladin
(d. 1193)

al-'Adil Muhammad
(d. 1218)

al-Afdal 'Ali
D: 1186–96

al-'Aziz 'Uthman
E: 1193–8

al-Kamil
Muhammad
E: 1218–38

al-Ashraf
Musa
D: 1229–37

al-Mu'azzam
'Isa
D: 1218–27

al-Salih
Isma'il
D: 1237
1239–45

al-Zahir Ghazi
A: 1186–1216

al-Mansur
Muhammad
E: 1198–99

al-'Adil
Abu Bakr
E: 1238–40

al-Salih Ayyub
E: 1240–9
D: 1245–9

al-Nasir
Dawud
D: 1227–9

al-'Aziz Musa
A: 1216–36

al-Mughith
'Umar
(al-Karak)

al-Mu'azzam
Turan–Shah
E, D: 1249–50

al-Nasir Yusuf
A: 1236–60
D: 1250–60

Key:
A: Aleppo
D: Damascus
E: Egypt

1   The Ayyubids of Egypt, Damascus and Aleppo

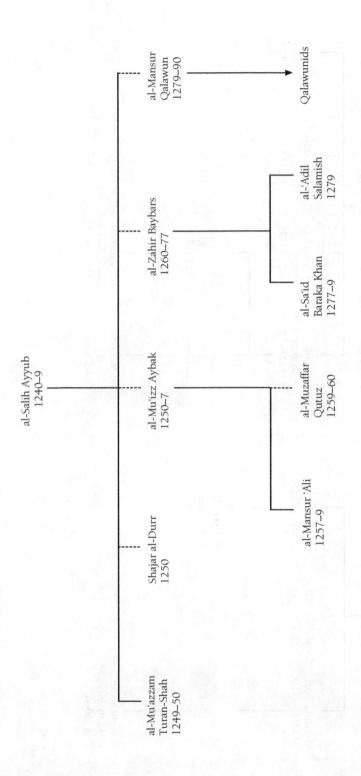

al-Salih Ayyub
1240–9

al-Mu'azzam
Turan-Shah
1249–50

Shajar al-Durr
1250

al-Mu'izz Aybak
1250–7

al-Mansur 'Ali
1257–9

al-Muzaffar
Qutuz
1259–60

al-Zahir Baybars
1260–77

al-Sa'id
Baraka Khan
1277–9

al-'Adil
Salamish
1279

al-Mansur
Qalawun
1279–90

Qalawunids

Key:

Son

Mamluk

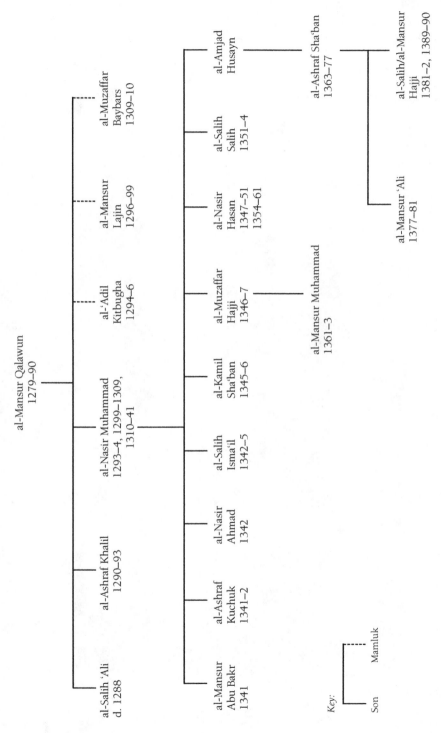

3 The house of Qalawun

1

Introduction

In this year [1096] there came a sequence of reports [telling] of the appearance of Frankish troops from the sea of Constantinople, the number of which was too great to be counted. News of that continued to arrive, and the people were disturbed to hear it and became alarmed as it spread.

(Ibn al-Qalanisi, 1983: 218)

Few historians would deny that the Crusades to the Middle East were of immense importance in the development of medieval Europe. From the thousands who marched east to the many more who were left behind to deal with the consequences of their departure, most people of medieval Europe felt the impact of crusading activities on some level. However, we should not forget that the Crusades also had a great impact on the peoples against whom they were waged. This book seeks to present the Crusades from the viewpoint of the Muslim peoples of the Levant, providing the reader with an understanding of the most significant issues that coloured their responses to both the crusaders from Europe and the descendants of these crusaders who were born and lived in the Latin Christian states that were created in the region. Through both a survey of the major topics that emerge from study of the period and the presentation of a wide range of sources that allow the people of the time to speak to us in their own voices, this book aims to act as a supplemental and counterbalancing work to the numerous books that tell the story of the crusading period from the European point of view, enabling readers to achieve a broader perspective on the period than they might do otherwise.

PREVIOUS WORKS ON THE MUSLIM SIDE OF THE CRUSADES

Study of the Muslim perspective on the Crusades is a relatively young scholarly field, and there are few major works that deal with the subject as a whole, particularly when compared with the immense number of works that tell the

European side of the story. A pioneering work is Emmanuel Sivan's *L'Islam et la Croisade*. Written in 1968, Sivan's book examines the development of the Muslim counter-crusade, thus presenting an important study of the topic, albeit one that only focuses on one aspect. A broader vision is found in Amin Maalouf's *The Crusades through Arab Eyes* (1984). This is an evocative, engaging treatment of the theme, though it self-consciously privileges story-telling over academic rigour. P.M. Holt's *The Age of the Crusades* (1986) is an excellent scholarly treatment of the history of the Levantine region at the time that concentrates primarily on the complex political developments that took place within the Muslim states of the region. Finally, the most important recent work is Carole Hillenbrand's magisterial *The Crusades: Islamic Perspectives* (1999 a). This weighty tome (704 pages) presents a detailed survey of the major themes and questions with which those seeking to study the period must grapple, providing a vivid illustration of the breadth of sources and wide range of lines of enquiry that require further exploration by modern scholars. At the time of writing a number of additional important studies are in press. Paul M. Cobb's *The Race for Paradise: An Islamic History of the Crusades* (2014) will examine the Muslim response to the Crusades in the Levant, Spain and Sicily. Alex Mallett's *Popular Muslim Reactions to the Frankish Presence in the Levant, 1097–1291* (2014 b) will discuss the responses of the 'non-elite' inhabitants of the Levantine region to the activities of the crusaders. Finally, Alex Mallet's edited volume, *Medieval Muslim Historians and the Franks in the Levant, 1097–1291* (2014 a), will provide a detailed overview of the Muslim sources for the crusading period.

Muslims and Crusaders aims to provide students, scholars and interested laypersons with a manageable and accessible entry into the topic of Muslim reactions to the Crusades, combining chronological narrative, discussion of important areas of scholarly enquiry and evidence from primary sources to give a well-rounded initial survey of the period, from which further study may proceed. Readers who want to know more about the subject after reading this work are encouraged to consult the texts mentioned above, as well as those highlighted in the *Further reading* sections at the end of each chapter in this book. Readers who would like to compare what is contained herein with works on the western side of the Crusades are encouraged to consult the extensive literature on the latter topic; excellent introductions to the current state of scholarship on the subject are *Palgrave Advances in the Crusades*, edited by Helen Nicholson (2005); and Norman Housley's *Contesting the Crusades* (2006).

THE LIMITATIONS OF THIS WORK

This is a short book, and as such it can only offer a brief introduction to the major topics that the student of the Muslim side of the Crusades might wish to consider. Modern scholarly understandings of the Crusades have expanded both the geographical and the temporal scope of the topic to encompass, for example, crusading activity in the Iberian Peninsula, but page limits will not allow us to address these here; thus we will be focused only on the Muslim response to the Crusades in the Levant during the 'core' period of crusading. In addition, again given the limits of space, we will, regrettably, not be able to consider the perspectives of the sizeable and important native Christian and Jewish communities that existed in the Middle East at the time that the Crusades were taking place. While our focus on the Muslim perspective might be regarded as one-sided, it is justifiable given the huge amount of attention that has been paid to the Muslims' opponents, the crusaders from Europe, and their descendants in the Latin East.

THE MUSLIM SOURCES FOR THE CRUSADING PERIOD

The Muslim sources, most of which are in Arabic, occupy a broad range of different genres, many of which had a long and distinguished history by the time that the Crusades themselves began, and we have sought to present a representative sample of these in English translation in the Documents section of this work. Chief among the Muslim sources are annalistic chronicles, intended to recount events on a year-by-year basis. Such chronicles take a number of forms, including universal chronicles that seek to present a history of the world from its origin to the author's own time, and city- or country-based chronicles, telling of events taking place in a particular location. Other works adopt a biographical basis: we have biographical and auto-biographical works focused on one individual; dynastic histories, telling of the lives of members of a particular family; and also (sometimes very large) bio-graphical dictionaries that seek to record the lives of individuals, collected on the basis of a shared theme, often a shared geographical origin, profession or importance to the Muslim community. We also have descriptive geographies and travel literature, including descriptions of the known world and accounts of journeys from one end of the Muslim lands to the other. There are also Muslim religious and legal texts, which take a variety of forms including, of course, the *Qur'an*, the Muslim holy book; the *hadith*, accounts of the sayings and actions of the Prophet Muhammad and his Companions, used to assist in understanding Islamic teachings; *fada'il* (merits), works praising the virtues of a place or activity, including particular books devoted to the *jihad* in all its legal and religious aspects; texts of *fatwas* (legal judgments); and records of treaties. It is worth noting that these enjoyed particular longevity of influence, and thus we find authors of the crusading period drawing heavily on works of these types from previous centuries. Other texts were intended to entertain or instruct their listeners, including works of poetry, folktales and epic sagas.

It should be noted that this is not an exhaustive list of the types of sources available for the crusading period, nor should the genres detailed above be seen as neatly divided from each other. In many cases sources combine genres; for instance, a legal text might have some of its ideas illustrated by quotations from the Qur'an and hadith, but also make use of poetry and historical anecdotes to prove its points. In theory at least, a cultivated Muslim nobleman of the time was expected to have, in addition to expertise in fighting and riding, a deep knowledge of the most important works of literature so that he could, where warranted, drop a Qur'anic or poetic quotation into a speech or conversation. The ability to compose literature was also highly respected; the Muslim emir Usama ibn Munqidh (d. 1188), although better known to modern historians for his anecdotes about the quirky characteristics of the crusaders, was most famous in his own time for his talents as a poet.

The Muslims referred to the crusaders and their Levantine descendants as the ifranj (Franks). Before the Crusades this term was used in a vague fashion, but it often referred to the inhabitants of the area of the world that corresponded roughly to the Frankish empire of Charlemagne (r. 768–814), thus occupying modern-day France and also parts of Spain, Germany and Italy. However, with the onset of the Crusades the term came to be used by the Muslim sources in a more widespread fashion, referring to western Europeans in general, a practice that persists in the sources even after the Muslim writers begin to show knowledge of the various different geographical origins of those about whom they write. In the sources the Franks are seen as being distinct from the rum (the Byzantines, though the term was also sometimes used to refer to eastern Christians), though they are usually recognized as sharing the same religion. That said, the Muslim sources do not dwell on the differences between the Christianity of the Franks, who were Catholic, and the Byzantines, who were Greek Orthodox.

Few of the Muslim sources take events of the wars with the crusaders as their primary subject matter. It is far more common to see Muslim inter-actions with the Franks forming part of a wider narrative. The Damascene chronicler Ibn al-Qalanisi (d. 1160), for example, has left us a history of the city in which he tells of the arrival of the crusaders and their subsequent activities in the Levant, but at the same time his perspective is limited, for his accounts of these are only a small part of a wider narrative in which he recounts various events that took place in and around the city. Sources such as these remind us of two things. First, for the inhabitants of the Muslim world as a whole, the impact of the Crusades was actually quite limited. We cannot deny that for those who lived in areas where such conflicts between

Muslims and Europeans were taking place – primarily the Levant and Spain – events could be at times politically, economically and personally devastating. However, at the same time the Muslim world stretched from the Iberian Peninsula and the Maghrib in the west to Central Asia and north-west India in the east; a Muslim merchant in Samarkand, for example, was probably unaware of or unconcerned by events in the Levant, assuming that they had no impact on his suppliers in the region. Even these events' impact on a city much closer to the Levant, such as the caliphal capital of Baghdad, was minimal, despite the feelings of some of its residents, as we will see. Second, given that they show that Muslim interaction with the Franks was a continuous process, rather than something that happened in distinct phases, the Muslim sources for the period are a salutary reminder that the neat division of the Crusades into numbered expeditions, like so many terms employed by historians, is a modern invention, a labelling used to impose a structure on the period in order to assist in discussions. No Muslim or crusader at the time numbered the expeditions that had been made from Europe to the Middle East, and for them terms such as 'Second Crusade' would have been meaningless. This in turn reminds us of the importance of seeking, as far as we can, to cast aside our own preconceptions and prejudices when we read the historical sources from the period, so that our understanding of them will be as unimpaired as possible. This will allow the writers of the past to speak to us on their own terms, permitting us to see their world as they would have us see it, rather than as we might wish to from our modern perspective.

2

The Muslim world before the Crusades

By the time that the crusaders arrived in the Levant, Islamic civilization was almost 500 years old. The Muslim faith had become a highly diverse tradition, practiced in a number of different ways; Muslim culture and science had become highly advanced; and the Muslim world itself had spread to cover the Iberian Peninsula, North Africa, the Middle East and parts of Central Asia and north-west India. Here we will provide a brief discussion of the history, theology and practices of Islam, before considering the state of the Levant before the Crusades.

A BRIEF HISTORY

Muslim tradition states that in 610, in a cave on the outskirts of the Arabian city of Mecca, an orphaned merchant named Muhammad began receiving divine revelations. He was instructed to preach to the people of Mecca, who were mostly pagans, encouraging them to abandon idolatry and worship only the one true God ('**Allah**' in Arabic), the same God worshipped by the Jews and Christians. The new faith was to be known as 'Islam', a word meaning submission of one's will to God, while the revelations themselves would eventually be gathered into the *Qur'an* (recitation), the Muslim holy book. Muhammad's message was not well received by the inhabitants of Mecca, which was an important trade centre that profited from pilgrims visiting the **Ka'ba**, the shrine of the Black Stone, at the time a popular pagan religious site. In 622, in response to increasing pressure, Muhammad emigrated to Medina, about 200 miles to the north, where his message was more favourably received. Muhammad then fought an eight-year war with Mecca, culminating in his conquest of the city in 630. The Ka'ba was confirmed as the holiest site of Islam, being seen as a shrine built by Abraham and Ishmael (Abraham's oldest son and the ancestor of the Arabs) that had been taken over for pagan use, and most of the inhabitants of Mecca

Allah: The Arabic word for God, meaning the god worshipped by followers of all the major monotheistic faiths.

Qur'an (Koran): The Muslim holy book, believed to record the actual words of God revealed to Muhammad starting in 610 and ending shortly before the Prophet's death in 632.

Ka'ba: The shrine of the Black Stone at Mecca. The Ka'ba is believed to have been built by Abraham and Ishmael, and is the holiest site of Islam.

converted to Islam. By the time that Muhammad died in 632 his message had spread across the Arabian Peninsula, and most of the pagans of the region had converted.

An important teaching in Islam is that Muhammad was the last prophet, so no other Muslim could now take over this position. Leadership of the Muslim community passed instead into the hands of a succession of figures known as **khalifas** (**caliphs**, 'successors'). The first three of these were chosen by approximate consensus of the Muslim community, but the fourth, the Prophet's cousin and son-in-law 'Ali ibn Abi Talib (r. 656–61), faced opposition throughout his reign and was killed in the course of a civil war over the caliphate. Thereafter power passed under the control of a dynastic succession of caliphs, the **Umayyads** (r. 661–750), who ruled from Damascus. They were in turn ousted by the **'Abbasid** family, who founded the next caliphal dynasty and soon established their seat of power at Baghdad. In the meantime, the Islamic polity had continued to spread, through a mixture of armed conquest, acquiescence of local populations and voluntary conversion. By the time of the 'Abbasid takeover in 750, the Muslims had dismantled the Persian Empire, taking over territories as far east as Transoxania and northwest India; had conquered much of the Levant, North Africa, and Spain; and had even conducted raids into what is now France. At the same time, many of the administrative structures of the state had been set up, including the establishment of Arabic as the major language of the administration and the standardization of the coinage into a distinctive form bearing Arabic inscriptions and no iconography.

The early 'Abbasid caliphs enjoyed a heyday of power, and the first century of their rule saw the Muslim world prosper economically and intellectually. Lucrative trade networks were established across the Muslim world and to places beyond. Literature, both prose and poetic, flourished, and advances were made in science, law, philosophy and theology. Scholars took works from the Classical, Persian and Indian traditions and translated them into Arabic; many of both these texts and books by the scholars who worked on them subsequently passed into Europe, mainly through the Iberian Peninsula. However, this age of prosperity did not last, for the 'Abbasids at least. Economic problems, rebellions and the increasing domination of the caliphs by their troops starting in the later ninth century resulted in many of the provinces becoming independent from Baghdad's control. The final insult, from the 'Abbasid point of view, came in the mid-tenth century when Baghdad itself was taken over by the armies of the **Buyids**, a **Shi'ite** clan from Persia. Forced to accept the Buyid conquerors as their 'deputies', the **Sunni** caliphs became for the most part figureheads, maintained in power only to give legitimacy to the decrees of their theoretical subordinates (for the distinctions between Sunnis and Shi'ites, see below).

Khalifa: See *Caliph*.

Caliph: Anglicization of the Arabic term *khalifa* (deputy, successor). The caliph was, in theory if not always in fact, the spiritual and political ruler of the Muslim world.

Umayyads: The first dynasty of caliphs to establish a hereditary succession. They reigned at Damascus from 661 until 750, and at Cordoba in Spain from 756 (taking the title of caliphs from 929) until 1031.

'Abbasids: Dynasty of Sunni caliphs reigning at Baghdad at the time of the Crusades. After the Mongol destruction of Baghdad in 1258 the caliphate was re-established, at Cairo, in 1261, and reigned there until the Ottoman conquest of 1516–17.

Buyids: Dynasty of Persian Shi'ites who ruled as caliphal 'deputies' (wielding effective power) at Baghdad from 945 to 1055.

Shi'ites: Followers of a variety of forms of Islam who trace their spiritual origins to early Muslims who advocated that a member of the family of the Prophet's cousin and son-in-law, 'Ali ibn Abi Talib (r. 656–61), should be the caliph.

Sunnis: Followers of the majority form of Islam, currently constituting about 85–90 per cent of the total Muslim population of the world. The name derives from the Sunna, a word used to refer to the sayings and actions of the Prophet and his Companions, which act as a guide to Muslim conduct and are preserved in the *hadith*.

The late tenth century saw the beginning of the immigration into the Muslim world of large numbers of Turks from Central Asia. Most of these converted to Sunni Islam, and one Turkish clan, the **Seljuks** (Saljuqs), led their armies in a series of campaigns that enabled them to take control of much of the Middle East. In 1055 Seljuk troops took control of Baghdad, and the Buyid caliphal deputy was now replaced by a Seljuk one, known as the **sultan**. Although the caliph now had a Sunni deputy, this did not mean that the caliph regained significant power, and periodic conflicts between the caliphs and the sultans would take place in the twelfth century.

The Seljuk armies were largely composed of two major groups: *mamluks* (slave-soldiers) and **Turkmen** (**Turcomans**, free nomadic Turks). The *mamluks* were normally used as the backbone of the Seljuk armies, while the rather less disciplined Turkmen, who brought their families and flocks with them, were used in a supporting role or allowed to engage in their own raids, which could prove to be a convenient way to distract enemies from major Seljuk campaigns. During the reign of the Seljuk sultan Alp-Arslan (r. 1063–73), Turkmen tribesmen conducted raids against Byzantine territory in Asia Minor and northern Syria. Tensions between Alp-Arslan and the Byzantine emperor Romanus Diogenes (r. 1068–71) mounted, and in 1071 they met in battle at Manzikert (Malasjird), near Lake Van. The Byzantine army was defeated and the frontier collapsed. The Turkmen raids into the region now became a flood of immigrant settlers, and a relative of Alp-Arslan set up a new sultanate, based at Nicaea (Iznik); this became known as the Seljuk Sultanate of **Rum**, to distinguish it from the so-called Great Seljuk Sultanate that we saw established previously. In the meantime, the Byzantine emperors sent appeals for aid to western Europe, contributing to the build-up of support for the crusade that would eventually manifest itself in military action at the end of the eleventh century.

CORE BELIEFS AND PRACTICES

The Muslim faith centres on the belief that there is only one God, omnipotent, omniscient and with no associates, partners or offspring. This is the same God as that of the Christians and Jews, who are presented in the *Qur'an* as having received the divine revelation previously, but also as having mis-understood or distorted it. Thus the scripture that was revealed to Muhammad is seen as a corrective and clarification. Muhammad himself is understood to be the last and 'Seal' of a long line of prophets, including Adam, Abraham, Moses, David and Jesus (who is regarded as having been born of a virgin by divine will, and is explicitly noted as being a great prophet but not the son of God).

Seljuks: Clan of Sunni Muslim Turks who entered the Muslim world in the late tenth century. In 1055 they ousted the Buyids from Baghdad and took control of the 'Abbasid caliphate, subsequently establishing two sultan-ates based in Persia and Asia Minor.

Sultan: Arabic: 'power'. Originally used by the Seljuk 'deputies' of the 'Abbasid caliph, the term 'sultan' came to be used as an honorific mark of political power by a number of Muslim rulers, with or without caliphal approval.

Mamluk: Arabic: 'owned'. A slave. The term is used in particular for slave-soldiers. The capitalized term is also used to refer to the Mamluk Sultanate, the sequence of rulers who controlled Egypt and Syria from 1250 to 1517.

Turkmen: Free nomadic Turks who served in the armies of the Seljuks and later dynasties. They generally travelled with their families and flocks, at least initially, though many then settled in the new lands taken by the Seljuks. They were esteemed for their abilities as highly mobile horse-archers, though they were also often seen as undisciplined.

Turcomans: See *Turkmen*.

Rum: The Arabic word for the Byzantines. The term was also used to refer both to eastern Christians and to Asia Minor.

Muslims believe that at a time known only to God all who have lived will be resurrected and a Last Judgement will take place. All will be judged individually according to their good and bad deeds. Those who are judged worthy will then achieve the lush gardens of Paradise, while those who are not will be condemned to the burning fires of Hell. Thus Muslims should seek as far as possible to be righteous in their beliefs and actions. The first source of wisdom for Muslims is the Qur'an, understood to be the words of God, dictated to the Prophet. It contains material addressing a wide range of topics, including accounts and explanations of the stories of the prophets, vivid depictions of Paradise and Hell, stern injunctions to right belief and good conduct, and practical teachings on social and personal interactions. Muslims expand their understanding of the Qur'an through examination of the **hadith**, accounts of the sayings and actions of the Prophet and his Companions, who are seen as the foremost interpreters of the Qur'an's teachings. Over the centuries following the death of the Prophet, a number of groups of scholars of Islamic law came into being, each of which developed its own understanding of Islamic teaching depending on its own interpretation of the Qur'an and hadith. The four most prominent of these schools of Islamic law are the Sunni schools known as the **Hanafis**, the **Malikis**, the **Shafi'is** and the **Hanbalis**. Muslim religious scholars also developed other methods for interpreting Islamic teaching when even the hadith did not yield a clear answer, including the use of analogy and the establishment of consensus (of the Muslim community, or of particular groups within it).

Probably the most distinctive Muslim ritual practices are the five so-called 'Pillars of Islam':

1. *Shahada* (profession of faith): Muslims use a two-part declaration of faith, 'There is no god except God, and Muhammad is the Messenger of God', in various ritual practices. For example, the *shahada* is recited when converting to Islam.
2. *Salat* (ritual prayer): Most Muslims perform ritual prayers five times per day, at dawn, noon, mid-afternoon, dusk and in the evening. Prayer is preceded by ritual ablutions and involves changes in bodily posture, from standing, to kneeling, to prostration, accompanied by ritual recitations and invocations. A mosque is a place specially designated for prayer, but the *salat* can be performed anywhere, though it should be conducted facing Mecca if possible; in mosques, a niche called a **mihrab** indicates to worshippers the direction in which they should face. Travellers may perform an abbreviated prayer, even doing so while in their seats if necessary. Muslims are encouraged to go to the mosque on Friday for the noon prayer, when the communal practice of prayer is supplemented with a *khutba* (sermon).

Hadith: Accounts of the sayings and actions of the Prophet Muhammad and his Companions. The *hadith* are used alongside the *Qur'an* to assist in understanding the holy book's teachings.

Hanafis: Followers of the Sunni legal school named after Abu Hanifa (d. 767). Well-known Hanafis from the crusading period include Sibt ibn al-Jawzi (d. 1257) and the Zangid sultan Nur al-Din (r. 1146–74).

Malikis: Followers of the legal school of Malik ibn Anas (d. 795). While there were a significant number of Maliki scholars in the Levant in the crusading period, the school was much more prominent in Spain and North Africa.

Shafi'is: Followers of the legal school of Muhammad ibn Idris al-Shafi'i (d. 820). The most famous Shafi'i of the crusading period is Saladin (r. 1169–93).

Hanbalis: Followers of the Sunni legal school of Ahmad ibn Hanbal (d. 855). Probably the most famous Hanbali scholar of the crusading period is Ibn Taymiyya (d. 1328).

Pillars of Islam: Five major ritual practices that characterize the religious observances of a Muslim: (1) *shahada* (profession of faith); (2) *salat* (ritual prayer); (3) *zakat* (almsgiving); (4) *sawm* (fasting); and (5) *hajj* (greater pilgrimage).

Shahada: Profession of faith. A 'pillar of Islam'. The two-part declaration of faith, 'There is no god except God, and Muhammad is the Messenger of God', is spoken regularly by Muslims as part of their ritual observances.

Salat: Ritual prayer. A 'pillar of Islam'. Most Muslims perform the *salat* five times a day, at dawn, noon, mid-afternoon, dusk and in the evening.

Mihrab: A prayer niche in a mosque, oriented towards Mecca and hence indicating the direction of prayer.

Zakat: Almsgiving. A 'pillar of Islam'. Muslims are required to donate a portion of their wealth to suitable charitable causes each year. The money is used, for example, to support the poor and travellers, and to ransom prisoners.

Sawm: Fasting, especially fasting during Ramadan, which is a 'pillar of Islam'. Muslims, except for those for whom dispensations are made due to age or illness, fast from dawn until sunset during the Muslim month of Ramadan. This commemorates the first revelation of the *Qur'an* and ends with the 'Id al-Fitr (feast of the breaking of the fast).

Ramadan: The ninth month of the Muslim year, and the month during which the revelation of the *Qur'an* to Muhammad began. Muslims observe the *sawm* (fast) during Ramadan in commemoration of this.

Hajj: Arabic: 'greater pilgrimage to Mecca'. A 'pillar of Islam'; every Muslim is expected to undertake the *hajj* at least once during their lifetime, if they are able.

Jihad: Arabic: 'striving'. A struggle undertaken on the behalf of the religion. This struggle is intended to be undertaken against one's own inner sinfulness, and to defend the faith with speech, writing or (if absolutely necessary) military action.

3. *Zakat* (almsgiving): Muslims are required to donate a portion of their wealth to good causes each year. Good causes include supporting the poor and travellers, or ransoming prisoners.

4. *Sawm* (fasting): Muslims fast from dawn until sunset during the Muslim month of **Ramadan**; this includes abstinence from food, drink, smoking and sexual activity. The fast is observed by all except children, the old, and others who are excused for health reasons (including pregnant women and the sick). Travellers may postpone their fast. The Ramadan fast commemorates the first revelation of the *Qur'an* and ends with the 'Id al-Fitr (feast of the breaking of the fast) on the first day of the Muslim month of Shawwal.

5. *Hajj* (greater pilgrimage): At least once during their life, if possible, every Muslim should perform the *hajj*, the greater pilgrimage to Mecca. This takes place on the 1st–10th of the Muslim month of Dhu'l-Hijja and involves a number of ritual activities, including circumambulating the Ka'ba and throwing stones at pillars representing Satan. The *hajj* ends with the 'Id al-Adha (feast of sacrifice), which is celebrated across the Muslim world and commemorates Abraham's near-sacrifice of his son Ishmael (as opposed to Isaac in the Judaeo-Christian version). An important part of the celebrations is the slaughter of animals, with the meat being eaten and distributed to the poor.

An often-misunderstood concept in Islam is **jihad**, striving on behalf of the faith. The term is frequently translated as 'holy war', a translation that only conveys one aspect of the teaching. The *Qur'an* itself demonstrates a mixed attitude towards violence. A survey of its verses shows that at times the text seems to encourage forbearance from the Muslims in the face of opposition, while at other times it advocates warfare, albeit within limits (for examples see **Doc. 1.i**). Muslim scholars resolved the apparent contradictions in the text using theories of abrogation, whereby one teaching was seen as being superseded by another, and in the case of warfare they related the various teachings to various stages of the Prophet's career, during which he was initially encouraged to turn away from conflict, but was later allowed to engage in defensive and then offensive warfare as the ongoing conflict between Mecca and Medina developed. After the death of Muhammad, the Muslim campaigns out of the Arabian Peninsula were fought in the name of the military *jihad*. However, as the pace of conquest slowed, the obligation to fight for the faith became less of a universal concern and instead began to take the form of periodic raids made on enemy territory, often by volunteers living on the borders of the Muslim state. At the same time, under the influence of Muslim religious scholars, *jihad* teaching became increasingly sophisticated. Various regulations became formalized, including the prohibition of attacks on non-combatants or destruction of property, and guidelines on who was obliged to take part and under what circumstances. The former bipartite division of the world into **dar al-islam** (the Abode of Islam) and **dar al-harb** (the Abode of War) came to be nuanced with the addition of **dar al-'ahd** (the Abode of the Treaty) or **dar al-sulh** (the Abode of Peace), non-Muslim territory that remained autonomous provided that its people recognized Muslim authority and paid tributes. Peace agreements with states in the *dar al-harb* were also made, facilitating trade and diplomatic exchanges (Hillenbrand, 1999 a: 98). While fighters in the holy war were promised Paradise if they were killed in action, deliberate self-destruction was forbidden as part of the wider prohibition of suicide in Islam. In addition, by the twelfth century a number of Muslim religious scholars, particularly **Sufis** (Muslim mystics), had conceived a division of the *jihad* into *al-jihad al-akbar* (the greater *jihad*) and *al-jihad al-asghar* (the lesser *jihad*). The military *jihad* was viewed as the lesser of the two; the greater *jihad* was a spiritual struggle waged both externally – speaking or writing in defence of the faith – and above all internally – against one's own inner sinfulness – something that was seen as a prerequisite before one undertook the lesser *jihad*. Although the timing is a matter of some debate, the doctrine was probably crystallizing during the first decades of the crusading period (Morabia, 1993: 256–7 and 293–336; Cook, 2005: 32–48; Bonner, 2006: 13–14 and 169–70).

From the earliest days of Islam it was recognized that the Muslims could not realistically expect all people to convert to their faith. Indeed, the validity of some other religions is explicitly noted in the *Qur'an*. However, it was also recognized that there would be conflict with members of these other faiths; indeed, Muhammad himself had to deal with opposition from three of the Jewish tribes inhabiting Medina. The *Qur'an* again provided some guidance; for example, *Qur'an* 9: 29 states the following:

> Fight those who believe not in Allah nor in the Last Day, nor hold that forbidden which hath been forbidden by Allah and his Messenger, nor acknowledge the Religion of Truth, from among the People of the Book, until they pay the *jizya* with willing submission, and feel themselves subdued.
> [Doc. 1.i.g]

On the basis of passages like this the Muslim leadership gradually developed a policy stating that Christians and Jews could remain in the Muslim community, and enjoy rights of protection by the Muslim rulers, in exchange for acknowledging Muslim authority, paying a poll tax and accepting certain social restrictions such as wearing distinctive dress, not bearing arms or riding horses, and not building new places of worship. As the Muslim conquests proceeded, this policy was extended to followers of other faiths who could

Dar al-Islam: Arabic: 'the abode of Islam'. Territory where Islam is the dominant religion, and in particular the religion of the rulers.

Dar al-Harb: Arabic: 'the abode of war'. In Islamic law, *dar al-harb* is non-Muslim territory, against the inhabitants of which Muslims were expected to fight.

Dar al-'Ahd: See *Dar al-Sulh*.

Dar al-Sulh: Arabic: 'the abode of peace'. Also known as *dar al-'ahd* (the abode of the treaty), *dar al-sulh* is non-Muslim territory, the inhabitants of which are allowed to retain their autonomy, provided that they pay tribute and recognize Muslim authority.

Sufi: A Muslim mystic. Sufis seek to gain a direct, higher-state experience of God through a variety of means, including asceticism and group rituals involving prayer, chanting, music or dance.

Jizya: Poll tax paid by non-Muslims living in Muslim territory.

not practically be expected to convert *en masse* to Islam. Non-Muslims under Muslim rule became known as *ahl al-dhimma* (the People of the Pact) or *dhimmis*. The enforcement of these social restrictions on *dhimmis* was uneven, and treatment of them was highly variable; at times non-Muslims rose to high ranks within Muslim courts or were even involved in the defence of cities against other Muslims or non-Muslims; at other times they suffered persecution or came under intense pressure to convert or emigrate.

Ithna 'Ashari Shi'ism: See *Twelver Shi'ism*.

Twelver Shi'ism: Forming the majority of the Shi'ites in the world today, Twelver Shi'ites maintain that history has witnessed a line of 12 *imams*, the last of whom has entered 'greater concealment' and will return as the *mahdi* at the end of time.

Imam: At the basic level, the Arabic term for a prayer-leader. It is also the term used to refer to the spiritual leader of the Muslim community, especially in Shi'ite Islam, where the identities and precise attributes of the *imams* are often defining features of each different strand of Shi'ism.

Mahdi: In both Sunni and Shi'ite Islam, a messianic figure who will return to restore truth and justice. Belief in the *mahdi* is particularly prominent in Twelver Shi'ism, where he is identified as the Twelfth *imam* Muhammad al-Muntazar, who is regarded as currently being in 'greater concealment'.

Fatimids: Isma'ili Shi'ite dynasty of caliphs. The Fatimids first established themselves in North Africa in 910, then in Egypt in 969, from the second of which they reigned until the abolition of their caliphate by Saladin in 1171.

SUNNIS AND SHI'ITES

Although most Muslims accepted the authority of the Umayyad caliphs after the death of 'Ali ibn Abi Talib in 661, many of his supporters continued to advocate for the right of the family of the Prophet, as represented by the line of 'Ali, to hold the caliphate, and they and their successors proved to be an ongoing source of opposition to the caliphs in the following centuries. They became known as *shi'at 'Ali* (the party of 'Ali), or Shi'ites. Over time the majority of Muslims became known as Sunnis, a word deriving from the Sunna, a term used to refer to the sayings and actions of the Prophet and his Companions (as depicted in the *hadith*) that act as a guide to Muslim conduct. As the centuries passed various different Shi'ite movements developed, each with its own distinctive theology and practices. Three were particularly prominent in the Levant on the eve of the First Crusade:

1. The ***ithna 'asharis*** (Twelvers, Imamis): The **Twelver Shi'ites** are so called because they acknowledge a dynasty of 12 *imams* (divinely inspired leaders; the word is also used among Muslims in general to mean a prayer-leader), of whom 'Ali was the first. Even though these *imams* did not hold political leadership in the Muslim world, they were still seen by their supporters as being the rightful leaders of the Muslim community. According to Twelver belief, in the tenth century the last of these *imams* went into 'greater concealment', from which he will return as the **mahdi** ('the rightly guided', a Messianic figure) at the end of time to restore peace and justice. On the eve of the Crusades Twelver Shi'ism was popular among both the Bedouin of the Levant and important members of the community in Aleppo.

2. The **Fatimids**: In the eighth century a major split occurred within Shi'ism as a result of the death of the *imam* Ja'far al-Sadiq (d. 765). Ja'far's son Isma'il, whom Ja'far had designated as his successor, had predeceased him, so the Shi'ites were unsure who their next *imam* should be. The group who would become the Twelvers claimed that the rightful *imam* after Ja'far was Isma'il's brother Musa al-Kazim (d. 799), but not all agreed. Some maintained

that Isma'il's son, Muhammad, was the rightful *imam* after Ja'far; even though Muhammad ibn Isma'il had also appeared to die, he had in fact been hidden by God and would eventually return as the *mahdi*. For these Shi'ites, who became known as Isma'ilis, Muhammad ibn Isma'il was the seventh *imam*, and so they were also referred to pejoratively by their opponents as 'Seveners'. The Isma'ilis gradually transformed into a hierarchical and highly secretive movement, with teachings that emphasized inner, hidden truths found in Islamic texts that were only taught to those who had attained an appropriate rank. They were very active as missionaries and attracted many converts.

In 910 an Isma'ili leader called 'Abd Allah (or 'Ubayd Allah) took control of Qayrawan, in modern-day Tunisia. 'Abd Allah was regarded by his supporters as the rightful Isma'ili *imam* and became the first caliph of a new, rival caliphate, reigning with the significant title of al-Mahdi (r. 910–34). The dynasty that he founded became known as the Fatimids, after Fatima, the daughter of the Prophet and wife of 'Ali ibn Abi Talib. The Fatimids quickly established a strong presence in North Africa, then in 969 they took control of Egypt. They built a new city, Cairo, which became the seat of the Fatimid caliphs in 973, and then concentrated their efforts on expanding their influence in the Holy Land, Syria and Arabia. In the meantime they allowed North Africa to slip from their control into the hands of the family who had formerly governed it on their behalf. Possibly the best known of the Fatimid caliphs was al-Hakim bi-Amr Allah (r. 996–1021), who is depicted by non-Fatimid sources as a dangerous eccentric. Al-Hakim caused resentment among some western Europeans after he ordered the destruction of the Church of the Holy Sepulchre in 1009, though this did not transform into a military response at the time [**Doc. 2**].

3. The **Nizaris**: In 1090 an Isma'ili missionary of Persian origin named Hasan-i Sabbah took control of the fortress of Alamut, to the south of the Caspian Sea. From there he and his supporters began a campaign of political assassination, aimed in the first instance at the Seljuks. Hasan and his followers became known by their critics as the *hashishiyya* ('hashish-users', or 'low-life'). This term, in its meaning of 'hashish-users', led to the circulation in medieval Europe of exotic tales of their use of this substance in training or operations, as well as forming the origin of the term '**Assassins**' used by modern historians to refer to the movement and in more general parlance to refer to killers (Daftary, 1994: 89–94). Soon after, at the time of the death of the Fatimid caliph al-Mustansir (r. 1036–94), the heir apparent to al-Mustansir's throne was the caliph's son Nizar. However, the caliph's vizier (deputy of the ruler), al-Afdal Shahanshah, instead installed Nizar's younger and easier to manipulate

Nizaris: Isma'ili Shi'ite movement that split from the Fatimids in 1094. In the twelfth and thirteenth centuries the Nizaris engaged in a programme of political assassination, as a result of which they are also sometimes referred to as the Assassins.

Assassins: See *Nizaris*.

brother, al-Musta'li (r. 1094–1101). Nizar was killed in the conflict that followed, but Hasan-i Sabbah and his followers maintained that Nizar's son had been brought to Alamut. Thus they now claimed to have the rightful caliph and *imam* in their midst. Hasan and his successors ruled as the deputies of the *imam*, who was never seen. In the meantime they extended their territory until they held a network of castles in Persia and Syria. The Assassins would prove to be a force with which the various other political factions in the Levant would have to come to terms as the period of the Crusades progressed.

THE FRANKS THROUGH MUSLIM EYES BEFORE 1096

A survey of the Muslim sources for the period before the Crusades suggests that the Muslims of the Levant knew very little about the Franks. Mentions of them in the Muslim sources are sporadic, and the most helpful passages tend to come from the Muslim tradition of geographical writing. As indicated previously, before the Crusades the Muslim writers use the term *ifranj* to refer principally to the inhabitants of the region roughly corresponding to the Frankish empire of Charlemagne, and the Frankish capital is variously identified as Rome or Paris. The Franks themselves are depicted as warlike and violent, and are sometimes described as a particularly unified people, while at other times they are represented as being divided and feuding with one another. At the same time, the Franks have a somewhat blurry relationship with the Byzantines, who are sometimes identified as their neighbours, and at other times seen as their overlords, with Frankish lands being part of the Byzantine Empire. Most sources agree that the Franks and the Byzantines have a shared religion, Christianity (Hillenbrand, 1999 a: 267–74; Christie, 1999: 10–27).

This image of ignorance is open to question, however. It is apparent from the Muslim sources that Frankish merchants and pilgrims visited Muslim lands, and we also know that Franks served in the Byzantine armies as mercenaries. We also have evidence of embassies exchanged between Frankish and Muslim rulers. Perhaps most telling are the two different accounts of the Franks given by the traveller and geographer al-Mas'udi (d. 956). In one of his works, *Muruj al-Dhahab wa-Ma'adin al-Jawhar* (Meadows of Gold and Mines of Gemstone; 1965–79), he gives us an account of the Franks that is unusually well informed, even to the point of providing a list of the Frankish kings [**Doc. 3.i**]. However, in another of his works, *Kitab al-Tanbih wa-l-Ishraf* (The Book of Instruction and Supervision; 1894), he presents an account that gives a radically different depiction of the Franks, presenting a rather

Ifranj: Arabic: 'Franks'. The term used by the Muslim sources to refer to the Europeans.

fanciful image of them as sluggish, blue-skinned brutes [**Doc. 3.ii**]. Given that the *Kitab al-Tanbih* was written after the *Muruj*, it would be nonsensical to suggest that al-Mas'udi's knowledge of the Franks got worse. Instead, it would seem that al-Mas'udi wished to convey a sense of Muslim superiority over the uncivilized, non-Muslim barbarians, and to do this he exploited stereotypes of bestial nature and religious inferiority through his presentation of the Franks. Al-Mas'udi's position is in some ways a salutary reminder for us of the wider tendency of medieval sources to privilege moral messages over factual accuracy, as well as the fact that most of the Muslim writers were first and foremost religiously trained scholars, which naturally affected the emphasis of their literary output. Thus before the Crusades the Franks often only appear in Muslim sources when including them serves the agendas of the writers, and such appearances are sparse enough to suggest a level of ignorance that may actually be over-estimated.

THE MUSLIM LEVANT ON THE EVE OF THE CRUSADES

In the wake of the aforementioned Seljuk takeover of Baghdad, as the Seljuks and their allies spread their influence further west, the area known to Muslim writers as **Bilad al-Sham** (or simply **al-Sham**, roughly corresponding to modern Syria, Lebanon, Jordan, Israel, the Palestinian autonomous areas and the edge of south-east Turkey) became contested between the Seljuks and the Fatimids. It is important to note that this conflict had religious as well as political dimensions. This was not merely a conflict over territory fought between two Muslim powers. The Seljuks, as Sunnis, sought to present themselves as the defenders and promoters of the true faith against dangerous heretics who had taken control of a disturbingly large amount of territory and posed a real threat to the 'Abbasid caliphate; indeed, a pro-Fatimid general had briefly taken control of Baghdad, imprisoning the 'Abbasid caliph, in 1057–58. The Fatimids, in the meantime, saw *themselves* as the representatives of the true line of caliphs, and saw the Seljuks as supporting a heretical pretender whose ancestors had usurped power in the eighth century. Thus the Levant was the site of a struggle between two powers, each of which regarded the other as a legitimate target of holy war fought on behalf of Islam.

The regional instability resulting from this conflict was exacerbated when a number of strong leaders died at the end of the eleventh century. In 1092, the famous Seljuk vizier Nizam al-Mulk was killed by the Assassins as their first high-profile 'hit'. His death was followed about a month later by that of Malik-Shah (r. 1073–92), the son and successor of the Great Seljuk sultan Alp-Arslan; Malik-Shah's death marked the end of Seljuk unity, and as the

Bilad al-Sham: Arabic: 'the country of Syria'. The term used in the Arabic sources to refer to, approximately, modern Syria, Lebanon, Jordan, Israel, the Palestinian autonomous areas and the edge of south-eastern Turkey. Sometimes the region is simply referred to as *al-Sham*.

Al-Sham: See *Bilad al-Sham*.

various Seljuk claimants to the sultan's throne fought with each other, the Great Seljuk state fragmented. The major cities of Syria and the Holy Land passed into the hands of either the governors who had been appointed to them, who set up their own dynasties there, or young Seljuk princes whose affairs were overseen by military regents, known as **atabegs**, some of whom subsequently usurped the thrones of their charges. At the time the Seljuk Sultanate of *Rum* was also not an entirely secure realm; its rulers shared Asia Minor with a Turkmen dynasty, the Danishmendids, who had established themselves in the region in the wake of Manzikert, and with whom the Seljuks of *Rum* had mixed relations.

Atabeg: Turkish: 'father-lord'. *Atabegs* were military regents, ruling on the behalf of a (usually underage) Seljuk prince. They were normally originally *mamluks*. Needless to say, in a significant number of cases *atabegs* usurped power from their charges.

The power vacuum also extended to Egypt. In the mid-eleventh century factional fighting within the Fatimid army had caused devastation in Cairo and the countryside. Some degree of order was restored in 1074 when the Fatimid caliph al-Mustansir called in the governor of Palestine, Badr al-Jamali, to be his new vizier, but in the process of taking firm control Badr al-Jamali reduced the caliph to an effective figurehead like his 'Abbasid rival. Both Badr al-Jamali and al-Mustansir died in 1094, and one of the first actions of Badr al-Jamali's son and successor, al-Afdal Shahanshah, was to set aside the heir apparent, Nizar, in favour of the latter's younger brother al-Musta'li, as described above. This schism within the Fatimid caliphate only further damaged the power of the state. The instability in Egypt was also exacerbated by repeated outbreaks of plague in the country at the turn of the twelfth century (Hillenbrand, 1999 a: 37–8).

In our survey of the Muslim Levant it is also important to remember that the region was one in which populations were ruled by people who were in the minority, and often ethnically or religiously different from them. In Egypt, the Fatimids, who were **Isma'ili Shi'ites**, ruled over a population that was mostly Sunni Muslim, Christian or Jewish. The Fatimid armies, in the meantime, consisted of a mix of Nubians, Berbers, Turks and Armenians, all of whom had been imported at one point or another and thus were foreigners in the eyes of the Egyptian population. The Sunni Muslim Turkish Seljuks, in the meantime, based their power above all on Turkish *mamluk* and Turkmen troops, using them to maintain power over a population that in the Levant consisted largely of Sunni and Shi'ite Muslims, Christians and Jews from a wide range of ethnicities including Turks, Kurds and Arabs. In taxing their territory the Seljuks made use of a system inherited from the Buyids, in which a Muslim emir would be assigned an **iqta'**, the right to collect taxes from a particular area of land in return for military service from himself and his retinue. The result of this was that the populations of areas assigned as *iqta's* would have mixed feelings towards their overlords, who would on the one hand tax them heavily but on the other provide them with security. Given the fact that in both Seljuk and Fatimid territory the

Isma'ili Shi'ism: Isma'ili Shi'ites support Muhammad ibn Isma'il's claim to be the rightful *imam* of the Muslim world. At the time of the Crusades, the Isma'ilis were a hierarchical, secretive movement.

Iqta': Arabic: 'assignment'. A grant to an emir of the right to collect taxes from a particular area of land, given in return for a promise of military service.

populations often had religious or ethnic affiliations that differed from those of their rulers, concerns about security and levels of taxation probably had the most impact on the loyalties that the common people would feel towards them. This meant that the amount of support that any given ruler could expect from the majority population of the territory that he controlled was limited.

Given the prevailing instability in the Levant on the eve of the Crusades, coming just as the Muslim calendar was approaching the year 500 (1106–7), it is not surprising that we see some hints of apocalyptic sentiment among the Muslims of the time. Some saw in astral phenomena indications of impending misfortune; some felt that the Day of Judgement was approaching; and others awaited the appearance of a figure who would renew the faith (Hillenbrand, 1999 a: 36–7). It was into this unstable social, religious and political environment that the crusaders would make a startling intrusion.

FURTHER READING

Not surprisingly, given that this chapter covers a historical period of almost 500 years, the scholarly literature for the topics that we have addressed in this chapter is plentiful and wide-ranging. A clear and accessible overview of the Muslim faith in both its historical and modern forms is Andrew Rippin's *Muslims: Their Religious Beliefs and Practices* (2011). On *jihad* in particular, see David Cook, *Understanding Jihad* (2005) and Michael Bonner, *Jihad in Islamic History: Doctrines and Practice* (2006). On Shi'ism, the classic overview is Heinz Halm's *Shiism* (1992), but see also Moojan Momen's *An Introduction to Shi'i Islam: The History and Doctrines of Twelver Shi'ism* (1985) and two works by Farhad Daftary: *The Assassin Legends: Myths of the Isma'ilis* (1994) and *The Isma'ilis: Their History and Doctrines* (1990). For the history of the period in general, readers may wish to consult Vernon O. Egger's *A History of the Muslim World to 1405* (2004) or, for a more detailed account, Hugh Kennedy's *The Prophet and the Age of the Caliphates: The Islamic Near East from the Sixth to the Eleventh Century* (2004). For more on the Middle East immediately before the Crusades, see, in addition to Carole Hillenbrand's *The Crusades: Islamic Perspectives* (1999 a), Taef Kamal el-Azhari's *The Saljuqs of Syria during the Crusades, 463–549 A.H./1070–1154 A.D.* (1997); and David Morgan's *Medieval Persia, 1040–1797* (1988).

3

The First Crusade and the Muslim response, 1095–1146

I n this chapter we will examine Muslim reactions to the arrival of the First Crusade and the subsequent establishment of the four Latin states in the Levant. In the process we will discuss the tension between Muslim religious ideology and realpolitik that affected the development of the Muslim counter-crusade, before considering the role played in the latter by 'Imad al-Din Zangi (r. 1127–46), regarded by both contemporaries and some later scholars as the first great leader in the military *jihad* against the Franks.

CHRONOLOGICAL OVERVIEW

According to the Aleppine chronicler al-'Azimi (d. after 1161), the first inkling that the Muslims of the Levant had of the arrival of the First Crusade was when the Byzantine emperor Alexios Komnenos (r. 1081–1118) wrote to the Muslims in 1096 to inform them of the impending arrival of the Franks (al-'Azimi, 1984: 358). Whatever the truth of this, the first major encounters that took place between Muslims and crusaders occurred when the Seljuk Sultanate of *Rum* was repeatedly raided by the forces of the People's Crusade (or Peasants' Crusade) in the autumn of 1096. The Seljuks of *Rum* dispatched them easily and without mercy, wiping most of them out in less than a month.

The Seljuk sultan of *Rum*, Kilij-Arslan I (r. 1092–1107) may have considered the People's Crusade to be simply a continuation of previous Byzantine raids into his territory. Franks had, after all, served in the Byzantine armies before. Thus he may have under-estimated the magnitude of the threat when the major armies of the First Crusade began to gather at Constantinople in late 1096 and early 1097. In any case, he was unable to defeat this second wave of crusaders in battle when they advanced on his capital of Nicaea, and the city fell to them in June 1097. Two more Seljuk defeats followed, at Dorylaeum (Eskişehir) and Heraclea (Ereğli), and then the crusaders fought their way to Antioch, besieging it in October 1097. The city fell to the crusaders in June 1098, and they subsequently beat off an army led by Kerbogha, the *atabeg* of Mosul (r. 1095–1102). In the meantime, a contingent of crusaders under Baldwin of Boulogne had already taken control of the Armenian city of Edessa (Urfa) in March 1098, inaugurating the first Latin Christian state in the Levant. Antioch, now the second of the Latin states, came under the control of Bohemond of Taranto (r. 1098–1111). In December 1098 the crusaders took Ma'arrat al-Nu'man, and the Muslim sources emphasize the fact that the Franks slaughtered many of its people. At the same time it is striking that they do not mention the reports of cannibalism found in European sources, which one might expect to be included in the Muslim sources' portrayals of the Franks if they had been aware of them (see, for example, Ibn al-Athir, 2006: 17–18). The psychological effect of the conquest of Ma'arrat al-Nu'man was very great, however, and it is notable that a number of Muslim rulers came to terms with the crusaders as they continued their march south towards Jerusalem.

By the time that the crusaders reached it in June 1099, Jerusalem was in Fatimid hands, having been taken by them from its Seljuk-appointed Turkmen ruler the previous year. Fatimid tenure of the city was brief; it fell on 15 July, after a crusader siege lasting little more than a month. Both the European and the Muslim sources emphasize the magnitude of the massacre of Muslims and Jews alike that took place at the holy city after the crusaders broke through the walls (for two Muslim accounts, see **Doc. 4**). The Fatimids sent an army to rescue the city, but it was defeated at Ascalon in August 1099. Jerusalem soon became the capital of a Frankish kingdom, and over the years that followed the crusaders continued to expand their holdings in the Levant, including setting up their fourth state, the County of Tripoli, in 1109.

Many Muslims reacted to the Frankish invasion with shock and outrage, and poets and preachers issued emotional calls to both the local rulers in the Levant and the Great Seljuk sultan of the east for aid against the European interlopers. While the Egyptians sought to mount some opposition to the crusader expansion, such calls went mostly unheeded by the Muslim rulers in *Bilad al-Sham*, many of whom quickly realized that they could form alliances with the Frankish rulers against their Muslim or Frankish rivals. However, after the fall of Tripoli the Great Seljuk sultan Muhammad (r. 1105–18) was moved to act. Between 1110 and 1115 a number of expeditions were launched against the Franks at his direction. These were not received favourably by the Muslim rulers in the Levant, who probably feared a re-assertion of Great Seljuk power in the region, and after the last expedition was opposed by a coalition of Frankish and Muslim rulers and defeated by a Frankish army from Antioch at Danith in September 1115, the sultan Muhammad refocused his attention east, abandoning the Levant to its fate.

The year 1119 witnessed the first major Muslim victory against the Franks when the Turkmen ruler of Mardin, Ilghazi (r. 1108 or 1109–22) defeated and killed Roger of Salerno, the regent of Antioch (r. 1113–19), at the Battle at Balat, a Frankish loss that was so complete and bloody that it became known to the Latin chroniclers as *Ager Sanguinis* (the Field of Blood). Ilghazi did not capitalize on his success, however, and he died in 1122. It fell to others, the best known of whom is the ruler of Mosul, 'Imad al-Din Zangi (r. 1127–46), to pursue the war against the Franks. Zangi spent much of his time pursuing his own political ambitions in the Levant and Iraq, including repeatedly attempting to take control of Damascus, but he also prosecuted periodic campaigns against the Franks. Most famously, towards the end of 1144 he took advantage of the fact that Joscelin II of Edessa had been called away from his capital, conquering the city on 24 December and thus bringing the first of the capitals of the crusader states under Muslim control. Zangi himself died two years later, assassinated in September 1146; according to some sources, he was killed by a Frankish slave while he lay incapacitated by over-indulgence in alcohol. His territories were divided between his sons, principally between Sayf al-Din Ghazi (r. 1146–49), who received Mosul and his father's lands in the east, and Nur al-Din Mahmud (r. 1146–74), who received Aleppo and his father's holdings in *Bilad al-Sham*.

THE PROBLEM OF THE SOURCES

Gaining insight into Muslim reactions to the First Crusade is difficult, primarily due to the distribution of the sources and the agendas that affect their works. The earliest major chronicles, by Ibn al-Qalanisi and al-'Azimi, were written decades after the First Crusade and also well after Zangi's conquest of Edessa, when counter-crusading sentiment was much more prominent in the Levantine region than it had been at the time. The few sources that date from the period between the First Crusade and the conquest of Edessa consist of some works by professional poets (for examples, see **Doc. 5**) and, most importantly, a treatise on *jihad* by a Damascene religious scholar named 'Ali ibn Tahir al-Sulami (d. 1106) [**Doc. 6**]. The poets' works include laments for the fall of Jerusalem, emotional calls for the counter-crusade and above all panegyrics intended to flatter their patrons and ensure that they continued to support them. Al-Sulami's work, entitled *Kitab al-Jihad* (the Book of the *Jihad*) is intended first and foremost as a call to the rulers of *Bilad al-Sham* in general, and Damascus in particular, to unite and engage in the *jihad* against the crusaders. Al-Sulami draws on the *Qur'an* and *hadith* to provide precedents that encourage his audience (al-Sulami's work was composed in public and subsequently read aloud at public gatherings) to wage the military *jihad* against the Franks; he lays out practical and spiritual regulations regarding how the *jihad* should be conducted; and he severely criticizes rulers who neglect to engage in the holy war. Thus the earliest sources for the period give us some insight into how the Frankish attacks were perceived among some poets and religious scholars, but these works are far less useful in helping us understand the reactions of the politico-military elites, who were most able to mount opposition to the crusaders. Instead we are forced to rely on the testimonies of later writers; this poses significant problems when we seek to trace the origins of the Muslim counter-crusade, since these later writers were strongly aware of their audiences and the impact that their works might have upon them. This had a number of effects on their works, the most important of which, as we have indicated previously, is that later writers, many of whom were religious scholars, used their works as a means by which to teach moral lessons. Such agendas are as present in works that a modern reader might expect to be objective (such as chronicles) as they are in works that adopt a more explicitly pietistic stance. Thus, for example, later chroniclers have a tendency to attribute motives of *jihad* to any figure who went out to fight against the first crusaders (see for example **Doc. 4.i**), regardless of whether or not this was actually the reason for the given individual's actions; in doing so, they seek to teach their audiences the value of the *jihad* and encourage them to take part in it. Being forced to read these works through their pietistic lenses, the modern historian finds it difficult to tell to what extent the facts have been skewed to fit the writer's agenda, and hence treats the sources with great scepticism.

MUSLIM VIEWS OF THE CRUSADERS' MOTIVES

Why did the crusaders come? The Muslim sources express what seems to be a considerable amount of confusion regarding the motives of the Franks. Our earliest datable source, the *Kitab al-Jihad* of al-Sulami, which was composed in 1105, provides us with the most accurate assessment of the Franks' intentions, noting that they were fighting a *jihad*, sought to take control of Muslim territory and had the ultimate objective of Jerusalem [**Doc. 6**]. Al-Sulami also sees their campaign as part of a wider western Christian offensive against Muslim lands that had already manifested itself in the form of the *reconquista* in Spain and the Norman conquest of Sicily, a claim that Paul E. Chevedden has recently argued we should take seriously, although the question remains debated (2008: *passim*). Al-Sulami presents the Franks as having been surprised by the extent of their success, but also encouraged, as a result of the reluctance of Muslim leaders to engage them in battle, to pursue even greater destruction and material and territorial gains in the region. At the same time al-Sulami also sees the Frankish conquest in teleological terms, in that he presents it as a punishment for Muslim behaviour and a test from God, intended to reveal which of the Muslims will return to righteousness and become steadfast defenders of their faith, and which will not. Divine support and both earthly and spiritual rewards, including the spoils of war, divine approval and a place in the heaven reserved for martyrs, are offered to those who return to right conduct and undertake the *jihad*, while those who do not are criticized for their neglect and threatened with the fires of Hell (Christie, 2007 b: *passim*; for some elements of this discussion, see **Doc. 6**). Elsewhere in his work al-Sulami also suggests that the Franks have been sent to fulfil a prophecy whereby a group of Muslims will re-conquer Jerusalem, then go on to take Constantinople and Rome (Christie, 2007 a: *passim*). Thus the Franks are ultimately tools of the divine, intended to bring the Muslims back to good conduct and provide opportunities for them to demonstrate their piety and reap the benefits offered.

Returning more directly to the question of the Franks' motives, al-Sulami's ideas are recalled in the views of other Muslim sources. His view that the crusader conquests in the Levant formed part of a wider offensive is echoed in the works of a number of other writers (Hillenbrand, 1999 a: 51–4). His comments on the destructive tendencies of the Franks and his critique of the laggardness of Muslim rulers are paralleled in the work of the Syrian poet Ibn al-Khayyat (d. 1120s) [**Doc. 5.i.b**]. Meanwhile, his views on the ongoing territorial and material ambitions of the enemy resonate with comments made by Usama ibn Munqidh, who suggests that continued crusader activity was motivated by the lure of Baghdad [**Doc. 5.iii**]. Naturally, we should not assume that these later writers were drawing specifically on the work of al-Sulami; it is far more likely that all of the authors, including al-Sulami, drew on a common pool of ideas that were circulating at the time. By the same token, al-Sulami's views do not represent the sum total of suggestions that were made regarding the crusaders' motives. Al-'Azimi suggests that the Frankish attack was in fact undertaken in revenge for the killing of Frankish and Byzantine pilgrims who sought to visit Jerusalem [**Doc. 5.ii**]. Meanwhile, an anonymous poet quoted by the later historian Ibn Taghri Birdi (c. 1410–70) depicts the Frankish offensive as an attempt to propagate an impure, debased form of Christianity by force [**Doc. 5.i.c**]. Thus Muslim writers ascribed a wide range of motives to the crusaders, ranging from desire for plunder and an urge to spread Christianity to a simple love of violence.

It is striking that of all these sources, only al-Sulami uses the term '*jihad*' to describe the crusaders' activities, thus stating that they are conducting a form of religious warfare analogous to the military *jihad* of the Muslims.

How can this be explained? Was al-Sulami the only Muslim writer of the early twelfth century who knew that the crusaders were fighting an 'official' holy war? It is clear that as the twelfth century progressed, the Muslims became increasingly aware of a religious motivation behind the Franks' activities (Kedar, 1996: 347–50), but it is only in the latter half of the century that we see other Muslim writers using the same word to describe the crusaders' activities; one particularly striking example is found in the universal chronicle of the Mosuli historian Ibn al-Athir (1160–1233) [**Doc. 5.iv**]. We might be tempted to see al-Sulami as being unusually perceptive for his time, with it taking a long time before another Muslim author had the same insight, but Ibn al-Athir's depiction of the Frankish *jihad* suggests a different inter-pretation. In his account the crusaders are depicted as placing greater value on glory, material gain and political concerns than on pious recovery of the holy city; thus the Frankish *jihad* is a debased one that would definitely not meet with the approval of his Muslim readers. In this way Ibn al-Athir is careful to devalue the crusade even as he uses the word '*jihad*' to refer to it. This suggests that Muslim writers who became aware of the crusade doctrine wrestled with the problem of describing it on the one hand but also avoiding granting it any legitimacy on the other. It is thus possible that the absence of the term '*jihad*' in earlier Muslim sources stems from a desire to avoid using a word that might suggest that the crusaders' operations were in some way legitimate; referring to the crusaders' activities as a Christian equivalent of the Muslim *jihad* would make it harder to represent them as unequivocally malicious and hence valid targets for the Muslim counter-crusade (Christie, 2006: 66–70).

Ibn al-Athir actually provides two possible reasons for the arrival of the crusaders in the Levant, of which the debased *jihad* referred to above is the first. He also suggests that the Franks attacked the region because they were invited to by the Fatimids [**Doc. 5.iv**]. Ibn al-Athir, as a Sunni Muslim, saw the Fatimids as heretics and their claims to the caliphate as invalid, so he calls them merely 'the 'Alid rulers of Egypt'. He suggests that the Fatimids, intimidated by the Seljuks, invited the Franks to take control of Syria, thus driving a wedge between them and their Sunni enemies. It might be tempting to write off Ibn al-Athir's account as a slur cast against the Egyptians, but as Carole Hillenbrand has argued, it is possible that the Fatimids did indeed seek to make an alliance with the Byzantines and crusaders against their Seljuk rivals. The Fatimid conquest of Jerusalem in 1098, while their enemies were distracted by the crusaders to the north, would make particular sense if one were to assume that they expected the Franks to leave it in their hands; al-'Azimi's account of the letter sent in 1096 by the Byzantine emperor to the (unspecified) Muslims could be seen, then, as a record of communication between the Fatimids and the Byzantines. However, if the Fatimids had any such hopes, they were dashed when it became apparent that the crusade's ultimate target was the holy city, and thus we see them quickly coming into conflict with the crusaders afterwards (Hillenbrand, 1999 a: 44–7).

THE FIRST SIGNS OF THE COUNTER-CRUSADE

The possible Fatimid collaboration with the Franks, mentioned above, in some ways epitomizes the major factor that hindered the prompt development of widespread counter-crusading sentiment among the Muslims of the Levant. Many Muslim rulers were more interested in pursuing their political and territorial ambitions at the expense of other rulers, and it soon became apparent that many Frankish leaders were only too willing to take part in such alliances. Thus the crusaders swiftly became enmeshed in a political environment where realpolitik often trumped religious or political scruples about dealing with the enemy. The failure of the counter-crusading expeditions in 1110–15 authorized by the Great Seljuk sultan Muhammad was ultimately due to political concerns; the Muslim rulers of *Bilad al-Sham* preferred independence and alliances with non-Muslims to having to accept the re-imposition of Seljuk authority that would come with the sultan's aid.

Sultan Muhammad's expeditions were prompted by public unrest in Baghdad in the form of impassioned calls to the military *jihad* against the Franks. If the later sources are to be believed, such appeals began in 1098, *before* the fall of Jerusalem to the crusaders, and they reached their height in 1111, when a group of religious scholars, Sufis and merchants from Aleppo, led by a descendant of the Prophet, disrupted Friday prayers in both the Seljuk sultan's mosque and the caliphal mosque, thus challenging both the secular and the spiritual leaders of the Sunni Muslim community to fulfil their duty as defenders of the faith (Ibn al-Jawzi, 1992: Vol. 17, p. 43; Ibn al-Qalanisi, 1983: 276–7; Hillenbrand, 1999 a: 79). As we saw previously, the sultan had already begun to authorize campaigns against the Franks by this time, but the protests of 1111 proved a particular spur to these, even though the opposition of the rulers of *Bilad al-Sham* to interference from the sultan ultimately led to their failure.

In the meantime, calls to the *jihad* against the Franks were also being made within the Levant itself. As indicated above, al-Sulami made one such call in 1105, seeking to provoke, and if necessary shame, the local rulers of the region into taking up arms against the crusaders. While al-Sulami's call was directed first and foremost at the politico-military elite who could undertake a military response to the Franks, he also saw the defensive *jihad* as an obligation that was incumbent on all Muslims who were free, adult, male and sane. In line with earlier tradition, he presented the *jihad* as both a *fard 'ayn* (individual obligation) and *fard kifaya* (obligation of sufficiency). In other words, the duty was imposed on all eligible Muslims until enough undertook it to ensure its success. At the same time, the political leaders of the day were required to provide leadership in the endeavour, making them all the more worthy of criticism for their neglect (Christie, 2007 b: 4–6). Al-Sulami urged his listeners to prioritize the greater *jihad* against the self over the lesser *jihad* against the enemy, seeing the former as a prerequisite for the latter [**Doc. 6**]. In this way he reflected contemporary developments in *jihad* teachings; indeed, he may well have met and been influenced by the great Muslim theologian Abu Hamid Muhammad ibn Muhammad al-Ghazali (d. 1111), one of the principal thinkers involved in the development of the doctrine of greater and lesser *jihad*, who visited Damascus in 1095–96 (Christie, 2007 b: 5–6 and 10–11).

As we have previously noted, al-Sulami presented a number of motivations to his listeners; thus at times we find him describing the delights of Paradise to his listeners in glowing terms, while at other times he provides lengthy, workmanlike discussions of how plunder should be distributed. This is in some ways symptomatic of the wider multi-faceted nature of the text, which is simultaneously an anthology of sections from the *Qur'an* and *hadith*, a sermon, a legal text on *jihad*, a *fada'il* work on Jerusalem and Damascus, a grammatical treatise and a collection of relevant poetic quotations. As indicated in our Introduction, knowledge of a wide range of literature and the ability to deploy it appropriately were marks of a cultivated Muslim.

Fada'il: Arabic: 'merits'. Texts praising the merits of their subjects. Muslim writers wrote *fada'il* works on a range of topics, including places (e.g. Damascus, Jerusalem) and activities (e.g. *jihad*).

It is not clear how much of an impact al-Sulami made on his listeners or his wider society. The part of al-Sulami's work that deals most explicitly with the Franks was composed in public in May–June 1105. It is striking that in October–November of the same year the *atabeg* of Damascus, Zahir al-Din Tughtigin (r. 1105–28) fought the Franks and took strongholds that they were building near Damascus; then in 1106 he took Busra al-Sham, some 70 miles south of Damascus, from political rivals who had previously formed an alliance with the Franks against him. However, we should be wary of assuming that Tughtigin's activities were a response to calls from al-Sulami and others like him; it is far more likely that Tughtigin undertook these operations to further his own political ambitions, although if they helped to assuage public opinion in Damascus, that would also have been of benefit to him. Thus it is more likely that, as Hillenbrand asserts, al-Sulami's ideas circulated among the religious scholars of the region but did not provoke an immediate reaction from its political leaders (Hillenbrand, 1999 a: 108).

Hillenbrand sees the Battle of Balat in 1119 as a marker for growth in Muslim enthusiasm for the *jihad* against the Franks. According to the Aleppine

Qadi: A judge or magistrate, versed in Islamic law. *Qadis* were primarily expected to apply the existing body of legal rulings to cases that needed to be considered, rather than to develop new rulings through delivering legal opinions. The latter was the function of legal experts known as *muftis*.

historian Kamal al-Din ibn al-'Adim (1192–1262), present at the battle was the influential Twelver Shi'ite **qadi** (judge) of Aleppo, Ibn al-Khashshab (d. 1133 or 1134). Before the fighting began, he preached to Ilghazi's troops from his saddle, holding a spear and urging them to fight (Ibn al-'Adim, 1951–68: Vol. 2, pp. 188–9). Engagement by religious scholars in the military *jihad* had a long pedigree by this time. Some of the earliest writers on *jihad*, such as 'Abd Allah ibn al-Mubarak (d. 797) and Ibrahim ibn Muhammad al-Fazari (d. 802 or later) were enthusiastic fighters on the Muslim–Byzantine frontier (Bonner, 1996: 109–25). The presence of a religious scholar seems to have generated some initial reservations among Ilghazi's troops at Balat, but his eloquence apparently moved his listeners to tears. Admittedly, this reaction to preaching is a frequent topos in such accounts, but we might suggest, assuming that we can at least partially trust Ibn al-'Adim's account, that the completeness of the Muslim victory at least resulted to a certain extent from the enthusiasm that Ibn al-Khashshab generated with his preaching. Ilghazi did not follow up his victory at Balat with the conquest of Antioch; the sources accuse him of having instead chosen to spend the following week celebrating with an extended drinking binge, though it seems that he actually directed his attentions more usefully to the conquest of territory between Aleppo and Antioch. Meanwhile, the following decades saw other religious scholars issuing equally passionate calls to the *jihad* (Hillenbrand, 1999 a: 109–10; see also Paul Cobb's forthcoming *Race for Paradise*).

Another potential source of information in tracing the beginnings of the Muslim *jihad* against the Franks is epigraphic evidence found on tombs, mosques, religious colleges and other buildings. Such inscriptions have an advantage over historical chronicles in that they often include dates indicating when they were made, and were frequently created during or shortly after the lifetime of the person about whom they record information. Hillenbrand notes that from 1099 to 1146, the only monumental inscriptions found throughout the Muslim world that include mention of the *jihad* are those found in Syria. Thus the inscriptions found on the tomb of Balak, the nephew of Ilghazi, who died in 1124 and was interred at Aleppo, describe him in clear terms as a martyr and fighter in the *jihad*. She argues that the appearance of such language in inscriptions, specifically in the region neighbouring the Frankish states and at the time that the Muslims began to inflict defeats on the Franks in battle, testify to a rise in *jihad* spirit in the region, or at least increased propaganda using such ideas, as well as the beginnings of an informal alliance between the political and religious classes, the second of which probably composed the texts of the inscriptions in question (Hillenbrand, 1994: 63–9; Hillenbrand, 1999 a: 100–11). Hillenbrand's argument is disputed by Yaacov Lev, who maintains that in the political language of twelfth-century Syria, the term *jihad* was used for any military encounter with the Franks but was not intended to be understood as implying any deeper commitment to a holy war; thus the inscriptions under discussion merely indicate that conflict with the Franks was a common occurrence in the area, rather than conveying a particular religious or political ideology (Lev, 2008: 229–30).

ZANGI: THE FIRST GREAT COUNTER-CRUSADER?

'Imad al-Din Zangi is often regarded as having been the first of the great Muslim counter-crusaders, a reputation that is based on his conquest of Edessa in 1144. However, it is difficult to establish how far he himself took an interest in the *jihad* against the Franks; indeed, it seems far more likely that territorial and political ambitions were the primary motives behind his actions. Zangi himself had been brought up in a violent and ruthless political environment. His father Aq Sunqur, a Turkish *mamluk*, had served both Alp-Arslan and Malik-Shah, including acting as the governor of Aleppo from 1087 to 1092, but in the conflict over the Great Seljuk Sultanate that followed Malik-Shah's death he had been killed in 1094, when Zangi was about 10 years old. Thereafter Zangi was brought up by another of Malik-Shah's *mamluks* in Mosul and began his career there. After holding a number of governorships in Iraq, he was appointed governor of Mosul, as well as *atabeg* for two Seljuk princes, in 1127. He quickly extended his territory in northern Iraq, then in 1128 he negotiated the handover of Aleppo. He then divided his attention between east and west, expanding his territory in northern *Bilad al-Sham* at the expense of either the Franks or other Muslims, including several attempts to take control of Damascus, and intervening in the politics of Iraq and increasing his holdings there. The taking of Edessa was arguably an act of opportunism, with Zangi acting only because he could take advantage of the fact that its ruler and much of its army were absent.

Zangi was certainly seen as a great **mujahid** (*jihad* fighter) by those around him. Both during his lifetime and afterwards, poets and historians praised his zeal in fighting against the Franks; the caliph rewarded him for his conquest of Edessa with numerous honorific titles; and monumental inscriptions proclaimed his devotion to the holy war. However, Zangi himself spent more time increasing his territory and fighting fellow Muslims in both Iraq and the Levant than he spent pursuing campaigns against the Latin states, and it is not clear that he was seriously concerned with the *jihad*, except in so far as it helped him further his political ambitions. In addition, numerous sources attest to the brutal and uncompromising manner in which he dealt with his

Mujahid: One who strives in the *jihad*. The term is used in particular for fighters in the military *jihad*. A number of rulers included it among their titles as a way of asserting (genuinely or not) their devotion to the *jihad* against the Franks.

subjects and opponents. His troops, whom he ruled with an iron fist, were terrified of him. According to the sources, his cruel acts included killing, enslaving, mutilating and torturing prisoners, Muslim as well as Frankish; breaking promises of safe conduct; and once, when drunk, divorcing his wife and ordering that she be raped by stable-hands. At the same time, some depict him as seeking to preserve military discipline and public morality through his uncompromising approach (Hillenbrand, 1999 a: 112–16, 2001: 115–27). Yet whatever they thought of him beforehand, in the eyes of the Muslim writers Zangi's conquest of Edessa was his salvation, gaining him forgiveness for all his misdeeds. Ibn al-Athir, in his admittedly partisan history of the **Zangids**, tells the story of a pious man who saw Zangi in a dream after the latter was killed; the man said, '[He was] in the best condition, and I said to him, "How has God treated you?" Zangi answered, "He has granted me pardon." I asked, "On account of what?" and he responded, "On account of the conquest of Edessa"' (Ibn al-Athir, 1963: 70).

Zangids: Family of 'Imad al-Din Zangi (r. 1127–46). Members of the Zangid dynasty ruled territories in Syria until the second half of the twelfth century, and in Iraq and the Jazira until the mid-thirteenth century.

CONCLUSION

As we have seen, Muslim reactions to the arrival of the First Crusade were ones of shock, hostility and, if the varied comments of the sources are to be taken at face value, confusion regarding why the crusaders had come. These quickly transformed into emotional appeals for a Muslim counter-offensive that issued in the first instance from the lips of religious scholars and court poets. At what point these calls provoked a reaction in the politico-military leaders of *Bilad al-Sham* is unclear, but from the textual and epigraphic evidence we might suggest, tentatively, that the early twelfth century witnessed a gradual growth in the number of Muslim rulers who saw value in pursuing the military *jihad* against the Franks. Whether they did so from genuine piety or a recognition of the propaganda value of such ideas is of course impossible to tell and remains a matter of scholarly debate; indeed, the German scholar Michael Köhler has contended that the large number of alliances and treaties made between Muslim and Frankish rulers both at this time and later indicates that *jihad* propaganda was used by Muslim rulers purely to advance their own political, social and economic ambitions. He reinforces his argument when he notes that such treaties were even made by later figures widely regarded as proponents of the Muslim military *jihad*, such as Nur al-Din and Saladin (r. 1169–93) (Köhler, 1991: *passim*, esp. 429–31). Nevertheless, in employing such *jihad* ideology the Muslim rulers of the period under discussion in this chapter set in motion the gradual re-conquest of the Muslim territory that had been taken by the crusaders, as well as setting the stage for much wider use of *jihad* propaganda by their successors.

FURTHER READING

Carole Hillenbrand's *The Crusades: Islamic Perspectives* (1999 a) provides a detailed discussion of the Muslims' reactions to the First Crusade, as well as the beginnings of the Muslim counter-crusade. At the time of writing, Michael Köhler's valuable work on Muslim–Frankish alliances is in the course of being published in English translation (2013) as *Alliances and Treaties between Frankish and Muslim Rulers in the Middle East*. On the activities of Muslim poets, see also Hadia Dajani-Shakeel's article 'Jihad in Twelfth-Century Arabic Poetry: A Moral and Religious Force to Counter the Crusades' (1976); and Carole Hillenbrand, 'Jihad Poetry in the Age of the Crusades' (2010). On al-Sulami, see the various articles by Niall Christie in the select bibliography of this book, as well as his *The Book of the* Jihad *of 'Ali ibn Tahir al-Sulami (d. 1106): Text, Translation and Commentary* (Al-Sulami; in press at time of writing). For discussion of the evidence of inscriptions, see Carole Hillenbrand, 'Jihad Propaganda in Syria from the Time of the First Crusade until the Death of Zengi: The Evidence of Monumental Inscriptions' (1994) and Yaacov Lev, 'The Jihad of Sultan Nur al-Din of Syria (1146–74): History and Discourse' (2008). For an assessment of 'Imad al-Din Zangi, see Carole Hillenbrand, '"Abominable Acts": The Career of Zengi' (2001). Finally, a useful overview of historical developments in the major Seljuk centres of *Bilad al-Sham* at the time may be found in Taef Kamal el-Azhari's *The Saljuqs of Syria during the Crusades* (1997), while more information on Fatimid Egypt may be found in Paul E. Walker, *Exploring an Islamic Empire: Fatimid History and its Sources* (2002); and Yaacov Lev, *State and Society in Fatimid Egypt* (1991).

4

Nur al-Din and Saladin, 1146–74

H ere we will examine developments in the Levant in the wake of the fall of Edessa, including an examination of the Muslim perspective on the Second Crusade. Then we will consider the career of Zangi's son Nur al-Din, discussing in particular the *jihad* propaganda campaign that he sponsored as he expanded his influence over Syria. Our attention will then turn to Saladin, paying particular attention to the breakdown of relations between Nur al-Din and Saladin that followed the latter's assumption of power in Egypt and almost resulted in a direct military confrontation between them.

CHRONOLOGICAL OVERVIEW

As we have seen, in the wake of the death of Zangi his domains were divided between his sons. Relations between the primary inheritors, Sayf al-Din and Nur al-Din, were for the most part cordial, with the result that Nur al-Din, based at Aleppo, was able to concentrate his attention on affairs in *Bilad al-Sham*, without being distracted by events further east; however, he also suffered from the disadvantage of not having unlimited access to the resources of his father's eastern territories (Holt, 1986: 42).

Nur al-Din was immediately faced with the challenge of consolidating his hold on his inheritance. A Frankish attempt to retake and hold Edessa was foiled, with the native Christian population of the city being bloodily suppressed. There was also conflict over territory with Damascus, eventually resolved through a diplomatic agreement made in 1147. The next year witnessed the arrival of the forces of the Second Crusade in the Levant. The crusaders did not threaten Nur al-Din's holdings, but instead decided to attack Damascus, hoping to prevent closer relations between its rulers and Nur al-Din (Phillips, 2002: 75). When the crusaders besieged the city, its military governor, Mu'in al-Din Unur (d. 1149), sent requests for aid to Sayf al-Din and Nur al-Din, who set out for the city from the north. Learning of the approach of the relief force, the crusaders withdrew.

In some sense the crusaders provoked what they had feared, for their actions at Damascus led to closer co-operation between Nur al-Din and Mu'in al-Din; in June 1149 the two Muslim rulers assembled a combined force that defeated and killed Prince Raymond of Antioch at Inab, leaving the Principality of Antioch temporarily leaderless and vulnerable. While Nur al-Din passed through the principality and bathed symbolically in the Mediterranean, he sent Prince Raymond's head to the 'Abbasid caliph of Baghdad to attest to his victory in the military *jihad*. In the following years Nur al-Din continued to consolidate his territories, primarily in the former County of Edessa. Meanwhile he also sought as far as possible to win over the Muslims in general and the people of Damascus in particular through a propaganda campaign, presenting himself as a ruler who was pious, dedicated to the *jihad* and just to those under his command.

While Nur al-Din was expanding his influence in Syria, Fatimid Egypt was in decline. The death of the Fatimid caliph al-Hafiz (r. 1131–49) was followed by the accession of the 16-year-old al-Zafir (r. 1149–54), the first of a succession of caliphs who were minors when they came to the throne. In the meantime, power passed into the hands of the military leaders, who spent much of their time fighting each other for the position of vizier, weakening the stability of the state and the government. As a result, the Fatimids were unable to prevent the Franks from conquering Ascalon in 1153. Ascalon was a major loss for the Egyptians, as it had acted as forward defence against the Kingdom of Jerusalem, and so they lost both a major obstacle to Frankish land-based attacks on Egypt and a staging-post for Fatimid naval operations against the coastal cities of the Frankish states.

In 1154 Nur al-Din's propaganda campaign bore fruit when he took control of Damascus. The last Burid ruler of Damascus was unpopular with his subjects, who had become increasingly inclined towards the pious promises of Nur al-Din, and when the latter besieged the city agents within it, with whom he had been secretly communicating for some time, opened the gates to him. There was minimal resistance, and Nur al-Din subsequently continued to assert his Islamic credentials with the foundation of religious and public institutions in the city, most notably the **dar al-'adl** (House of Justice), a building where he or his representatives would appear twice a week to hear and address the grievances of the people (Hillenbrand, 1999 a: 127).

The fall of Ascalon in 1153 had signalled a shift in focus for both the Franks and Nur al-Din. The sickly state of the Fatimid caliphate was becoming increasingly perceptible, and it was becoming equally apparent that control of Egypt could be the key to military superiority in the Levant. Arguably the major factor that led to Nur al-Din's takeover of Damascus,

Dar al-'Adl: Arabic: 'the house of justice'. A building where the ruler or his deputy would appear regularly to hear and address the grievances of his subjects. Probably the best known example is that of Nur al-Din (r. 1146–74) established in Damascus after his takeover of the city in 1154.

along with the fact that the Second Crusade had made its inhabitants pain-fully aware of the proximate danger of the Franks, was that after the fall of Ascalon the city found itself increasingly cut off from potential aid from Egypt and caught between the Frankish states and the territory of Nur al-Din; thus its leaders were forced to choose which side they would align themselves with. Over the course of the 1160s both King Amalric of Jerusalem (r. 1163–74) and Nur al-Din sent forces to intervene in Egyptian affairs. In 1163 the Egyptian vizier Shawar was ousted by a rival, Dirgham, and fled to Nur al-Din. Amalric took advantage of the instability to launch an invasion of Egypt that was held off by the Egyptians, while Nur al-Din sought to remain aloof. However, he was eventually persuaded to become involved by his loyal Kurdish vassal Asad al-Din Shirkuh. Shirkuh was entrusted with an army and set out in 1164 with Shawar to reinstate the latter in the vizierate. They were accompanied by Shirkuh's nephew Salah al-Din Yusuf, better known to modern historians as Saladin, who at the time was in his twenties. Dirgham was driven out and killed and Shawar restored to his position, but the latter then refused to hand over a third of the grain revenues of Egypt, the sum that had been agreed between Shawar and Nur al-Din (Lyons and Jackson, 1984: 7–8). When Shirkuh refused to withdraw, Shawar negotiated assistance from the Franks, and after some manoeuvres an agreement was made whereby both the Franks and Shirkuh's forces left Egypt in return for payments.

Shirkuh, however, had not ceased to train his sights on Egypt, and in 1167 Nur al-Din allowed him to take another army there. Shawar again called in Frankish aid. Shirkuh negotiated the handover of Alexandria by its inhabitants but was unable to persuade Shawar to switch sides and join him in fighting against the Franks. In March 1167 a major battle was fought between a combined Frankish–Egyptian force and the army of Shirkuh at al-Babayn in Middle Egypt, in which Saladin acted as a commander. The Frankish–Egyptian coalition was soundly defeated, and Shirkuh marched north to Alexandria, where he installed Saladin as governor with a small garrison before setting out again to face the regrouped allies. Alexandria was now besieged by the allies, while Shirkuh menaced other cities, but eventually a peace agreement was made, and the Franks and Syrians evacuated Egypt in August.

Amalric attacked Egypt again the following year. While Shawar tried to negotiate with the Franks, the Fatimid caliph al-'Adid (r. 1160–71) appealed directly to Nur al-Din for help. Shirkuh set out for a third time in December 1168, and Amalric withdrew soon after, so that Shirkuh entered Egypt largely unopposed. In January 1169 Shirkuh had an audience with the Fatimid caliph, and shortly afterwards Saladin arrested Shawar, who was killed at the caliph's orders. The caliph appointed Shirkuh as his new vizier, a position that he did not hold for long; Shirkuh was well known for his gluttonous habits, and on 23 March 1169 he died when he took a hot bath after a huge meal. He was succeeded as vizier by Saladin, who seems to have been a compromise candidate from among the various emirs of Shirkuh's army (Lyons and Jackson, 1984: 20–9).

Saladin spent the next two years consolidating his position, including eliminating the old Fatimid army and replacing it with one loyal to himself. Then in 1171, responding to mounting pressure from Nur al-Din, he officially abolished the Fatimid caliphate; almost immediately afterwards the now-deposed caliph al-'Adid died, in circumstances that remain somewhat murky, and the remaining members of the Fatimid family were 'kept from women lest they breed' (Eddé, 2011: 49; Lyons and Jackson, 1984: 47). Meanwhile, the authority of the 'Abbasid caliph was acknowledged in the mosques and Egypt was thus restored to the fold of Sunni Islam. Immediately afterwards Nur al-Din required Saladin to take part in joint operations with him against Transjordan. Saladin attacked Shawbak (Crac de Montréal) but soon retreated, claiming that he needed to deal with Fatimid conspiracies in Cairo. A similarly abortive collaboration took place in 1173, and the following summer the resentful Nur al-Din began to gather his troops to bring his recalcitrant vassal to heel. However, on 15 May 1174, after a brief illness contracted while playing polo, Nur al-Din died, and the expedition against Saladin was never launched.

THE SECOND CRUSADE THROUGH MUSLIM EYES

Numerous explanations for the failure of the Second Crusade were given by the western chroniclers, including bribery, disunity or religious impurity among the crusaders, and blame of either the Templars and Hospitallers or the Greeks (Phillips, 2002: 76). The Muslim sources also suggest a number of reasons for the failure of the attack on Damascus. Ibn al-Qalanisi, who was in the city at the time, ascribes the failure of the siege to the crusaders retreating when they heard of the approach of the Zangid relief force, though he is also careful to emphasize that the Damascenes had by then already turned the tide of battle and were inflicting great losses on the Franks. To emphasize the deserved nature of the Frankish defeat, Ibn al-Qalanisi suggests that before the attack they had arrogantly already divided up the territory that they anticipated conquering between themselves [Doc. 7.i]. The Baghdadi historian and religious scholar 'Abd al-Rahman ibn al-Jawzi (c. 1116–1201) also comments on the involvement of both the Damascene armies and the Zangid reinforcements in repelling the Frankish attack, though

he ascribes the actual departure of the Franks to divine favour in the face
of a show of penitence on the part of the people of the city, who gathered
around a copy of the Qur'an from the time of the caliph 'Uthman ibn 'Affan
(r. 644–56, credited with having compiled the standard text), bared their
heads and prayed to God for help. He also emphasizes the fact that the
Franks expected to take the city with the following story:

> There was with them a tall priest with a white beard, riding a roan
> donkey, with a cross hanging from his throat, a cross hanging from the
> throat of his donkey, and carrying two crosses in his hand. He said to
> the Franks, 'The Messiah promised me that I would take Damascus and
> no-one would resist me.' So they gathered around him and approached,
> heading for Damascus. When the Muslims saw him they demonstrated
> their zeal for Islam and attacked him all together. They killed him and his
> donkey, took the crosses and burned them.
>
> (Ibn al-Jawzi, 1992: Vol. 18, pp. 63–4)

In this way Ibn al-Jawzi contrasts the penitent piety of the Muslims with the
arrogant sense of entitlement of the Christians, in the process demonstrating
the superiority of Islam over Christianity.

Ibn al-Athir, while also commenting on Frankish overconfidence, provides a more nuanced understanding of the events in his historical works,
suggesting that Mu'in al-Din of Damascus exploited the differences between
the newly arrived Franks and the ones who were resident in Syria to bring
about the failure of the siege. He informed the newly arrived crusaders that
he had called in the aid of Sayf al-Din of Mosul and was prepared to hand
the city over to him, which would not bode well for them. Meanwhile, he
threatened the resident Franks, saying that if the newly arrived crusaders
took Damascus they would also seize the coastal lands from the resident
Franks, and again threatening to hand the city over to Sayf al-Din. According
to Ibn al-Athir, this enabled Mu'in al-Din to drive a wedge between the two
Frankish factions, with the result that the resident Franks persuaded the
German King Conrad III (r. 1138–52; Ibn al-Athir does not mention the
French participants in the crusade) to call off the siege, in return for which
Mu'in al-Din rewarded them with the castle of Banyas [See Doc. 7.ii]. Ibn
al-'Adim provides a much briefer account, stating only that the German king
withdrew from Damascus after Nur al-Din joined forces with Mu'in al-Din.
However, he follows this immediately with an account of a dispute over
Tripoli between Bertrand, the grandson of Raymond of Poitiers who had
accompanied Conrad III, and Count Raymond II of Tripoli (r. 1137–52). As
Ibn al-'Adim notes, since Bertrand's grandfather was Raymond of Poitiers,
who had taken Tripoli in 1109, he also had a claim on the city. Bertrand took

control of al-'Urayma (Arima) from its Frankish rulers, in response to which Raymond formed an alliance with Nur al-Din and encouraged him to take the castle from his rival (Ibn al-'Adim, 1951–68: Vol. 2, pp. 291–2); in this way Ibn al-'Adim, like Ibn al-Athir, draws attention to tensions between resident and newly arrived Franks. It is worth noting that the same incident is described in more detail in the *Kamil* of Ibn al-Athir, although the Mosuli author does not indicate an awareness that Bertrand took al-'Urayma from Frankish rulers (Ibn al-Athir, 2007: 22–3). Nonetheless, both authors show a strikingly detailed awareness of Frankish internal politics.

What are we to make of these varied accounts? The common themes that emerge from the narratives are the arrogance of the Franks, as contrasted with the humble piety of the Muslims; the divisions between the Franks who had lived in the Latin states for some time and the newly arrived crusaders; and the alliance between Mu'in al-Din and the Zangids that rescued Damascus from the Frankish siege. Arrogance is a vice that is periodically ascribed to the Franks in the Muslim sources, and given that this vice is condemned in the *Qur'an*, being associated with the stiff-necked refusal of pagans to turn to the true faith, while humility is lauded, such ascription is evidence of both the moralizing tendencies and the propagandistic intentions of the Muslim sources; the Christian Franks are deliberately associated with the unbelievers of old, while the humble Muslims are celebrated for their piety in the true faith. Meanwhile, the detailed descriptions of the divisions between the Franks in the works of Ibn al-Athir and Ibn al-'Adim (who based their accounts on earlier works) tell us that by the mid-twelfth century at least, Muslims had begun to achieve a detailed understanding of the internal affairs of the Latin states. Finally, the alliance between the Zangids and Mu'in al-Din is one example of a recognition on the part of the Muslims that unity was the key to defeating the Franks. It was upon this idea of Muslim unity against the Franks that Nur al-Din was to base his propaganda campaign as he expanded his influence over the Muslim Levant.

NUR AL-DIN: 'LA PLAQUE TOURNANTE'?

Emmanuel Sivan refers to Nur al-Din as 'la plaque tournante' (the pivot), viewing his reign as a decisive period that saw the *jihad* become a major factor in the spiritual and political life of Syria and, to a lesser extent, the surrounding regions (Sivan, 1968: 59). Certainly Nur al-Din employed *jihad* propaganda in a widespread manner in his efforts to expand his power and territory in the region; indeed, devotion to the *jihad* was a major characteristic through which he sought to assert his position as a pious Muslim ruler who was deserving of popular support.

Before embarking on an examination of the various methods that Nur al-Din used to promote his Islamic credentials, it is worth placing them within the wider context. As indicated in Chapter 2, in 1055 the Sunni Seljuks ousted the Shi'ite Buyids from power, thus replacing the Shi'ite caliphal 'deputy' with a Sunni one. Under the Buyids, Shi'ites had enjoyed considerably more freedom of worship than they had previously, receiving official recognition and support. In the tenth century other Shi'ite dynasties had also established themselves as rulers in various parts of the Muslim world, including, as we have seen, the Fatimids in Egypt, and in the eastern Muslim world a struggle for supremacy was taking place between Sunni and Shi'ite rulers and scholars. As a result, when they advanced westwards the Seljuks found themselves drawn into this struggle, patronizing Sunni scholars and institutions in what is commonly termed the 'Sunni revival' of the eleventh century. Of particular importance were **madrasas** (religious colleges), where Sunni Islam was studied and promoted, and which became the standard institutions for the education of religious scholars and state officials. With the support of the new rulers, these and other Sunni religious institutions spread across the Great Seljuk Sultanate. However, the inter-necine conflict that followed the death of Malik-Shah distracted the political classes from their support of religious institutions, with the result that the revival slowed, though in some cities such as Damascus we continue to see the foundation of *madrasas* and other religious buildings (Tabbaa, 2001: 19–21).

Madrasa: *Madrasas* were colleges where various subjects were taught, but especially Islamic religion, theology and law. Under the Seljuks Sunni *madrasas* proliferated and became the standard institutions where prospective state officials and religious scholars received their education. *Madrasas* continued to be founded by the Zangids, Ayyubids and Mamluks throughout the crusading period.

Soon after taking power, Nur al-Din embarked on a propaganda campaign that acted as a 'revival of the Sunni revival', seeking to promote Sunni Islam in his domains and advocate for Muslim unity against the Franks. This campaign expressed its aims in a number of ways. Like his Seljuk predecessors, Nur al-Din sponsored the foundation of numerous religious institutions, including *madrasas* in particular. Lev has noted that during Nur al-Din's reign 56 *madrasas* were founded in the territories that his domain eventually encompassed; before his reign there were only 16 (Lev, 2008: 275). These were, naturally, not the only religious institutions that Nur al-Din sponsored. In addition to *madrasas*, there were also lodges and convents for Sufis, shrines, mosques and, in particular, the celebrated *dar al-'adl* mentioned above, which was built in Damascus in about 1163; Ibn al-Athir sees the foundation of this institution as so representative of the piously just activity of Nur al-Din that he devotes a section of his dynastic history of the Zangids to it (Ibn al-Athir, 1963: 168). In addition to building mosques, Nur al-Din also added to or restored a number of older mosques, in particular building several minarets between 1165 and 1170. This included adding minarets to a number of small mosques in Damascus that would not normally have had them. These minarets, towering over the urban landscape, acted as witnesses to the Islamic identity of the cities in which they were built and testified to Islam's dominance there, and in the case of Damascus they also emphasized its role as Nur al-Din's centre of *jihad* propaganda (Tabbaa, 1986: 235–6). As Tabbaa has shown, the foundation of these various religious institutions was also accompanied by careful consideration of the ways that they should be decorated. In line with earlier precedents, vegetal and geometric ornament (arabesque) was used, through the naturalistic but also geometrically ordered shapes that it employed, to make allusions to the garden of Paradise and the divinely ordered universe. Meanwhile *muqarnas* (stalactite or honeycomb) vaulting, reflecting Baghdadi models, reinforced Nur al-Din's ties with the 'Abbasid caliphate while also invoking both the heavens and the idea of an atomistic universe under divine control. At the same time, new, more legible cursive forms of Arabic script were employed for inscriptions, thus making their texts easier to read and hence more effective as communicators of messages. In addition, the scripts were clearly different from Fatimid ones and reflected 'Abbasid precedents, again reinforcing Nur al-Din's demonstrations of loyalty to the 'Abbasid caliphs (Tabbaa, 2001: *passim*).

As Tabbaa has noted, the inscriptions that were made on monuments sponsored by Nur al-Din show important differences from those made for his father. In particular, Nur al-Din largely abandoned his father's use of Turkish titles and opted instead for purely Arabic ones, in order to emphasize his position as the ruler of an Arab state. The most prominent of his titles were *al-'adil* (the just) and *al-mujahid* (the wager of *jihad*) (Tabbaa, 1986: 226). Thus Nur al-Din sought to emphasize both the just nature of his rule and his devotion to the *jihad*. Probably the best known of the monuments that Nur al-Din patronized was a **minbar** (pulpit), which he commissioned around 1168, probably with the intention of placing it in the Aqsa Mosque in Jerusalem once he had reconquered the holy city (Plate 2). Nur al-Din did not live long enough to see his wish fulfilled, but the *minbar* was subsequently placed in the mosque by Saladin, where it remained until it was destroyed by a Christian fanatic in 1969. Among its inscriptions is the following:

Minbar: A pulpit in a mosque, from which speeches and prayers are given, including the *khutba* (sermon) at the Friday noon prayer.

> The slave needy of [God's] mercy, the one who is thankful for His favour, the *mujahid* for His cause, the one stationed to fight against the enemies of His faith, al-Malik al-'Adil [the Just King] Nur al-Din [Light of the Faith], the pillar of Islam and the Muslims, the establisher of the rights of the oppressed against oppressors, Abu'l-Qasim Mahmud ibn Zangi ibn Aq Sunqur, the helper of the Commander of the Faithful [the caliph], commissioned the construction [of this *minbar*]. May God honour his victories and preserve his power. May He exalt his signs and spread his standards and banners to the east and west. May He strengthen the supporters of his state and abase those who are ungrateful for his favour. May He grant him

conquest with His help and gladden his eyes with victory and closeness
to Him. At Your mercy, O God of the Worlds! That took place in the
months of the year 564 [1168–9].

(*Matériaux pour un Corpus Inscriptionum Arabicarum*, 1925: 394;
Tabbaa, 1986: 233; Lev, 2008: 271)

If this inscription were to be taken at face value, it would seem that Nur
al-Din was hoping to achieve great victories in the military *jihad* in his own
lifetime, and if we accept that the *minbar* was made for the Aqsa Mosque,
then it would also seem that Nur al-Din's primary target was Jerusalem. It is
also worth noting that the language used emphasizes Nur al-Din's desire to
achieve closeness to God and to receive God's support (Tabbaa, 1986: 233).
Thus we see Nur al-Din fusing his assertions of piety and obedience to God
with his military *jihad* against the Franks, with a particular focus on Jerusalem.

The increasing importance of Jerusalem in the Muslim counter-crusading
consciousness is also discernible in the literature and other written documents that we have from Nur al-Din's reign. Particularly tantalizing is a letter
written by Nur al-Din to the 'Abbasid caliph that is quoted by the historian
Abu Shama (1203–67), in which Nur al-Din himself identifies Jerusalem
as his primary goal (Hillenbrand, 1999 a: 151). Also of particular relevance
is the *fada'il* literature relating to Jerusalem. As indicated previously, *fada'il*
works concentrated on the merits of a particular place or practice. Such merits
were normally articulated principally through the collection of quotations
from the *Qur'an* and *hadith* that illustrated the virtues of the place or practice
about which the author was writing, with the author often adding commentary and explanations thereof. Even before the Crusades, *fada'il* works on
Jerusalem had been written by a number of authors; the earliest known work
in this regard is *Fada'il al-Bayt al-Muqaddas* (The Merits of Jerusalem) written
in 1019 by Muhammad ibn Ahmad al-Wasiti, a religious scholar from the
Shafi'i school who preached in the Aqsa Mosque [**Doc. 8**]. During the latter
half of the twelfth century, the number of works of this type being written or
disseminated grew rapidly, and continued to do so in the following centuries
(Hillenbrand, 1999 a: 162–3). Al-Wasiti's work itself was used in both
preaching and writing by a number of later scholars including such distinguished figures as Ibn al-Jawzi, mentioned above, and the Damascene Ibn
'Asakir (1105–76), who were important figures in the propagation of Nur
al-Din's propaganda. In particular, Sivan credits Ibn 'Asakir with the revival
of the genre (Dajani-Shakeel, 1986: 206; Sivan, 1968: 62–70).

Why was Jerusalem so important? As Hadia Dajani-Shakeel has demonstrated, the city was important to the Muslims of the time for a range of
reasons, which can be grouped under three major themes. First, Abraham,
regarded as the first Muslim, the builder of the Ka'ba and the father of

Ishmael, lived in Jerusalem before he moved to Mecca, and many traditions linked the two cities and suggested that Muslims had the right to control them both. Jerusalem was also home to other prophets and Hebron, nearby, was the site of Abraham's grave. Second, Jerusalem was both the original direction of prayer for the Muslims and the city to which the Prophet Muhammad travelled on his *isra'* (miraculous night journey), subsequently rising on his *mi'raj* (ascension) to visit the heavens and meet with God, with the Dome of the Rock being seen as marking the actual place from which he ascended. Thus it was an important pilgrimage destination. Finally, Jerusalem was regarded as the future site of the Last Judgement, and being buried there was regarded as being particularly meritorious (Dajani-Shakeel, 1986: 206–13). Thus in giving prominence to the city in propaganda, Nur al-Din and his successors drew on a powerful symbol that loomed large in Muslim views of their sacred past, present and future.

The heightened atmosphere of *jihad* that existed during the reign of Nur al-Din also stimulated the production of other works on the topic. Poetic compositions by figures such as Ibn al-Qaysarani (1085–1154), Ibn Munir (1080–1153) and 'Imad al-Din al-Isfahani (1125–1201) praise Nur al-Din's virtues and devotion to the *jihad*. In addition to the *fada'il* works on Jerusalem, the period also sees the increased production of *fada'il* works on the topic of *jihad*, as well as other works in similar vein (al-Sulami's work, mentioned in Chapter 3, falls into this category); for example, Ibn 'Asakir himself produced, at Nur al-Din's request, a compilation of 40 *hadiths* on the topic of *jihad* that could be used to encourage the Muslim *mujahidin* and which proved to be highly influential in the centuries that followed (Mourad and Lindsay, 2007: 37–55, 2013: *passim*). Meanwhile in Aleppo, Nur al-Din's original capital, an anonymous author produced a work in Persian entitled *Bahr al-Fava'id* (The Sea of Precious Virtues). This work falls into a genre called '**Mirrors for Princes**', works that were intended to provide guides for good conduct to Muslim rulers. The Aleppine author devotes significant attention to the subject of *jihad*, in both its greater and lesser manifestations, as well as providing some less than positive impressions about Christianity (see Chapter 6); in this way his work seems to reflect the atmosphere of the times. It also seems likely that rousing *jihad* sermons, the texts of which have for the most part not survived, were being given in mosques throughout the lands held by Nur al-Din (Hillenbrand, 1999 a: 161–7).

Mirrors for Princes: A genre of Muslim literature that takes the form of books of guidance for rulers on good conduct and wise and just governance.

The sheer magnitude of the *jihad* propaganda campaign mounted by Nur al-Din is impressive, but to what extent can we regard it as proof that Nur al-Din was genuinely motivated by piety and a desire to wage the *jihad*, and to what extent should we regard it as a tool that he used to serve his political ambitions? Clearly a number of writers and architects of the time sought to portray Nur al-Din as devoted to the *jihad* and pious, just Muslim rule.

However, a number of modern scholars, including Michael Köhler, Taef El-Azhari and Yaacov Lev, have questioned Nur al-Din's apparent devotion to the holy war. As indicated earlier, Köhler regards Nur al-Din's use of *jihad* propaganda as simply a way of advancing his political ambitions (Köhler, 1991: 239). Lev concurs with Köhler and also argues that Nur al-Din's pro- motion of Sunni Islam was similarly motivated (Lev, 2008: 276–7). El-Azhari, in the meantime, points out that the propaganda call to Muslim unity for the *jihad* that Nur al-Din mounted when seeking to negotiate the takeover of Damascus was supplemented by an economic blockade aimed at starving the city into submission (El-Azhari, 1997: 264–70). Certainly it is also striking that Nur al-Din frequently waged war on fellow Muslims, which calls into question his concern for the welfare of the Muslim community. However, it is equally striking how *personally* involved Nur al-Din seems to have been in various activities related to the promotion and conduct of the *jihad* in its various forms, when at times he could arguably have delegated such activities to others; he often led his own armies, and he himself would appear at the *dar al-'adl* in Damascus to hear the grievances of his subjects. He is also said to have adopted a more pious, ascetic lifestyle after two bouts of illness and a defeat by the Franks in 1163. While such activities could be interpreted as careful public-relations exercises, they can also be seen as testifying to genuine piety. With regard to the wars that Nur al-Din waged against other Muslims, he may have recognized that in the fractious political environment of the Muslim Levant, unity in the military *jihad* against the Franks was something that could only be imposed by force.

Of course, given the complexities of human nature we should perhaps be wary of seeing Nur al-Din's activities (and those of later figures such as Saladin) in terms of a binary model that places religious piety and political ambition in opposition to one another. Nur al-Din may well have viewed his political and territorial aims as being appropriate within the context of his faith, with the gains that he made being his just reward from God for his piety and devotion. Thus his religious beliefs and worldly desires could be seen as inextricably linked rather than automatically opposed to one another. Ultimately it is impossible to tell to what extent Nur al-Din was motivated by religious zeal or political goals, but the end result of his efforts was that the Muslims of the region experienced a heightened atmosphere of Sunni piety and counter-crusading sentiment, with Nur al-Din himself at its centre.

SALADIN AND NUR AL-DIN

As indicated above, Saladin became the new Fatimid vizier after the death of Shirkuh in 1169. Nur al-Din seems to have expected Saladin to abolish the

Fatimid caliphate as soon as possible and rule Egypt as his deputy, but from early on Saladin seems to have shown signs of resistance that Nur al-Din found troubling. In spring of 1170 he sent his faithful vassal, Saladin's father Najm al-Din Ayyub, to Egypt, possibly to remind Saladin of his obligations, and then wrote to Saladin in June 1171 demanding that the latter establish 'Abbasid authority in Egypt, something that Saladin did only after a further delay of over two months (Lyons and Jackson, 1984: 38 and 45–6). Nur al-Din then ordered Saladin to join him in an attack on Transjordan. Saladin set out with an army and attacked Shawbak, forcing the surrender of its garrison, but then withdrew before meeting with Nur al-Din, claiming that there were disturbances in Cairo that had to be dealt with. Nur al-Din refused to accept Saladin's excuses and prepared to depose him, but relented when Saladin wrote to re-affirm his loyalty [Doc. 9]. A similar sequence of events took place in 1173, and the following year the exasperated Nur al-Din prepared an expedition to Egypt to bring Saladin to heel. However, he died before he could set out, and Saladin was spared his sovereign's anger.

Saladin's reluctance to co-operate with his master is perhaps understandable; he must have recognized the usefulness of having a Frankish 'buffer zone' between his territories and those of Nur al-Din, though as Lyons and Jackson note, it is unlikely that he was so obtuse as to need this to be pointed out to him, as Ibn al-Athir asserts. By the same token, by avoiding meeting with Nur al-Din he also avoided being removed from his position as ruler of Egypt by his lord, which enabled him to consolidate his position and establish his independence there (Lyons and Jackson, 1984: 48). As a result of this, he was well placed to expand his influence into Syria after Nur al-Din's death.

CONCLUSION

The period covered by this chapter sees the seeds of *jihad* sentiment that we saw planted in the previous chapter grow, under Nur al-Din's patronage, into a wide-ranging and dynamic propaganda campaign. Through a variety of means Nur al-Din sought to promote both Muslim unity, under his command, in the military *jihad* against the Franks and, in a more widespread fashion, a revival of Sunni Islam. This campaign included not only the propagation of his image as the *mujahid* par excellence in both written texts and architecture (including architectural decoration and inscriptions), but also the return of Egypt to the fold of Sunni Islam through the destruction of the Fatimid caliphate.

In the meantime, the Muslims were also learning more about the Franks, to the point that they seem to have been able to exploit the divisions between them. This, in combination with increasing Muslim unity, enabled the Muslims to mount more effective resistance to the crusaders. Elisséeff sees the defeat of the Second Crusade at Damascus as the turning point in the history of the Latin states, in that to him it foreshadowed the eventual victory over the Franks of a unified Syro-Egyptian polity (Elisséeff, 1967: Vol. 2, p. 426). It is that eventual unification and victory, as well as their aftermath, that we will trace in the next chapter.

FURTHER READING

The standard work on Nur al-Din is Nikita Elisséeff's monumental study, *Nur ad-Din: Un Grand Prince Musulman de Syrie au Temps des Croisades (511–569 H./1118–1174)* (1967). On Nur al-Din's career and propaganda campaign see also Carole Hillenbrand, *The Crusades: Islamic Perspectives* (1999 a); Yaacov Lev, 'The *Jihad* of Sultan Nur al-Din of Syria' (2008); and (on poetry), Hadia Dajani-Shakeel, '*Jihad* in Twelfth-Century Arabic Poetry' (1976). On Ibn 'Asakir in particular, see Suleiman A. Mourad and James E. Lindsay, *The Intensification and Reorientation of Sunni Jihad Ideology in the Crusader Period: Ibn 'Asakir of Damascus (1105–1176) and His Age, with an Edition and Translation of Ibn 'Asakir's* The Forty Hadiths for Inciting Jihad (2013); their 'Rescuing Syria from the Infidels: The Contribution of Ibn 'Asakir of Damascus to the *Jihad* Campaign of Sultan Nur al-Din' (2007); and James E. Lindsay (ed.), *Ibn 'Asakir and Early Islamic History* (2001). For further discussion of religious life in the period, see Daniella Talmon-Heller, *Islamic Piety in Medieval Syria: Mosques, Cemeteries and Sermons under the Zangids and Ayyubids (1146–1260)* (2007 a). On architecture and inscriptions see Yasser Tabbaa, 'Monuments with a Message: Propagation of *Jihad* under Nur al-Din (1146–74)' (1986); and *The Transformation of Islamic Art during the Sunni Revival* (2001). Taef Kamal el-Azhari's *The Saljuqs of Syria during the Crusades* (1997) contains discussions of the impacts of the Second Crusade and Nur al-Din's takeover on Damascus. Further reading on the career of Saladin will be provided in the next chapter, but on the Egyptian period see in particular Yaacov Lev, *Saladin in Egypt* (1999).

5

Victory and stalemate, 1174–93

W e will now turn our attention fully to the career of Saladin. After our initial chronological overview, we will discuss the problems that historians face when seeking to uncover the true face of the sultan. Subsequently we will examine the means through which he established and articulated power in the Muslim Levant. Then we will consider his victory at Hattin and conquest of most of the Frankish states, followed by his struggle to defend these conquests against the forces of the Third Crusade.

CHRONOLOGICAL OVERVIEW

Nur al-Din's only son and successor, al-Salih Isma'il, was only 11 when his father died, and there immediately ensued a dispute over who was to serve as regent. Power was quickly established at Aleppo by a triumvirate of Nur al-Din's emirs, the foremost of whom was called Gümüshtigin. They secured the transferral of al-Salih Isma'il to Aleppo and ruled there in his name. Although he did make an immediate profession of loyalty to his young overlord, Saladin did not intervene directly in the establishment of the regency. He was occupied in Egypt, in particular with defending Alexandria against an attack made by Sicilian forces in July–August 1174. However, in October he responded to appeals for help from the emirs ruling in Damascus and Busra, setting out for Syria with an army. Both Busra and Damascus surrendered to Saladin; the latter's citadel put up a brief resistance before also capitulating, but otherwise the takeover occurred without difficulty.

Saladin's takeover of Damascus was in some senses a prelude to what would turn out to be 12 years of periodic conflict between Saladin and his supporters on the one side and Saladin's opponents, principally the Zangids of Mosul and Aleppo, on the other. Over the next two years Saladin took control of much of southern Syria and also conducted campaigns against his opponents in the north, repeatedly besieging Aleppo and defeating the Zangids twice in battle, at the Horns of Hamah on 13 April 1175 and at Tall al-Sultan on 22 April 1176. A peace agreement was concluded on 29 July 1176, but the death of al-Salih Isma'il on 4 December 1181 gave Saladin the pretext to intervene again at Aleppo, which he claimed was meant to pass to him after al-Salih's death, in accordance with caliphal decree. Saladin set out for northern Syria again in May 1182. Over the next year he took control of a number of strongholds and cities in the region, and on 11 June 1183, after a three-week siege, he finally achieved the handover of Aleppo. Three years later, after another long campaign during which he almost died of illness, Saladin secured a treaty with Mosul that included recognition of his authority and a guarantee of military support. In addition to his other diplomatic and military ventures in northern Syria, Saladin had by this time also sent emirs to conquer both Yemen and much of North Africa, so his authority was now recognized from Tawzar in the west to Mosul in the east, and from Akhlat in the north to Aden in the south (Eddé, 2011: 67–89).

It was during this early period that Saladin also came to terms with Rashid al-Din Sinan (d. 1192 or 1193), the 'Old Man of the Mountain', the head of the Syrian Assassins. The Assassins attacked Saladin twice, in January 1175 and May 1176, and after the second attack he would sometimes have a wooden tower or palisade built in his camp so that he could sleep more securely. He also attacked Sinan's fortress of Masyaf in August 1176, but broke off the siege after a week, in mysterious circumstances. Some sources maintain that the Assassins threatened Saladin's uncle Shihab al-Din, and he persuaded his nephew to abandon the siege. Others suggest that Saladin had to break off the siege to deal with other threats. An Isma'ili source claims that Saladin was frightened off by Sinan's supernatural powers (Eddé, 2011: 392–4). Whatever the truth of the matter, it is striking that thereafter Saladin and Sinan left each other alone, although the Assassins continued to strike at other targets.

While Saladin was expanding his authority beyond Egypt, he also concerned himself with the war against the Franks. The Sicilian attack on Alexandria, mentioned above, was but one of several raids that would be made by the Franks on Egypt in the 1170s and 1180s, and Saladin devoted a significant amount of resources to strengthening the fortifications of both Cairo and a number of the ports on the Egyptian coast, including Alexandria, Tinnis and Damietta. He likewise built fortifications to protect the routes linking Egypt and Syria through the Sinai Peninsula. Saladin also went on the offensive; in 1177 he launched a raid into southern Palestine, but despite some initial success his force was surprised and scattered by a Frankish counteroffensive at Mont Gisard, near Ramla, with Saladin himself barely escaping with his life. Later campaigns were more successful. In 1179 Saladin's troops defeated the Franks in battle twice, in the Jawlan (Golan) in April and again at Marj 'Uyun in June. In August he destroyed the castle of Bayt al-Ahzan, which was less than a year old, then raided the area around Tiberias, Tyre and Beirut before returning to Damascus (Eddé, 2011: 198–200).

Muslim forces made more raids on the Kingdom of Jerusalem in May–July 1182, but a new dimension was added to the conflict in 1183 through the belligerence of Reynald of Châtillon, lord of Kerak and Transjordan. In that year Reynald launched a naval raid into the Red Sea. His sailors plundered 'Aydhab and sank a pilgrim ship, attacked the Hijaz coast and captured a number of merchant ships. The precise objective of Reynald's expedition remains a matter of debate among modern scholars, but rumours circulated among the Muslims that he planned to attack the holy cities of Mecca and Medina, and perhaps even to steal the remains of the Prophet Muhammad. The Frankish fleet was quickly opposed by a Muslim one under the admiral Husam al-Din Lu'lu', who destroyed it and hunted down the survivors. The prisoners were transported to Cairo and Mecca, where they were publicly executed as punishment for their sacrilegious ambitions (Lyons and Jackson, 1984: 186–7; Eddé, 2011: 194–5). Saladin followed this up with two attacks on Kerak in October–December 1183 and August 1184, although its citadel was not taken in either case. After the second siege Saladin raided Frankish territories further north before returning to Damascus. The following year he agreed to a truce proposed by Raymond III of Tripoli (r. 1152–87), who at the time was acting as regent for the underage King Baldwin V of Jerusalem (r. 1185–6). This conveniently enabled him to concentrate his attention on the final conflict with Mosul.

Saladin was already preparing to renew the holy war against the Franks when Reynald of Châtillon gave him an excuse to re-open hostilities. In early 1187 Reynald seized a caravan travelling between Egypt and Syria and then refused Saladin's demands that he free the prisoners and return the goods that he had taken. Saladin, incensed, swore that he would kill Reynald if he ever got the opportunity and, using the broken truce as justification, mustered his troops. Initial raids were made on a number of points on the frontier with the Franks, then Saladin gathered his forces, which probably numbered about 30,000 men, at Busra. The Franks in turn mustered their army of about 20,000 men at Sepphoris (Saffuriyya) (Eddé, 2011: 206–8). On 2 July, in an effort to lure the Frankish army out, Saladin attacked and took Tiberias, trapping its remaining defenders, including Raymond of Tripoli's wife, Eschiva, in its citadel. That night the Franks met to decide on a response. What exactly happened in their discussion is unclear, but the following morning Guy of Lusignan, the king of Jerusalem (r. 1186–92), ordered the advance. The Frankish army marched towards Tiberias. Saladin abandoned the siege of the citadel of Tiberias and sent units of horse-archers

to harass the Frankish flanks, in the meantime surrounding the Frankish
army and cutting its access to sources of water. Thirsty and drained by the
heat, the army headed for the village of Hattin, which had plentiful springs
of water, but Muslim pressure prevented the Franks from reaching their goal
and they were forced to camp for the night.

On the morning of 4 July the Frankish army, harassed by Muslim skir-
mishers, attempted to march on to Lake Tiberias. In addition to maintaining
a constant hail of arrows, the Muslims started brushfires that only exacerbated
the heat and thirst that were already taking their toll on the Frankish army.
Raymond of Tripoli attempted to break the cordon by leading the vanguard
in a charge on the Muslim ranks, but the Muslims opened their ranks and
allowed the charge to pass through, shooting at the Frankish knights as they
passed. The remnants of the vanguard were allowed to escape and played
no further part in the battle. The Franks took refuge on the slopes of the
twin-peaked hill known as the Horns of Hattin, where they pitched the king's
red tent. Further attempts to charge the Muslim ranks failed, the Frankish
infantry were scattered and eventually the king's tent fell. The king and many
senior members of the nobility, including Reynald of Châtillon and Gerard
of Ridefort, the Master of the Knights Templar, were captured, and the relic
of the True Cross was taken. The Knights Templar and Knights Hospitaller,
implacable enemies of the Muslims, were put to the sword, as were the tur-
copoles, locally recruited, lightly armed horsemen considered traitors and
apostates by the Muslims. The remaining Frankish prisoners were enslaved,
and the market would subsequently become so flooded with them that their
value would collapse.

Saladin, meanwhile, had King Guy and Reynald brought to his tent.
Observing that the king was frightened and thirsty, he sought to calm him
and gave him iced water to drink. However, when Guy passed this on to
Reynald, Saladin hastened to point out that he had not authorized this and
was thus not bound by the laws of hospitality, which would have obliged
the sultan to spare his old enemy. Later he separated the two, reproached
Reynald for his crimes, and when the latter showed neither repentance nor
a willingness to convert to Islam, struck him in the shoulder with his sword.
Reynald was beheaded and dragged away past the king, who became convinced that he would be next. However, Saladin hastened to reassure him,
commenting (in the words of his army judge Baha' al-Din ibn Shaddad [d.
1234]), 'It has not been customary for princes to kill princes, but this man
transgressed his limits' (Ibn Shaddad, 2001: 75, but see also **Doc. 10**).

Without the field army to protect it, the Kingdom of Jerusalem was
swiftly conquered by Saladin. One after another, over the course of a year,
Frankish castles and cities fell to Saladin's forces, with the exception of Tyre,
which managed to withstand Saladin's siege. Jerusalem itself was besieged in

September 1187, and initially Saladin refused to give its inhabitants terms, intending to reciprocate for the crusaders' conquest of 1099. On 2 October, however, he was persuaded to accept the city's capitulation by its commander, Balian of Ibelin, who threatened to kill the Muslim prisoners therein and destroy its holy sites. The inhabitants were allowed to leave upon payment of a ransom, and chroniclers from both sides tell of the generosity with which Saladin excused many prisoners from payment or enslavement. In all, only about 16,000 Franks actually became slaves, out of a population of between 60,000 and 100,000 (Eddé, 2011: 218–20; **Doc. 10**).

By the beginning of 1189, all that remained of the Kingdom of Jerusalem were a few scattered fortresses, and the County of Tripoli and Principality of Antioch had also seen their territories significantly reduced. Then in August Guy of Lusignan, whom Saladin had freed the previous summer on the condition that he promise not to fight the Muslims, but who had been absolved from his vow by the Christian clergy, arrived with an army and a Pisan fleet at the now Muslim-held Acre and besieged the city. Saladin attempted to remove the besiegers, but he was having difficulty keeping adequate forces in the field after years of campaigning. Saladin's conquest of Jerusalem had caused dismay in Europe, leading to the departure of new armies on what modern historians call the Third Crusade. Both Philip II Augustus of France (r. 1180–1223) and Richard the Lionheart of England (r. 1189–99) had taken the cross and sailed east with their troops, landing at Acre and swelling Guy's forces there. As a result of the participation of these new European contingents, the siege became a long, drawn-out affair that concluded with the Muslims being forced to surrender the city to the Franks on 12 July 1191. Philip returned home again almost immediately after, but Richard remained to lead an attempt to take Jerusalem from Saladin.

The capitulation of Acre had been agreed on the condition that Saladin return the relic of the True Cross, pay a ransom of 200,000 *dinars* and free over 1,500 Christian prisoners, but Saladin delayed, and in August Richard lost patience and killed between 2,600 and 3,000 Muslim prisoners – an act that was greeted with great hostility by the Muslims. Richard then gathered his forces and marched south along the coast, heading for Jaffa. Saladin subjected the Frankish army to constant harassment, hoping to break its coherence, but when he was finally able to provoke a battle at Arsuf on 7 September, his forces were badly defeated and the crusaders were subsequently able to take Jaffa. Saladin, in an effort to prevent the enemy from having a secure base from which to launch an assault on Jerusalem, razed Ascalon and other fortresses on the road between Jaffa and the holy city while simultaneously building up the defences of the latter. In October the crusading force marched on Jerusalem but was forced to turn back due to bad weather and doubts about supporting the attack. Richard instead re-fortified Ascalon before heading north to deal with disputes within the Frankish kingdom. May 1192 saw him back again; Darum, to the south of Ascalon, was taken by Richard's forces on 23 May, and on 24 June he seized a caravan coming from Egypt. He then launched a second march on Jerusalem but was forced to turn back on 5 July, after having come within sight of the city, again due to concerns about adequately supporting the attack. Saladin almost took Jaffa on 30 July, but had barely secured its surrender when Richard's forces arrived by sea and drove the Muslim army away.

Throughout Richard's crusade there were periodic negotiations between him and Saladin, and by the end of the summer of 1192 both men had come to accept that they were at a stalemate. Richard could not adequately support an attack on Jerusalem, but Saladin could not muster enough forces to defeat the Franks completely. From 1 to 3 September a treaty was drawn up and sworn to: a truce was made for three years and eight months; Jerusalem was to remain Muslim, but Christian pilgrims would be allowed to visit; the coast from Jaffa to Tyre would remain in Frankish hands; the defences of Ascalon, Darum and Gaza would be demolished; Nazareth, Sepphoris and Ascalon would be Saladin's; and the revenues of Ramla and Lydda would be shared (Eddé, 2011: 268–9). After giving his agreement, Richard left for Europe on 9 October 1192. Saladin, meanwhile, visited Jerusalem and Beirut before returning to Damascus. In the following winter his health deteriorated and on 20 February 1193 he fell seriously ill. Despite the efforts of his physicians, he died on the morning of 4 March 1193. Baha' al-Din describes his grief at his master's passing:

> In God's name, I had heard from some people that they were desirous of ransoming those dear to them with their own lives, but I only ever heard such an expression as a sort of exaggeration or poetic license until this day, as I knew for myself and for others that, had the purchase of his life been acceptable, we would have paid for it with our own.
>
> (Ibn Shaddad, 2001: 244)

THE PROBLEM OF THE SOURCES

Sources for the life of Saladin are plentiful and wide-ranging in origin, for he is a prominent figure in both contemporary and later works by not only Muslim authors, but also eastern Christian and Frankish writers. Yet despite this, he remains an enigmatic figure, presented in various guises depending on the viewpoints and agendas of the writers in question. We have already seen hints that Ibn al-Athir's partiality for the Zangid dynasty made him critical of Saladin (see Chapter 4 and **Doc. 9**); the vehemence of his attitude is often exaggerated by historians in disregard of the occasions when he expresses respect and admiration for the sultan. However, we must likewise be suspicious of authors who do not express critical attitudes. We are fortunate to have information about Saladin from three individuals who knew him intimately. Al-Qadi al-Fadil (d. 1200) was a close friend and advisor of Saladin's, as well as the chief administrator of Egypt, and has left us hundreds of letters and documents that tell us much about both Saladin's policies and his personality. Al-Fadil was also the man who in 1175 employed a scribe and administrator known as 'Imad al-Din al-Isfahani (d. 1201), who soon became Saladin's personal secretary and has left us both poetic and prose works, including two that tell us about Saladin's campaigns [**Doc. 10**]. Finally, Baha' al-Din ibn Shaddad, mentioned above, was a well-known Mosuli jurist and *qadi* who entered Saladin's service in 1188 as judge of the army and soon became a close companion and confidant of the sultan; he is best known for his biography of Saladin, which includes an account of his master's virtues [**Doc. 11**]. This feature in Baha' al-Din's work typifies the issues that modern scholars face when working with these sources: all three men were close friends of Saladin, as well as being deeply involved in his efforts both to have his authority recognized in the Levant and to promote the *jihad* against the Franks, and thus we cannot regard their accounts as being objective and unbiased, yet at the same time their first-hand experience of the sultan and his activities make them of immense value for the historical details that they supply (Eddé, 2011: 4–9). In this way, the works of all four of the authors mentioned here are emblematic of the wider dilemma that historians face when studying the past in general; on the one hand, sources contemporary with their subjects are incredibly important as repositories of information, but on the other hand there is always the challenge of disengaging this information from the agendas of the people who recorded it. In the case of Saladin, a controversial figure, such agendas are emphasized and only hide the real face of the sultan all the more.

THE ARTICULATION OF POWER

Like Nur al-Din, Saladin employed a number of techniques in order to have his authority acknowledged in Egypt and *Bilad al-Sham*. As Hillenbrand has noted, Saladin adopted the same methods used by Nur al-Din to promote his image as an epitome of piety and consequently the natural leader in the holy war against the Franks, including the foundation and restoration of religious institutions, patronage of poets and religious scholars, and numerous calls for the Muslims to unify with him so that he might re-take Jerusalem for Islam (Hillenbrand, 1999 a: 175). However, what is striking is the magnitude of Saladin's efforts in this regard. His prolific correspondence included regular letters to the 'Abbasid caliph in Baghdad, expressing his loyalty and his dedication to the *jihad*, and seeking caliphal recognition of his right to rule the territories that he won from other Muslim rulers. By the same token, in the Levant he sought to win over both the politico-military and religious elites with his attestations of piety and devotion to the war against the Franks (Eddé, 2011: *passim*). Like Nur al-Din, he also sought to engender loyalty among his followers by becoming personally involved in the actions that he asked of them, leading armies himself, and even 'mucking in' with his men, carrying stones himself to help build up the defences of Jerusalem in 1192 (Lyons and Jackson, 1984: 347). He also sought to promote a reputation for accessibility and just rule similar to that of Nur al-Din by making himself available to commoners who might wish to appeal to his justice on a regular basis [**Doc. 11**].

Saladin also sought to capitalize on associations with Nur al-Din in other ways. On 6 September 1176 he married 'Ismat al-Din, who was both Nur al-Din's widow and a daughter of Mu'in al-Din Unur, though not the mother of al-Salih Isma'il. In this way he drew on a practice traditional among rulers to cement his position at Damascus and further lay claim to the heritage of Nur al-Din; the significance of this move is indicated by the fact that in 1182 the Zangid ruler of Mosul and Aleppo married al-Salih Isma'il's mother to strengthen his own claim to Nur al-Din's legacy (Eddé, 2011: 76–7). Even after the conquest of Jerusalem in 1187 Saladin continued to emphasize his links to his predecessor by placing the latter's *minbar* in the Aqsa Mosque in the holy city (see Chapter 4). Carole Hillenbrand has described the careers of Nur al-Din and Saladin as a 'continuum', forming the real turning point in the development of the Muslim counter-crusade (Hillenbrand, 1999 a: 195). It certainly appears from his multi-faceted propaganda campaign that Saladin wished them to be seen this way.

Naturally, in his dealings with both other Muslim rulers and the Franks Saladin employed the traditional two-pronged approach of force and nego-tiations. Attacks on the Franks were easy to justify as part of his efforts in the military *jihad* against them, but he has been criticized by both contemporary and modern scholars, including members of his own retinue, for his wars against other Muslims. Saladin justified his actions by arguing that the imperative of unification to fight the holy war against the Franks should be recognized and obeyed by all Muslim rulers, and that those who did not do so were more concerned with secular ambitions than the good of Islam, and hence had to be compelled (Eddé, 2011: 93–4). Saladin's negotiations with Muslims were naturally acceptable, but diplomatic dealings with the Franks likewise required justification, particularly given that he himself was fiercely critical of the Zangids for negotiating with them. Saladin and his propagandists were always careful to present his own dealings with them as being both within the *Qur'an*'s regulations and only undertaken when absolutely necessary; thus they sought to preserve his image as a pious *mujahid*, reluctantly driven to treat with the enemy when there was no way to avoid it (Eddé, 2011: 271–3). In fact, Saladin undertook diplomatic relations with both the Franks and the Byzantines whenever it suited his needs, thus following the precedents of many earlier Muslim rulers, including Nur al-Din.

In both his diplomatic activities and his conduct of war, Saladin successfully cultivated a reputation for generosity and clemency, even though occasionally he ordered acts of shocking brutality. Nevertheless, both Muslim and non-Muslim sources commented on these qualities, albeit in both positive and negative ways. His panegyrists naturally drew on Islamic tradition in representing this conduct as entirely fitting an ideal Muslim ruler, but both they and other authors also sometimes questioned the actual value of such qualities. 'Imad al-Din al-Isfahani, for example, expresses regret that Saladin's generosity at Jerusalem resulted in the loss of substantial wealth for his treasury, while Ibn al-Athir states that Saladin's habit of freeing Frankish prisoners taken in battle contributed directly to his failure to take Tyre in 1187, since the Franks freed by Saladin went there and swelled its garrison (al-Isfahani, 1965: 135; Ibn al-Athir, 2007: 337). Nonetheless, this reputation generally served Saladin well in negotiations with both Muslim rivals and Frankish opponents, easing the handover of fortresses and cities and helping to establish his reputation as a pious Muslim, and his financial generosity doubtless assisted him in expanding his supporter base.

Saladin's open-handedness is often seen as indicative of a wider lack of economic sense, an impression that is not helped by comments such as that made by Baha' al-Din, who states that Saladin's treasurers used to hide money from him to prevent him from spending it [**Doc. 11**]. Al-Qadi al-Fadil repeatedly expressed concerns about the extent of Saladin's spending and its impact on the economy, famously commenting that Saladin had 'spent the money of Egypt to conquer Syria, the money of Syria to conquer **al-Jazira** [the region covering modern south-eastern Turkey, north-eastern Syria and north-western Iraq], and the money of all of them to conquer the coast' (Eddé, 2011: 427). However, both Eddé and Lev have questioned the idea that Saladin was financially irresponsible. It is clear that as soon as he took power in Egypt he undertook a number of measures intended to improve the economic health of his state, including re-organizing the collection of taxes and the distribution of *iqta's*, reforming the coinage and endowing the incomes of properties to finance his construction projects (so-called *waqf* endowments) (Eddé, 2011: 418–26; Lev, 2007: *passim*). He also devoted attention to commerce, seeking to maintain the vibrant trade between Egypt and the Italian cities (which also helped to secure supplies of

Al-Jazira: Arabic: 'the Peninsula'. The region roughly covering modern south-eastern Turkey, north-eastern Syria and north-western Iraq. It is mostly bracketed by the Tigris and Euphrates rivers.

war materials such as wood and iron), safeguarding as far as possible the land trade between Syria, Egypt and the Red Sea, and attempting to ensure the smooth running of markets. However, wars are expensive, spending constantly outstripped income, and so finances remained an ever-present challenge (Eddé, 2011: 426–8 and 447–61).

The other pillar on which Saladin based his power was his family. Saladin himself had succeeded his uncle Shirkuh in Egypt, and under his rule the **Ayyubid** state effectively formed a family confederation with himself at its head. In the early years, his most prominent supporters were his brothers al-Mu'azzam Turan-Shah (d. 1180) and al-'Adil Muhammad (d. 1218) and his nephew Taqi al-Din 'Umar (d. 1191), all of whom were given key responsibilities in Saladin's state. Other family members were also appointed to supporting positions, and later his sons al-Afdal 'Ali (d. 1225), al-'Aziz 'Uthman (d. 1198) and al-Zahir Ghazi (d. 1216) were given important governorships in the state, even though they had not yet reached adulthood. Naturally not all Saladin's subordinates were family members, but they formed a core upon whom he relied for backing. For the most part this arrangement proved effective, provided that Saladin's family co-operated. However, the system did not always work; for example, Saladin was furious when it became apparent that Taqi al-Din had left the siege of Acre on 2 March 1191 to pursue territorial ambitions around Lake Van rather than simply to visit his holdings in the north, though the sultan's fury swiftly turned to grief when he learned of his nephew's death on 10 October of the same year (Eddé, 2011: 127–8).

Ayyubids: Term used to refer to the family of Ayyub ibn Shadhi (d. 1173), the father of Saladin (r. 1169–93). After Saladin's death, other Ayyubids took over his territories, ruling them until the mid-thirteenth century.

THE VICTORIOUS *MUJAHID*

One of the ongoing unanswered questions in crusade studies is what happened at the council of war held by the Franks on the night of 2 July 1187, a full understanding of which would explain why King Guy of Lusignan marched his army out to its defeat at the Horns of Hattin. Like the western sources, the Muslim ones provide differing opinions on the discussion that took place. Baha' al-Din states merely that when they heard of the Muslim conquest of Tiberias, the Franks 'could not bear not to give in to their impulsive zeal, but set out at once' (Ibn Shaddad, 2001: 73). Both 'Imad al-Din and Ibn al-Athir give prominence to Raymond of Tripoli in their accounts, but in contrasting ways. 'Imad al-Din presents Raymond of Tripoli as having been traumatized by the news that the outer city of Tiberias had been taken, urging the king to act and saying that if the city fell completely, then the rest of the Frankish lands would follow (al-Isfahani, 1965: 76). Ibn al-Athir, on the other hand, presents Raymond as having exhorted the Franks to withhold from responding to Tiberias' plight, on the grounds that it would be difficult for Saladin to keep his army in the field; however, he also presents Raymond as having been opposed by Reynald of Châtillon, who accused him of siding with the Muslims (Ibn al-Athir, 2007: 321). Naturally, the Muslim authors did not witness the council of war, and so their accounts must be based on hearsay and speculation, but both 'Imad al-Din's and Ibn al-Athir's versions reflect currents found in the Frankish sources (Lyons and Jackson, 1984: 258). Whatever the truth of the matter, as indicated above Saladin destroyed the Frankish field army at Hattin and went on to conquer a huge swath of Frankish territory.

In terms of propaganda impact, the conquest of Jerusalem was, undoubtedly, Saladin's crowning achievement, acting as justification for the military action that he undertook against other Muslims and confirming his claims that his ultimate ambition was the re-conquest of the holy city. Great celebrations ensued among nobility and common folk alike as a result of the conquest. Poets and preachers praised Saladin in joyful panegyrics and pious rhetoric; indeed, the opportunity to be the first to preach and extol the sultan in the Aqsa Mosque after the re-conquest was hotly contested. Saladin himself was careful to make the most of his victory, not only sending out letters to the caliph and other Muslim rulers announcing his success, but also waiting to make his triumphal procession into Jerusalem on the anniversary of the Prophet's *mi'raj* and thus invoking the memory of sacred history to enhance his own image of piety (Hillenbrand, 1999 a: 188–91). He also devoted significant resources to restoring the Muslim institutions of the city. 'Imad al-Din, in his chronicle *al-Fath al-Qussi fi'l-Fath al-Qudsi* (Qussian Eloquence on the Conquest of Jerusalem), which covers Saladin's campaigns from 1187 to 1193, provides an account of Saladin's efforts in this regard entitled 'A Description of the Good Works that the Sultan Initiated in Jerusalem, and the Evil Works that he Eradicated'. In it he notes that his master restored the Aqsa Mosque, including uncovering the *mihrab* (which, he claims, the Templars had turned into a granary or a latrine) and removing other buildings, including a church, that the Templars had added to the structure. As indicated above, Saladin also installed Nur al-Din's *minbar* in the mosque, thus helping to tie himself into his predecessor's legacy. In his work 'Imad al-Din goes on to note that Saladin also purified the Dome of the Rock, which the Franks had turned into a church, removing its Christian accoutrements and uncovering the sacred rock itself, with its imprint of the Prophet Muhammad's foot. The sultan also had a number of other Christian buildings converted into Islamic ones such as Sufi convents and *madrasas*. However, not all Christian buildings suffered this fate; a number of churches were spared including, most notably, the Church of the Holy Sepulchre (*kanisat al-qiyama* [Church of the Resurrection] in Arabic, though for centuries Muslim writers had nicknamed it *kanisat al-qumama*, a change of one letter [in

Arabic] that renamed it 'the Church of Garbage'). Some of Saladin's advisors did suggest that he demolish the church to remove its attraction for Christian pilgrims and crusaders, but others pointed out that the holy site itself, rather than the church building, was the attraction, and that the caliph 'Umar ibn al-Khattab (r. 634–44), who had first conquered Jerusalem in 638, had left it unharmed for the Christians (al-Isfahani, 1965: 137–46). As Eddé notes, 'Imad al-Din refrains from also mentioning that the Muslims could impose heavy fees on Christian pilgrims who visited the site (Eddé, 2011: 224). It is worth noting that the Christian presence in Jerusalem was not completely eradicated; thousands of eastern Christians, and even some Frankish ones, were allowed to remain once they had paid their ransoms (Eddé, 2011: 219 and 224). However, Saladin put in great efforts to restore a distinctively and perceptibly Islamic character to the holy city, in the process emphasizing his own dedication to the faith.

THE THIRD CRUSADE

While the re-conquest of Jerusalem was Saladin's greatest achievement, his failure to defeat the forces of the Third Crusade was probably his greatest frustration. Having come within sight of destroying the Kingdom of Jerusalem completely, the sultan found himself neither able to prevent the Frankish re-conquest of Acre nor able to score a decisive victory against the armies of Richard the Lionheart. Saladin's principal difficulty was holding sufficient manpower in the field. In 1189 he had been forced to allow his troops to disperse after years of campaigning, and thus he only had a reduced force available when Guy of Lusignan besieged Acre. Thereafter Saladin sent repeated appeals for aid to the rulers of the various cities that theoretically owed him support, as well as other Muslim rulers, but his calls, lacking the lofty goal of the conquest of Jerusalem and being made to men who were weary from years of conflict, received only patchy responses; he was never again able to command a great muster like that which had preceded the Battle of Hattin. From the caliph of Baghdad, in particular, he received what can only be understood as a diplomatic insult: two loads of *naft* (naphtha, Greek fire), five naphtha artificers, some spear-shafts and a note authorizing him to borrow a paltry 20,000 *dinars* from the merchants on the caliph's behalf. Relations between Saladin and the 'Abbasid caliph al-Nasir (r. 1180–1225) had been tense for years, and it is likely that the caliph was concerned about where Saladin might direct his attention if he defeated the Franks. The last part of the caliph's gift highlights the fact that by now financial shortages were also impeding Saladin's ability to field sufficient forces to neutralize the Frankish threat. Saladin himself remarked that he was spending more than 20,000 *dinars* a *day* to support the war effort (Lyons and Jackson, 1984: 310–11), and as we have already seen, his income was not sufficient to cover such requirements.

Meanwhile the Franks had been reinforced by large contingents from overseas, fired with enthusiasm for the crusade and zealous to ride to the rescue of the holy city from the infidel. In addition, the Franks were led by Richard the Lionheart, an expert general who was Saladin's equal on the battlefield. Perhaps this is best exemplified by the Franks' march south along the coast in 1191. Richard arranged his forces with the knights in a central column, supplied and protected by half the infantry, the baggage train and a fleet on the seaward side, and the other half of the infantry, including archers, protecting the column on the landward side (Riley-Smith, 1991: 64). The whole army maintained a disciplined formation and was hence able to avoid being broken up by the usual Muslim harassing tactics. At Arsuf Saladin was finally able to provoke a break in the Franks' formation, when two Hospitaller knights charged the Muslim lines, leading the remaining Hospitallers and the French contingent to follow them. Richard quickly ordered the remaining knights to charge and turned the army's broken formation into a victorious one (Phillips, 2002: 146).

Yet despite his difficulties, Saladin was able to fight Richard to a stalemate. Since he could not beat the Frankish army in a pitched battle, Saladin adopted a number of tactics to impede its advance on Jerusalem. As noted above, he destroyed fortresses on the route between Jaffa and the holy city that might be used as bases from which to attack it. He also destroyed the cisterns around Jerusalem, so that it would be difficult to ensure that there was enough water available for the crusading army. Finally, he mounted harassing attacks on the Franks' supply lines. Thus Saladin prevented the Franks from making an attack on Jerusalem by ensuring that they could not support it adequately (Lyons and Jackson, 1984: 352–4). Faced with this frustrating situation, and concerned about the state of his kingdom in Europe, Richard was forced to recognize the impasse and eventually a mutually acceptable treaty was negotiated.

As indicated above, the agreement made in September 1192 between Richard and Saladin represented the culmination of periodic discussions over the years that the former had been in the Levant. Saladin and Richard seem to have regarded each other with great respect, though they never met; Baha' al-Din notes that Richard repeatedly asked for a meeting, but Saladin always refused; the sultan explained his refusal by saying, 'Kings do not meet unless an agreement has been reached. It is not good for them to fight after meeting and eating together' (Ibn Shaddad, 2001: 153). Instead, Saladin's chief negotiator was his brother, al-'Adil Muhammad, with whom Richard seems to have enjoyed a close friendship, with interesting results; see what follows.

In some senses the major issues at stake in the negotiations are effectively summed up by an exchange of letters that took place between Richard and Saladin in October 1191, and which is recorded by Baha' al-Din [**Doc. 12**]. The principal point of contention was Jerusalem, along with the acceptable extent of Frankish territories and the relic of the True Cross. Supplementary concerns were the fate of prisoners, defensive structures and sources of income. Perhaps the most imaginative, if unrealistic, solution mooted at the time was Richard's proposal that al-'Adil marry his sister Joan, with the couple then ruling in Jerusalem, where Frankish clergy would be permitted to live but Frankish troops would not. Both al-'Adil and Saladin accepted the proposal, though the latter thought it was not likely to work out, and he was proved correct when the lady refused marriage to a non-Christian, a position in which she was supported by members of the Frankish nobility. Al-'Adil refused Richard's attempts to persuade him to convert, and after further discussions the idea fell through. As indicated above, the eventual solution focused on Jerusalem, the extent of Frankish territory, fortresses and income; prisoner concerns were not addressed in the final agreement, nor was the fate of the True Cross, which was sent after Saladin's death to the caliph of Baghdad and in the process passed out of the historical record (Eddé, 2011: 212 and 263–9).

CONCLUSION

To an even greater degree than with Nur al-Din, scholarly discussions of Saladin have often focused on the extent to which he was motivated by genuine piety, and how far his actions were actually driven by political aims. Opinions have ranged from one extreme to the other, with some arguing that Saladin was a true devotee of his faith and the military *jihad*, while others have insisted that he was an ambitious politician who cynically made use of religious propaganda to support his secular goals. There is certainly plenty of evidence to support both positions, but ultimately we can never know the absolute truth of the matter, and Eddé argues that the over-concentration of historians on this aspect of Saladin's career has until recently been an unwelcome and prevalent distraction from a full consideration of the period (Eddé, 2011: 615–19).

In the meantime, it is useful to consider the impact of Saladin's reign on the Muslim Levant, which attests to the greatness of his achievement, regardless of his motivations. Building on the military and propaganda foundations laid by Nur al-Din, Saladin unified an immense swath of territory under his banner, and then directed its resources and manpower to conquer the greater part of the Frankish states, including bringing the holy city of Jerusalem back under Muslim rule. Then, despite the difficulties that he faced in holding an effective fighting force in the field, he was able to blunt the Third Crusade sufficiently for the Franks to remain largely confined to a narrow strip on the Levantine coast, unable to re-take Jerusalem. By the time of Saladin's death the Muslim states of the Levant had become a unified confederation, mostly ruled by Saladin's family, that had proved to be an effective basis for opposition to the Franks. However, that unity would not continue under Saladin's successors.

FURTHER READING

Numerous books have been published on Saladin, the most comprehensive of which is Anne-Marie Eddé's recent detailed study, *Saladin* (2011). Another important work is Malcolm Cameron Lyons and David E.P. Jackson's *Saladin: The Politics of the Holy War* (1984), while Carole Hillenbrand's *The Crusades: Islamic Perspectives* (1999 a) provides a discussion of Saladin's *jihad* that includes a helpful comparison of Saladin and Nur al-Din. For a sense of the widely differing interpretations of Saladin's motives that exist, it is worth comparing H.A.R. Gibb's *The Life of Saladin* (1973) with Andrew S. Ehrenkreutz's *Saladin* (1972). Ehrenkreutz's work includes a number of useful discussions of Saladin's economic policies, and these are also the subject of Yaacov Lev's important article, 'Saladin's Economic Policies and the Economy of Ayyubid Egypt' (2007). On the Battle of Hattin see in the first instance Benjamin Z. Kedar's article, 'The Battle of Hattin Revisited' (1992) and R.C. Smail, *Crusading Warfare, 1097–1193* (1995). On Saladin and the Third Crusade in particular, readers of German will also appreciate Hannes Möhring's *Saladin und der Dritte Kreuzzug: Aiyubidische Strategie und Diplomatie im Vergleich vornehmlich der Arabischen mit den Lateinischen Quellen* (1980). On the establishment of the Ayyubid state, and the role played by Saladin's family in particular, see R. Stephen Humphreys, *From Saladin to the Mongols: The Ayyubids of Damascus, 1193–1260* (1977). On religious life, including preaching of the *jihad*, see Daniella Talmon-Heller, 'Islamic Preaching in Syria during the Counter-Crusade (Twelfth–Thirteenth Centuries)' (2007 b) and, again, *Islamic Piety in Medieval Syria* (2007 a).

6

War and peace in the twelfth-century Levant

This chapter presents an intermission in our examination of events in the Levant during the crusading period. Our focus now turns to a wider consideration of Muslim–Frankish interaction both on and off the battlefield. First, we will consider in general terms what the Muslims actually learned about the Franks during the period. Then we will discuss Muslim military tactics. Subsequently we will consider Muslim–Frankish relations off the battlefield, including the situation of Muslims under Latin rule, treaties and trade, before devoting closer attention to the opinions that Muslim writers present us with on some aspects of Frankish culture.

THE PROBLEM OF THE SOURCES

As we seek to explore the wider interactions between the Muslims and the Franks, we immediately encounter a difficulty in that the amount of source material that is available to us drops significantly. Many of the sources that we have been relying on so far are concerned above all with political history, telling us much about the activities of Muslim rulers, but the Franks normally only appear when they have a direct impact on the territories of these rulers. Aspects of Frankish internal politics do appear in the Muslim sources, but their deeper cultural characteristics are mostly ignored by them. The accounts of the battles that we have also tend to be presented only in simple terms, principally from a religious point of view rather than an expert military one; we read far more often about the role of the supernatural in victories won by one side or the other, and far less often about the particular strategic manoeuvres that carried the day (see, for example, **Doc. 10**). This is of course not surprising, since the majority of the writers of the Muslim sources tended to be religiously trained scholars rather than military officers.

However, the situation is not entirely gloomy. It is possible to glean a certain amount about Muslim–Frankish interactions from the anecdotes with which the Muslim writers adorn their narratives, and we do have a few cases of specialized works that give us a deeper understanding of the topics under discussion here. When we come to examine Muslim military tactics and the impact that the Franks had on these, we are fortunate that we have a number of military manuals from the twelfth and thirteenth centuries, which contain information on the various sorts of weapons that Muslim soldiers used and the tactics that they employed, although the extent to which such works present ideals rather than realities is of course something that we must bear in mind [**Doc. 13**]. These works can be supplemented with the evidence of both artistic works and other texts to give us greater insight (Hillenbrand, 1999 a: 432–9). Learning about Frankish–Muslim interaction off the battlefield is harder, as we of course do not have specialized ethnographic studies of the Franks written by Muslim authors, and so much of our evidence is anecdotal; this of course raises concerns about how far it is reliable and how far truth is subordinated to the literary or propagandistic aims of the writers in question.

A case in point is the *Kitab al-I'tibar* (Book of Contemplation) of the emir Usama ibn Munqidh, a work that has enjoyed perhaps disproportionate attention in the west due to both its uniqueness and its having been available in translation since the end of the nineteenth century. Born in his clan stronghold of Shayzar in northern Syria, Usama had a chequered career during which he spent periods serving as an officer under both a number of Sunni rulers in Syria and the Fatimid caliphs in Egypt; in many instances he had to move on after becoming involved in dangerous political entanglements! He eventually joined the court of Saladin, where he was initially warmly welcomed but seems to have become (or at least felt) neglected by his exalted patron. He died in 1188 at the age of 93, lamenting the loss of his youthful vigour (Cobb, 2005: *passim*). The *Kitab al-I'tibar*, which presents itself as the memoirs of the aging Usama, has been much celebrated by historians as giving an account of one Muslim's relations with the Franks, both in battle and in times of peace. Certainly Usama claims to have had friends among the Latins, including even the Templars, who apparently used to let him pray in a mosque next to their headquarters in the Aqsa Mosque on the Temple Mount (Usama, 2008: 147), and he describes his experiences of Frankish culture in a wide range of forms, including judicial proceedings, medical practices and their behaviour towards women [**Doc. 14**]. However, as a number of scholars have noted, we cannot take Usama's work at face value. As mentioned previously, Usama was well known for his literary skills, and his purported memoirs show a wealth of features that indicate that they are intended to be entertaining and didactic rather than a straightforward account of his experiences; in particular, following Qur'anic precedent they juxtapose contrasting examples that seek to teach readers how to live as a good and honourable Muslim in the face of the inevitability of divine decree (Irwin, 1998: 73–5; Cobb, 2005: 67–91). Thus when we read his work we must recall that it is one that is carefully constructed, and much of what he tells us is probably embroidered at the very least, if not at times complete fabrication; Usama was a talented storyteller who preferred not to let the facts get in the way of a good yarn, if it served his purposes. That said, at times he perhaps reveals more to us about Frankish–Muslim interactions than he intends, as will be discussed below.

THE 'FRANKS'

Despite the problematic nature of the sources, it is possible to detect a marked evolution in Muslim knowledge of the Franks during the crusading period. As we have indicated earlier, the Arabic term *ifranj* (along with similar permutations of the *f-r-n-j* root letters), which we translate as 'Franks', was originally used by Muslim writers to refer to the people of, roughly, the Frankish territories that emerged after the collapse of the Roman Empire and came under the sway of the Merovingians and their successors, the Carolingians. However, with the onset of the Crusades the term came to be used of western Europeans in general, without intending to refer to a particular part of the region. This generalized usage persisted as the decades passed, even though it is apparent that by the second half of the twelfth century the Muslims had gradually gained a deeper understanding of the differences between the origins of the various Franks whom they encountered. Ibn al-Qalanisi, writing in about 1145–60, was already distinguishing the Genoese from the rest of the Franks, though he also occasionally mixed up names and ethnicities, calling Conrad III of Germany (r. 1138–52), for example, by the name 'Alman', probably an Arabicization of the medieval French word *aleman* (German) [**Doc. 7.i**]. Later writers clearly distinguished between the ethnicities of the Franks, as well as seeing the Franks of the crusader states as being distinct from the Franks of Europe, even as they continued to use *ifranj* as an over-arching ethnic term (see, for example, **Doc. 7.ii**). Indeed, as we have noted (see Chapter 4), some writers suggested that Muslim exploitation of the distinction between 'local' and 'foreign' Franks played a part in the thwarting of the Second Crusade's attack on Damascus (Hillenbrand, 1999 a: 303 and 331–4; Christie, 1999: 63–71 and 187–90). By the same token, Usama gives us two (typically balanced) anecdotes through which he contrasts the rough nature of Franks who are newly arrived from Europe with the more refined character of those who have lived in the Levant for some time and have adapted to Middle Eastern ways, though he is careful to note that the latter 'are the exception and should not be considered representative' (Usama, 2008: 147 and 153–4; Cobb, 2005: 104–5; Christie, 1999: 69–71).

We also see Muslim writers singling out particular figures by name in order to express respect or condemnation; for example, the merits of Richard I the Lionheart of England, Louis IX of France and the Holy Roman Emperor Frederick II are all praised by Muslim writers, while Conrad of Montferrat (r. as King of Jerusalem, 1190–2) and above all Reynald of Châtillon are vehemently criticized (Hillenbrand, 1999 a: 336–47). Of course, often such praise is given with ulterior motives, not the least of which is the reflection of even greater praise on the Muslim heroes who fought or defeated such formidable opponents.

It is worth noting that the Muslim writers were undoubtedly aware from the outset that the Franks were Christians. The Muslims had been intimately acquainted with Christians living within their communities for centuries, as we have seen (see Chapter 2), and some of them knew a significant amount about Christianity. However, the Muslim sources play down this under-standing, instead emphasizing the (to them) heretical nature of the Christian faith, above all by using words such as **kuffar** (blasphemers or infidels) and **mushrikun** (polytheists) to refer to their enemies, and by regularly calling down God's curses upon them (see, for example, **Doc. 14.i**); this allows them to present the Franks firmly as enemies of both the Muslim inhabitants of the Levant and God Himself. We will return to the Muslim sources' presentation of Frankish Christianity below.

It is worth considering whence the Muslims probably derived their improving knowledge of the Franks. As we have seen, even before the arrival of the first crusaders the Muslims had encountered Franks, including those serving in the Byzantine armies and those who visited the east as merchants, ambassadors or pilgrims. It is clear that these interactions continued through-out the crusading period, although the Frankish troops whom the Muslims encountered were now usually fighting on their own behalf rather than that of the Byzantines, or even sometimes serving as mercenaries in Muslim armies (Nicolle, 1999: 208). With regard to diplomatic contacts, it is clear that Muslim rulers increasingly exchanged embassies with not only local Frankish rulers, but also more distant European monarchs and popes. The Italian trading powers had already been negotiating with the rulers of Egypt before the crusad-ing period, but in the latter half of the twelfth century Muslim–Frankish diplomacy expanded in volume and geographical range; early evidence of this includes letters exchanged between Saladin and both Frederick I Barbarossa and the papacy (Eddé, 2011: 244–5 and 302), and such diplomatic inter-actions expanded still further after the sultan's death. Muslim writers would also have encountered both Frankish converts to Islam and Frankish slaves who had been former prisoners of war; there were many of the latter in

Kuffar: Arabic: 'blas-phemers' or 'infidels'. A term applied by the Muslim sources to the Franks, whose claims that Jesus was the son of God were seen by the Muslims as blasphemous.

Mushrikun: Arabic: 'polytheists'. A term used by the Muslim sources of the Franks as a way of denigrating them.

particular, especially in the wake of the Battle of Hattin in 1187. Muslims and Franks also interacted socially; we have already noted that Usama described some Templars in Jerusalem as being his friends, and both he and other writers give accounts of Frankish festivals that they attended. Thus it is apparent that as the Crusades proceeded there were ever more opportunities for the Muslims and the Franks to gain a fuller understanding of each other's cultures and habits. There were, however, other factors that limited the extent to which such opportunities influenced the Muslim sources, as we shall see.

THE CONDUCT OF WAR

It is important to note from the outset that the armies with which the Muslims fought the Franks were diverse in composition and tactics, and every military encounter had its own particular circumstances and physical context, so that what follows is only a brief overview of the armies and tactics of the Muslim forces. When the crusaders arrived in the east, the Fatimid army was in the process of being reformed by the viziers Badr al-Jamali and al-Afdal Shahanshah. The core of the army was made up of infantry, including archers and javelin troops, who were supported by light cavalry and a range of other troops, including mercenary light infantry from Daylam in Persia, black African slaves serving as heavy infantry and Turkish *mamluks* and horse-archers. As a result of the reforms, the mercenary and slave contingents were expanded, though the core contingents remained the basis of Fatimid tactics, which required infantry and cavalry to co-operate effectively (Nicolle, 1999: 119–20, 2007: Vol. 2, pp. 39–42).

The forces used by the Seljuks and Zangids continued, broadly, to follow the earlier Seljuk model, being based around two core contingents, one consisting of Turkish *mamluks*, who fought equally effectively with bows and close-combat weapons, and the other consisting of Turkmen horse-archers. In the case of the Zangids, such forces were supplemented with free Kurdish cavalry. Thus their armies continued to emphasize mobility in their tactics. In the twelfth and thirteenth centuries the Seljuks of *Rum* expanded their forces to include a wider range of mercenary and allied contingents. Some of these consisted of European or Frankish troops, who seem not to have been criticized by western sources for 'fighting for the enemy', in contrast to the reaction that such mercenaries received when fighting for Muslim rulers of Syria or Egypt (Nicolle, 1999: 176–8 and 207–9, 2007: Vol. 2, p. 35; Holt, 1986: 42–3).

Saladin and his successors followed the Seljuk and Zangid model, basing their armies above all on cavalry, principally Turkish *mamluks* and free

Turkmen and Kurdish troops. Saladin did initially make use of infantry, but over time he and his successors placed an increasing emphasis on cavalry armies, with infantry being used only in siege actions. In addition, Saladin's successors reduced the prominence of Kurdish troops in their forces, instead expanding the *mamluk* contingents in their armies. The Ayyubids also made use of additional mercenary and allied contingents drawn from various parts of the Muslim world (Nicolle, 1999: 120–1, 2007: Vol. 2, pp. 42–5; Hillenbrand, 1999 a: 445).

It is important not to neglect the auxiliary troops who swelled the ranks of the Muslim armies. As indicated above, for sieges it would be necessary to employ infantry, and city militias could be drawn on to assist with this, thus acting as offensive as well as defensive troops; at times city militiamen were also even mounted on horses and used as cavalry. Bedouin Arabs also frequently served in Muslim armies, and charismatic rulers such as Nur al-Din and Saladin also attracted volunteer soldiers; Saladin's forces at the Battle of Hattin in 1187, for example, included a large contingent of ascetics and Sufis who had chosen to take up arms in the *jihad* against the Franks (Nicolle, 1999: 176–8, 2007, Vol. 2, p. 35; Holt, 1986: 42–3; Hillenbrand, 1999 a: 445).

It is clear from the above that the majority of the Muslim armies consisted mainly of cavalry, with mobility being the most prized quality in troops. On the battlefield, Muslim armies were normally divided into a centre and two wings, with the greater part of the cavalry being found in the centre; this formation could be supported with a vanguard and additional flanking units. Favoured tactics included harassment of the enemy by repeated waves of horse-archers, each of which would advance, shower the enemy with arrows and then retreat to make way for the next, which would arrive about ten seconds later; the attrition from such attacks was intended to weaken a force and make it vulnerable to a final, crushing cavalry charge. Related to this was the traditional Muslim tactic of *al-karr wa'l-farr*, a rotation system that enabled repeated attacks to be made, sometimes by different units of attackers. This is not to say that Muslim troops were not also capable of the more traditional military manoeuvres; the *mamluks* were known for the effectiveness of their shock charges, and also became increasingly skilled at standing, rapid-fire arrow volleys that enabled them to decimate more mobile foes like the Mongols (Nicolle, 2007: Vol. 2, pp. 122–50).

There is one Frankish military manoeuvre that attracted particular attention from Muslim chroniclers, and has also received much attention from modern scholars: the Frankish heavy cavalry charge. When describing the Frankish effort to take Damascus in 1148, Ibn al-Qalanisi notes that at one point the Frankish cavalry prepared to make the charge 'for which they are famous', though in this case without success (Ibn al-Qalanisi, 1983: 464).

Joshua Prawer has described the charge of the Frankish heavy cavalry, when launched, as 'pareil à un bloc de fer se mouvant à toute vitesse' (like a block of iron moving at full speed; Prawer, 1964: 178). The potential psychological impact and physical destructiveness of the Frankish cavalry charge was immense; it could shatter a battle line and punch a hole through an army. However, it was an attack of opportunity, requiring particular circumstances, rather than a manoeuvre that could be set up in advance, which made it difficult to deliver. In addition, the Muslims soon learned ways to neutralize its effectiveness, including avoiding presenting a static target or opening their ranks to allow the charge to pass through the gap; the charging unit could then be attacked in the flanks or rear (as seen at the Battle of Hattin in 1187; see Chapter 5). In response, the Franks sought to ensure that infantry cross-bowmen co-operated effectively with cavalry, protecting them from harassment until suitable opportunities to charge arose, but the Muslims became so skilled at minimizing such opportunities that the tactic eventually saw little use against them. The decline of the use by Muslim armies of infantry, the most obvious targets for such cavalry charges, was also a contributory factor (Nicolle, 2007, Vol. 1, pp. 65–8).

It is worth noting that pitched battles between Muslims and Franks were actually relatively rare. Forces for such encounters required considerable resources to mount, and they were incredibly destructive in terms of human lives and equipment. For the Latin states, which relied on careful co-operation of the Frankish field army and castles for their survival, engaging in major battles was a risky endeavour, for the destruction of the army would leave the strongholds and cities of the Latin states vulnerable to attack; this was exactly what happened in the wake of the Battle of Hattin in 1187. Thus most encounters between military forces tended to be skirmishes, often occurring as a result of forces from one side being sent out to repel enemy forces who had entered their territory to conduct raids. Given this situation, siege warfare was more decisive in determining the balance of power between Muslims and Franks.

Both the Franks and the Muslims built fortifications. The prevailing view of scholars thus far has been that the Franks were more skilled and innovative at building fortifications, something that resulted both from their already having superior techniques at their disposal when they arrived in the Levant and from the necessity of using networks of fortifications to ensure the survival of the Latin states (Hillenbrand, 1999 a: 468 and 502–4). However, this view has recently been challenged by a number of scholars, including David Nicolle and Kate Raphael; Nicolle, for example, has pointed out that many of the first castles built by the crusaders were erected on the foundations of earlier Muslim strongholds, and that it was from the Muslims that the Franks learned to build cisterns in castles to store water, a vital requirement in withstanding a siege (Nicolle, 2007: Vol. 2, p. 204). The situation is further complicated by the fact that both the Muslims and the Franks would often restore and re-use fortifications that they took from each other, sometimes extending or modifying them, and both sides also built on even earlier structures; for example, Saladin's brother al-'Adil Muhammad based the citadel of Busra al-Sham on a Roman theatre, to which he added concentric walls between 1202 and 1218 (Hillenbrand, 1999 a: 500; Nicolle, 2007: Vol. 2, p. 218). It is also clear that both the Franks and the Muslims were influenced by other cultures of the area, such as the Byzantines and Armenians. An early example from the Muslim side is the massive *Bab al-Futuh* (Gate of Conquests; see Plate 3) in Cairo, which was completed in 1087, shortly before the arrival of the crusaders, at the orders of Badr al-Jamali, the vizier of the Fatimid caliph, who was himself Armenian and employed fellow Armenian architects in the task; it is not surprising, then, that it shows similarities to contemporary Greater Armenian architecture (Ettinghausen and Grabar, 1994: 186). Thus we cannot make neat comparisons between the Muslims and Franks in terms of superiority or inferiority in their military architecture.

We can, however, detect a different emphasis in the military architecture created by the Muslims and the Franks. While the Latins built primarily castles, the Muslims devoted most of their attention to strengthening the defences of cities. This is not to disregard the importance or quality of the castles built by Muslim rulers; for example, both Nicolle and Raphael have drawn attention to the castle at Ajlun, built in the Jordan valley at the orders of Saladin in 1184–5, which is superior in design and layout to the nearby crusader castle of Belvoir (Nicolle, 2007: Vol. 2, p. 218; Raphael, 2011, 11–51; see Plate 4). However, Muslim rulers spent far more time and resources on strengthening the walls and citadels of towns and cities, something that Carole Hillenbrand ascribes to the tendencies of the Muslims of the region to see cities as their natural places of shelter, with the citadels providing fortified strongholds in time of need (Hillenbrand, 1999 a: 473). Saladin, for example, spent considerable resources strengthening the walls and citadels of a number of Muslim cities; perhaps the best-known surviving example of this is the Citadel in Cairo, which was begun at his orders in 1176. The Citadel's fortifications were completed after his death by his brother al-'Adil Muhammad, and the complex was further expanded by subsequent rulers of Egypt in the centuries that followed (Hillenbrand, 1999 a: 478–9; see Plate 5).

The equipment and weapons used by both Muslims and Franks were, on the whole, the same. Both attackers and defenders would use swing-beam mangonels (initially pulled by hand but later by a counterweight), crossbows and bows to shoot projectiles (both regular and incendiary) at each other and (in the case of the attackers' mangonels) to damage fortifications. Defenders would also use rocks, javelins, incendiaries and anything else suitable that came to hand to repel those trying to get into the stronghold being attacked. Attackers would use various forms of rams to damage walls and gates. Likewise, they would use wheeled, wooden shelters and siege towers to attack walls and protect those operating rams or conducting sapping operations, though it seems that the Muslims made less use of these; Nicolle ascribes this both to the fact that the Muslims were expert in the use of incendiaries, including naphtha (Greek fire), and hence were aware of how easy such constructions were to destroy, and to the fact that wood was always in short supply (Hillenbrand 1999 a: 523–9; Nicolle, 2007: Vol. 2, p. 237).

Naturally, the means used to prosecute sieges varied. Many of the weapons mentioned above were intended to batter fortifications and their defenders, both to create breaches through which to gain entry, reducing the number of capable defenders in the process, and to intimidate the enemy into surrendering. Sappers would dig tunnels under walls, which they would then fill with incendiary materials and set fire to; the resultant conflagration would create a weakness in a wall's foundations that could cause it to collapse. Of course, if the enemy became aware of the sapping attempt, they might dig a moat or counter-tunnel to intercept the sappers, which could lead to furious battles being fought in the tunnels. Other means might be used to harm enemy morale, including playing drums during assaults to create an intimidating noise or forging letters from the defenders' allies or military superiors telling them to surrender. Naturally, the besiegers would attempt to cut off supplies to the stronghold that they were attacking, to weaken their enemies both physically and psychologically. At times bribery or trickery led to the surrender of fortresses. Taking a city or castle by storm was probably the least-preferred option, as it would be very costly in terms of casualties and damage to the edifice in question, requiring a leader to rebuild both his forces and also the defences of the stronghold, if he wanted to re-use it (Hillenbrand, 1999 a: 529–33; Nicolle, 2007: Vol. 2, pp. 220–41).

Before concluding our discussion of warfare, we should give brief consideration to the role of Muslim navies in the war with the Franks. From the outset the crusaders outclassed the Muslims at naval warfare. When the Franks arrived in the Levant, the only political power there with any naval might was the Fatimid caliphate. However, while Fatimid fleets had been prominent in the eastern Mediterranean in the tenth and eleventh centuries, by the time that the First Crusade arrived the Fatimid navy was in decline and was unable to contribute significantly to the effort to prevent the Franks, who were supported by fleets from the Italian cities, from taking most of the ports on the coast of Syria and Palestine and hence securing a major tactical advantage. Saladin attempted to revive the Egyptian fleet with some success, even securing trade deals with the Italian city-states for raw materials, but was not sufficiently expert in naval warfare to use his ships effectively against the Franks, in the Mediterranean at least; as we have seen, his maritime activities in the Red Sea were more successful. His successors and their political heirs, the Mamluks (see Chapters 7 and 8) on the whole did not seek to recover a naval advantage against the Franks. As we shall see, the Mamluk solution to the problem was to adopt a general policy of razing the ports that they took from the Franks, so that they could not be used again as bridgeheads for crusading forces (Hillenbrand, 1999 a: 561–77; Nicolle, 2007: Vol. 2, pp. 256–68).

Yet we must not be too hasty to criticize the Muslim rulers of the time for their neglect of the maritime aspect of warfare. Admittedly, Muslim rulers could have made more efforts to prosecute the maritime military *jihad* against the Franks, but there were also a number of other factors that hindered the Levantine Muslim leaders from establishing a serious military presence in the Mediterranean Sea. As we have already noted, wood was always in short supply, and so were iron and wax, and given that the major source of these valuable resources for the Levant was Europe, their importation was periodically interrupted whenever military conflict led to a suspension of trade. In addition, both ships and their crews were expensive, and in many cases rulers' coffers were already drained from assembling land-based armies. As Nicolle notes, the Muslims actually exceeded the Franks in terms of their theoretical expertise in shipbuilding and maritime activity; however, they did not translate this into practical dominance of the Mediterranean's waters (Hillenbrand, 1999 a: 558–9 and 576–7; Nicolle, 2007: Vol. 2, pp. 256–68, esp. 256–7).

Let us return to our main question: to what degree were Muslim military tactics and technology influenced by the presence of the Franks? We have already touched on debates among scholars about the extent to which crusader military technology outstripped that of the Muslims, thus enabling the success of the First Crusade and the survival of the Frankish states for almost two centuries. Lynn White in particular described the Crusades as 'implemented by the world's best military technology', and scholars seeking to understand the eventual demise of the crusader states generally explained it as having been a result of the Muslims outnumbering the Franks, rather than superior Muslim strategy or other causes (White, 1975: 97–112, esp. 111; France, 1997: 163; Hillenbrand, 1999 a: 578–9). However, more recently a number of scholars have argued for other factors playing a prominent part, in particular a lack of desire and capacity on the part of the Muslims to resist or extirpate the Franks; Carole Hillenbrand has noted that the Mamluks, who eventually swept the Franks from the coast (see Chapter 8), were distinctive in having 'the expertise, resources and will to conduct [. . .] a series of sieges and to uproot the Franks definitively' (Hillenbrand 1999 a: 580).

In the meantime other scholars, including John France and David Nicolle, have shown that the Muslim forces were not actually inferior, in terms of their technology and structure, as has previously been assumed. As Nicolle has noted, the small but significant contingents of heavy cavalry that were used in Muslim armies during the period were actually, at least until the end of the twelfth century, more heavily armoured than the western knights, wearing both lamellar and mail armour and also using horse-armour; the latter in particular was only adopted by European cavalry in the thirteenth century. Likewise, the flow of influence with regard to gunpowder and incendiary weapons was probably from east to west, with Muslim ideas influencing Frankish and European ones. Meanwhile, as we have seen, there was probably also a mutual exchange of ideas in military engineering as better ways of resisting and prosecuting sieges developed (France, 1997: 163–76; Nicolle, 2007: Vol. 2, p. 293; Nicolle, 1994: 31–2 and 45).

MUSLIMS UNDER FRANKISH RULE

Despite the hostility and resentment that they aroused, the Frankish conquests of Muslim territory did not result in mass-migrations of Muslims from the lands that had fallen into Latin hands. Certainly there were many who fled the Frankish attacks, particularly from cities in the aftermath of massacres like the ones that took place at Ma'arrat al-Nu'man in 1098 and Jerusalem in 1099. However, it is clear that for most Muslim peasants, once the dust of the First Crusade had settled, life did not change significantly, except that they were now paying taxes to Frankish rather than Muslim overlords. It was neither practical nor desirable for the Franks to expel the Muslim inhabitants of their new territories, for the former were few in number and could not import serfs of their own to work abandoned fields. The Franks became, on the whole, a ruling minority reigning over the majority inhabitants of the region, who as we have noted were a mixture of Muslims, eastern Christians and Jews (Prawer: 2001: 46–93). Frenkel has argued that there was a significant change in the lives of the Levantine peasantry, in that the Franks' fusion of the pre-existent *iqta'* system with European feudal institutions led to them becoming serfs under Latin rule, and then remaining so under Saladin and his successors when they maintained the Frankish practices after they conquered their lands (Frenkel, 1997: *passim*). It is, however, very difficult to make generalizations about Frankish treatment of the peoples whom they conquered, as there was a great deal of variation from place to place, and every situation was different.

Why did most of the Muslim peasants acquiesce to Latin rule? It is of course important to bear in mind that for peasants at the time, in both Europe and the Levant, the decision to abandon one's lands and move to another place was not an easy one, and was often not practical simply because in doing so one was giving up one's means of survival. However, it does seem that when faced with the complex ethnic and religious composition of the Levant, the Franks chose on the whole to enact only limited changes to the social structures that they encountered, enough to impose and maintain their ruling position but not to disrupt the established order any more than necessary. The Franks allowed the subject populations to practise their own religions and did not generally seek to convert them to Catholic Christianity, although of course they did appropriate a number of Muslim religious buildings, including the Dome of the Rock and the Aqsa Mosque in Jerusalem. A number of Muslims did convert, and some even rose to positions of prominence in their conquerors' governments and military, but some Frankish lords found it more profitable to discourage or even prevent conversion of their non-Christian subjects, since non-Christian slaves who converted to Christianity were legally entitled to their freedom (Kedar, 1997 a: 190–3). Muslims were treated as inferior to Christians (including eastern Christians) in matters of law, and taxation was heavy, but Muslim peasants were taxed heavily by their Muslim overlords too, and in some cases this actually resulted in Muslims under Frankish rule being taxed less heavily than their neighbours under Muslim rule (Kedar, 1990: 153–74). The Spanish Muslim Muhammad ibn Jubayr (1145–1217) travelled through Frankish lands on the way back from performing the *hajj*, which he had apparently undertaken in remorse at having drunk seven cups of wine (Ibn Jubayr, 2001: 15); in his record of his travels he expresses his outrage at the sight of Muslims preferring Frankish to Muslim rule:

> Our entire route passed through uninterrupted landed estates and orderly settlements, of which all of the inhabitants were Muslims, [living] in a state of contentment with the Franks. We take refuge with God from this temptation, which is that they give the Franks half their produce at the time that it is harvested, and a poll-tax for each person of one dinar and five qirat, and [the Franks] do not trouble them any more than that. [. . .] The hearts of most of them have become dominated by this temptation, because of what they see of their brethren among the people of the Muslim regions and [how they are treated by] *their* governors, for the latter are in a state that is the contrary to theirs with regard to contentment and comfort. This is one of the calamities that is descending on the Muslims: the Muslim people complain of the tyranny of their co-religionist ruler and cherish the conduct of their opponent and enemy, the Frank who rules over them, being used to his justice.
>
> (Ibn Jubayr, 1907: 301–2)

Ibn Jubayr thus criticizes both the Muslim peasants who choose to stay under Frankish rule and the Muslim overlords whose own behaviour makes this the more attractive option. Ibn Jubayr's piety of course influenced his outlook, and as a foreigner he would not have been likely to have understood the nuances of the local interactions between Muslims and Franks that made this situation acceptable. It is also clear that the situation that he indignantly describes was not universally true (Kedar, 1990: 168).

A particularly well-known case of a significant number of Muslims fleeing Frankish rule is that of the Hanbalis of the Nablus region, about 30 miles north of Jerusalem, who emigrated to Damascus in 1156. This case has been studied in detail by Joseph Drory. According to the account of Diya' al-Din Muhammad al-Muqaddasi (1173–1245), a member of the Qudama family, which led the exodus, the Frankish lord under whom the Muslims of the region lived, Baldwin of Ibelin, used to levy inflated taxes on his Muslim subjects, as well as mutilating the legs of some of them. The emigration was led by Ahmad ibn Qudama, a religious scholar who fled to Damascus because Baldwin planned to kill him and because of the oppressive conditions under which he and his fellows lived, which he felt included a lack of religious freedom. Ahmad subsequently sent a call to his family to follow him, perhaps seeing better opportunities for himself and his family in Damascus, where the Sunni revival was taking place under Nur al-Din. The obligation to emigrate from infidel territory was in line with Hanbali religious teaching, being seen as a form of imitation of the Prophet Muhammad, who emigrated from Mecca to Medina to avoid having to live with infidels. When Ahmad ibn Qudama issued his call, it was enthusiastically received by some of the inhabitants of nine villages under Baldwin's rule; we have the names of 139 people who subsequently emigrated to Damascus. Others, however, rejected the call and attempted to prevent the migrants from departing, even inform- ing the Frankish authorities of what was taking place, though the latter were unable to prevent the exodus. The Qudama family subsequently played a small role in the preaching and prosecution of the military *jihad* against the Franks (Drory, 1988: *passim*).

It is striking, of course, that Ahmad ibn Qudama's call received only limited support, and indeed those who rejected it sought to prevent those who accepted it from leaving, even to the point of calling in the help of the Franks. Even if one accepts Diya' al-Din's accounts of Baldwin's misdeeds as true (and they are probably exaggerated), one can still understand the reluctance of those who did not flee both to depart and to allow others to do so; we have highlighted above the economic and survival implications of abandoning one's lands, and given that the inhabitants of medieval villages operated as unified communities, ploughing together, sowing together and reaping together, the Muslim peasants of the Nablus region must also have been unwilling to allow the manpower of their villages to become reduced. In any case, migrations such as the one described above were the exception rather than the rule.

The experience of Muslim prisoners in Frankish hands was rather different. They could be treated well, or they could be handled harshly, tortured or even killed. It is clear that they were an important element in the economic and especially military life of the Frankish territories; enslaved Muslims were often put to work, and in particular were used as manpower in the ongoing castle-building activities of the Franks. Among Muslims, ransoming prisoners is seen as a pious act; as we have seen, it is one of the uses to which the *zakat* is put, and at the time both private individuals and political figures devoted additional funds and efforts to redeeming prisoners. Indeed, Usama ibn Munqidh makes a point of mentioning the many prisoners whom he personally ransomed (Hillenbrand, 1999 a: 549–52; Kedar, 1997 b: 139–40, 1990, 152–3; Usama, 2008: 93–5).

As Hadia Dajani-Shakeel notes, the Muslims were particularly unsettled by the prospect of their womenfolk being taken prisoner by the Franks and possibly molested; indeed, it was assumed by both Muslims and Franks that women captured by the opposition would be unable to keep their virtue intact (Dajani-Shakeel, 1995: 206; Friedman, 1995: 81–5). Such molestation was seen as harmful not only to the woman in question, but also to the honour of the family, since it threatened the purity of the family bloodline (Cobb, 2005: 80–1). The Muslim poets who called for a response to the First Crusade certainly played on this concern, highlighting the distress that Muslim women were suffering as a result of the Franks' activities [**Doc. 5.i**]. In his *Kitab al-I'tibar* Usama includes a number of stories that draw attention to this fear; perhaps the most striking is the one that describes the attitude of a member of the garrison of the bridge defences of Shayzar:

> In the garrison of the Bridge was a Kurdish man called Abu al-Jaysh, who had a daughter named Raful, who had been carried off by the Franks. Abu al-Jaysh became pathologically obsessed with her, saying to everyone he met, 'Raful has been taken captive!'
>
> The next morning we went out to walk along the river and we saw a form by the bank of the river. We told one of the attendants, 'Swim over there and find out what that thing is.'
>
> He made his way over to it, and what should the form be but Raful, dressed in a blue garment. She had thrown herself from the horse of the Frank who had captured her and drowned. Her dress was caught in a willow-tree. In this way were the pangs of despair of her father silenced.

(Usama, 2008: 162)

For Raful and her father, as for many among both the Muslims and the Franks, a woman's capture and the assumed rape that would follow were a fate seen as literally worse than death, to be avoided at all cost. Usama likewise speaks with great admiration of his mother who, when Shayzar was attacked by Nizari Isma'ilis in March 1114, took his sister to a high balcony and was ready to push her off to her death rather than see her fall into the hands of the enemy. This did not mean that women who had been captured were not ransomed back by the Muslims, but it was expected that every effort should be made to avoid such an occurrence in the first place (Usama, 2008: 136–7; Friedman, 1995: 83–4; Christie, 1999: 87–8, 2004: 76 and 81; Cobb, 2005: 13).

It is important, of course, to give some consideration to Muslim treatment of Frankish prisoners, which in many ways reflected that of Muslim prisoners by the Franks. Frankish prisoners taken in battle by the Muslims faced the same uncertainty about their future. Some were tortured or killed out of hand, while others were enslaved and put to work. Some were given the choice of conversion to Islam or death, while others were simply released. We have already noted that in the wake of the Battle of Hattin in 1187 so many Frankish prisoners were sold into slavery that the market collapsed. As we have also seen, Saladin otherwise often let prisoners go free, which prompted criticism from Muslim authors who felt that in doing so he was allowing them to reinforce the Frankish armies (see Chapter 5). Of course, it is important to remember that feeding prisoners was a drain on resources, and for a sultan like Saladin, who was often short on cash, it must have been preferable to dispense with the burden, even if it swelled the enemy's ranks. He could at least be satisfied with the potential impact that the arrival of defeated, dispirited soldiers might have on enemy morale.

High-ranking Frankish prisoners were likely to be held for ransom, sometimes for long periods. Raymond III of Tripoli and Reynald of Châtillon respectively spent 7 and 15 years in captivity, during which they probably learned Arabic and gained some awareness of Muslim culture. Not all Frankish leaders were so lucky, though, and the Muslim sources are full of stories of grisly fates inflicted on them by principally Turkish Muslim leaders. Perhaps one of the most gruesome examples concerns the death of Gervase of Basoches, the Frankish ruler of Tiberias; apparently, after capturing him in 1108, Tughtigin opened up his prisoner's skull while the latter was still alive, scooped out its contents and drank wine from it. Gervase allegedly only died an hour later. Naturally, such stories contain a fair amount of exaggeration; as Carole Hillenbrand has noted, this probably reflects the fact that the Muslim writers saw the Turks as impious and barbaric (Hillenbrand, 1999 a: 552–3; consider also the story of Ilghazi's drinking binge mentioned in Chapter 3). It is also possible that the circulation of such stories was actually encouraged by the Turkish rulers in the region, since it made rebellion against them an intimidating prospect, thus reinforcing their positions.

TRUCES AND TRADE

As will by now have become apparent, it is clear that the official state of hostility that was meant to exist between the Muslims and the Franks did not prevent them from making peace agreements and allying with each other as the circumstances required (see, for example, **Doc. 7.ii**). Indeed, as Frenkel has noted, the traditional vision of the Crusades as a period of conflict between Christians and Muslims has created a skewed impression in modern minds, when in fact the real situation was 'one of fighting side by side with commerce and negotiations' (Frenkel, 2011: 29). Yvonne Friedman has traced approximately 109 treaties successfully made between Franks and Muslims between the years 1097 and 1291 that are noted in the sources for the period, and there were undoubtedly more, the records of which have not survived (Friedman, 2011: 232). Treaties and alliances were undertaken by most of the factions active in the region at the time and allowed for both joint military activity and more peaceful forms of interaction, including not only a cessation of bloodshed but also agreements about division of territory, exchanges of prisoners and in particular trade, which flourished in the region at the time.

By the crusading period Muslim scholars had given detailed consideration to the question of peace treaties. Precedents for making peace with non-Muslims are found in the *Qur'an* and the biographies of the Prophet, and agreements are permitted under almost all circumstances, including from positions of military strength, to avoid further bloodshed or to allow the Muslims an opportunity to bring in reinforcements or supplies; from positions of military parity, to allow for the use of alternate means to resolve the conflict; and from positions of military weakness, to allow the Muslims to adapt to the needs of the current situation (Friedman, 2011: 231). The popular view is that the duration of peace agreements can range from a few days to a maximum of ten years, but as Gideon Weigert has shown in an important article, most Muslim scholars have actually agreed that peace treaties can have an unlimited duration, and it is clear that many Muslim rulers throughout history also took this view. Muslims are expected to abide by the terms of the treaties that they make, and the decision to break a peace treaty with the enemy should not be undertaken lightly; in particular, the Muslims should announce their intentions to the enemy to give the latter the opportunity to prepare for the coming conflict (Weigert, 1997: 401–4).

Despite the clear legal authorization that existed for making peace with the Franks, Muslim rulers were still aware of the potential impact that their treaties and alliances might have on the way that they would be regarded by their subjects, particularly if they were simultaneously seeking to be viewed as great heroes of the *jihad*. Many were thus careful to ensure that they had publicized widely the justifications that they were using for their diplomatic relations with the Franks. Saladin, for example, even though he criticized other rulers who made alliances with the Franks, himself frequently came to agreements with the latter, of which his peace treaty with Richard I is but one example. He always ensured that his peacemaking fell within the requirements of Islamic law, and in his official propaganda he always justified these agreements on various grounds: a treaty might be presented as having been made to allow his troops time to rest and re-arm for the next phase of conflict; it might be described as a device to encourage the enemy to disperse without a fight, on the understanding that it would be difficult for them to gather their forces again in the future, especially if the forces in question were crusaders from abroad; or it might be depicted as having been made out of generosity because the Franks, in the face of humiliating defeat by the Muslims, were pleading for peace. Peace agreements with the Franks of course also allowed Saladin to concentrate on extending his political power within Muslim lands or consolidating his territorial gains, although naturally his propagandists did not dwell on this (Eddé, 2011: 271–3). Thus Saladin was careful to ensure that his negotiations with the Franks would not tarnish his image as a suitable leader of the Muslims by presenting them as having been undertaken out of unavoidable necessity or the clemency befitting a pious *mujahid*.

As indicated above, Islamic legal teaching requires Muslims to adhere to the terms of the peace agreements that they make, and the Muslims of the time clearly expected the same of the Franks. This is not to say that Muslim rulers never reneged on the treaties that they agreed to (with the Franks or other Muslims), but it is striking that one particular feature of the Franks that we see condemned repeatedly in the Muslim sources is treachery, a condemnation that becomes especially vehement when the Franks break truces without warning. Naturally, the benefits to be gained from not warning one's opponents before making a raid upon them must have made such actions attractive, but given that on the whole the Franks generally adopted a similar approach to treaties with the Muslims, including usually warning them if they were going to break agreements, the occasions when this did not occur particularly offended the Muslim writers (Christie, 1999: 77–80 and 194–6; Dajani-Shakeel, 1993: 212–13). The Muslim sources seem to have seen these treacherous tendencies as even having led the Franks to deceive and work against one another for their own gains. We have seen that Ibn al-Athir, for example, describes the failure of the Second Crusade's siege of Damascus as resulting from the Franks of the Levant collaborating with the Muslims of Damascus by withdrawing support from their brother-crusaders from Europe and encouraging the latter to give up the siege, for which they were rewarded with the castle of Banyas [**Doc. 7.ii**]. Thus the Franks' predisposition to treachery is something that the Muslim sources depict as affecting not only the Muslims, but also others with whom they interact, including themselves (Christie, 1999: 108–9 and 211). That said, this feature of the Frankish personality is exaggerated by the sources for dramatic and propagandistic effect; both Muslims and Franks seem on the whole to have abided by the agreements that they made with one another, including the customary practices that were associated with their abrogation (Dajani-Shakeel, 1993: 211–13).

One of the major benefits of the peace treaties that the Muslims made with the Franks was vibrant trade between Europe and the Levant. As we have seen (see Chapter 2), there was already trade between the two regions before the launching of the First Crusade, and during this period, encouraged by the Frankish occupation of ports on the coast, such trade flourished. When he was not fighting the Franks, Saladin sought to nurture trade links with Europe, recognizing the lucrative gains that the Mediterranean trade routes offered (see Chapter 5). Other rulers adopted a similar approach, despite the 'official' state of war that existed between the two sides, and commerce boomed. Indeed, it is clear that incidents of conflict between the Muslims and the Franks caused only temporary hiatuses; for example, trade was suspended in the summer of 1187 in the wake of Saladin's Hattin campaign, but resumed as early as the spring of 1188 (Eddé, 2011: 451).

Muslim rulers could justify their support of trade activities through Islamic legal teaching, which permits trade with the enemy provided that Muslim merchants do not supply them with war materials (such as weapons, armour and, according to some interpretations, horses, slaves and food) or prohibited substances (such as pork and wine). Importation of war materials is permitted, and foreign merchants are welcomed, provided that they pay customs duties on the goods that they sell (Khadduri, 1955: 223–30).

Foreign merchants were accommodated in *funduqs* (trade hostelries) located in Muslim cities and specifically designated for this purpose. These were constructed with the approval of local Muslim rulers and were subject to regulations governing how they operated, which presumably helped the Muslim authorities to control the foreigners visiting their lands. A late example of such regulations comes from the account of the Irish pilgrim Symon Semeonis, who visited Alexandria in 1323; he notes that foreign merchants were locked in their *funduqs* at times, a measure that seems to have been intended to control their movements when the Muslim rulers

Funduq: The Arabic word for a trade hostelry where merchants could stay and store goods, derived from the Greek *pandokheion* (inn). *Funduq* is used in modern times to refer to a hotel.

saw fit, such as at night and during Friday prayers (Semeonis, 1960: 51; Constable, 2003: 124).

Probably the most important trade centre in the Levant was indeed Alexandria, which was the main channel for goods passing from the Indian Ocean through the Red Sea to the Mediterranean. As we have noted, Italian merchants had been trading in Alexandria even before the onset of the Crusades, and such trade only expanded as the period progressed. Acre also became a major mercantile centre in the late twelfth and early thirteenth centuries, and to a degree the two ports were interdependent, with trade between them forming an important part of the commercial activities of the eastern Mediterranean (Abulafia, 1995: *passim*; Runciman, 1965: Vol. 3, p. 355).

East and west had much to offer each other. Western merchants bought both basics and luxury products including spices (especially pepper and ginger), embroidered and patterned rugs and textiles, dyes, glassware, porcelain, metalwork, gold and base metal ores. In return, they supplied eastern markets with silks, woollen cloth, cereals, silver and above all slaves, wood and iron (Hillenbrand, 1999 a: 404–7; Atiya, 1962: 182–6; Abulafia, 1994: 7–12). In providing these last three western merchants were effectively supporting the Muslim war effort; as we have seen, wood and iron were instrumental in the construction of siege weapons and ships, and many of the slaves became *mamluks* in the Muslim armies. While this state of affairs suited the Muslims, it generated significant resentment among the popes, who periodically tried to ban European merchants from trading with the Muslims, at times prohibiting trade completely and at others forbidding trade specifically in war materials. Even though the popes threatened excommunication of any who engaged in trade with the Muslims, their efforts were largely unsuccessful, for there was simply too much money to be made (Hillenbrand, 1999 a: 404–5).

It is worth noting that the Crusades were contemporary with significant developments in European intellectual culture, in particular the so-called 'twelfth-century Renaissance', which was based on the continued translation into Latin of both Arabic translations of Classical texts and the works that Muslim scholars produced as they synthesized and built upon these. However, the principal channels for such works seem to have been Iberia and Sicily, with the Latin states of the Levant playing only a secondary role (Irwin, 1995: 235). It is, on the other hand, possible to trace the transfer of some more practical innovations through the Latin states: for example, it was returning crusaders who brought the precise technique for making paper to Europe, and through obtaining Syrian techniques and materials in 1277 Venice was able to establish a virtual monopoly on glass production that lasted into the seventeenth century. Ceramic, leatherworking, metalworking and wood carving methods also seem to have been copied by western artisans from Middle Eastern models during this period (Atiya, 1962: 205–50).

MUSLIM VIEWS ON FRANKISH CULTURE

We will now turn our attention to some aspects of Frankish culture as they are represented in the Muslim sources, considering how the Muslim writers portray their Frankish opponents. Space dictates that this will of necessity be a brief discussion, and readers are encouraged to consult the *Further reading* section at the end of this chapter for more extended treatments of the topics addressed here. In conducting our investigation we will be drawing particularly heavily on the data provided to us by Usama ibn Munqidh, who, as we have commented above, has been lionized by scholars as the major source for 'anthropological' information on the Franks, though we will naturally also be calling on the evidence of other writers where appropriate.

Religion

As indicated above, it is clear that the Muslim writers were aware that the Franks were Christians, but the extent of their familiarity with the specifics of the Catholic Christianity followed by the Franks is far more difficult to determine. In any case, it is also clear that they were keen to depict the Franks' religious beliefs in as negative terms as possible. The Muslim writers considered their understanding of God's wishes for and from humanity to be superior to that of the Franks; they were, after all, the recipients of the *Qur'an*, which was understood as being among other things a corrective to the misunderstandings that had crept into the religious practices of the earlier recipients of the religion of Abraham. This sense of superiority was then accentuated by the fact that the Muslims were at war with the Franks, with the result that the Muslim writers emphasize the points of conflict between Christianity and Islam and for the most part disregard the features shared by the two faiths.

As an example, Muslim writers are strongly critical of the Christian belief that Jesus, to Muslims a prophet secondary only to Muhammad, is God incarnate. When recalling how a Frank showed him an icon of Jesus and Mary, describing it as an image of 'God when He was young', Usama reacts with indignation, saying, 'May God be exalted far beyond what the infidels say!' (Usama, 2008: 147–8). Usama's disapproval is positively mild when compared to that of the anonymous writer of the *Bahr al-Fava'id*, who sometime between 1159 and 1162 noted the following:

> They believe in this utter iniquity, that their God came forth from the privates of a woman and was created in a woman's womb, and that a woman was made pregnant by their God and gave birth to him [. . .] Anyone who

> believes that his God came out of a woman's privates is quite mad; he
> should not be spoken to, and he has neither intelligence nor faith.
>
> (*The Sea of Precious Virtues*, 1991: 232)

The author of the *Bahr al-Fava'id* is similarly contemptuous of Christian
belief in the crucifixion and the trinity, although with regard to the latter
the author distorts even the *Qur'an*'s misunderstanding of the trinity as consisting of God, Jesus and Mary (see, for example, *Qur'an* 5: 116–17). He
expresses incredulity at such ideas:

> The most amazing thing in the world is that the Christians say that
> Jesus is divine, that he is God, and then say that the Jews seized him and
> crucified him. How then can a God who cannot protect himself protect
> others? [. . .] The Christian sects do not dispute (the belief) that Jesus is
> not (God's) servant, but God, and divine, that he created the earth, that
> he is pre-existent, creator, and sustainer. He descended from Heaven,
> joined with Mary, and Jesus and Mary became one God; he was crucified
> and buried, and after three days he rose and ascended to Heaven.
>
> (*The Sea of Precious Virtues*, 1991: 231–2)

It is worth noting the vital position that both Jesus and Mary occupy in
Muslim views of their salvation history. Mary, as the one chosen by God to
bear the prophet preceding Muhammad, is held in enormous esteem (indeed,
Maryam [Mary] is an immensely popular name given to baby girls in the
Muslim world). Jesus, likewise, is immensely respected, and Muslim understandings of the end of his time on earth state that he was *not* crucified, but
was instead taken up to Heaven by God and will return in the end times to
slay the Antichrist. Here the author of the *Bahr al-Fava'id* focuses deliberately
and exclusively on the points where Islam and Christianity disagree, in order
to promote the superiority of Islam over Christianity at a time when followers of the two faiths were at war.

Most Muslim writers do not engage with Frankish Christianity on such
a detailed theological level, and reading the Muslim sources one almost gets
the impression that the writers saw the Franks as blasphemers worshipping
God incorrectly in often unspecified ways, pagans worshipping multiple
gods (the trinity), or idolaters worshipping cross-shaped idols. The cross
in particular recurs again and again in the works of the Muslim sources as
a symbol of the Franks' religious deviancy; as we have seen, the anonymous
poet cited by Ibn Taghri Birdi describes crosses set up in the *mihrabs* of
mosques [**Doc. 5.i.c**]. Likewise, Ibn al-Athir takes considerable satisfaction
in describing the removal of the cross from the Dome of the Rock after
Saladin's conquest of Jerusalem in 1187:

On top of the Dome of the Rock was a great gilded cross. When the Muslims entered the city on the Friday, several men climbed to the top of the dome to displace the cross. When they did so and it fell, everyone in the city and outside, both Muslims and Franks, cried out as one. The Muslims shouted, 'God is great!' in joy, while the Franks cried out in distress and pain. People heard a clamour so great and loud that the earth well-nigh shook under them.

(Ibn al-Athir, 2007: 334)

In this way the Muslim writers associate the Franks with the pagan idolaters who opposed Muhammad's mission in the early days of Islam, thus marking the Franks as enemies against whom the Muslims are obliged to fight, rather than merely misguided recipients of a previous revelation about the faith that the Muslims themselves follow.

Carole Hillenbrand has highlighted the particular link made by the Muslim sources between Frankish Christianity and ideas of pollution. This link is rooted in the fact that from the Muslim point of view the Franks were already physically unclean. Part of this was because they ate pigs, animals considered unclean according to Muslim teachings, but they were considered personally unhygienic as well. Ibn Jubayr, who as we have noted was not a neutral observer, states of Acre, 'Blasphemy and oppression blaze [there], and pigs and crosses abound. [It is] filthy and squalid, completely filled with dirt and excrement' (Ibn Jubayr, 1907: 303), thus highlighting both the porcine and human uncleanliness associated with the Franks. Usama relates the story of a Frankish knight who, in a bungled attempt to adopt Middle Eastern customs, behaved with considerable lack of decorum in a Muslim bath-house in Ma'arrat al-Nu'man; not only did he omit to wear the customary loin-cloth that would have protected his modesty, and removed that of the bath attendant, but he also had his wife brought into the bath-house, against the customary practice of women and men using the bath-houses on different days to preserve appropriate social divisions between the sexes. Usama also highlights the fact that both the knight and his wife needed to have their pubic hair shaved, with the knight in particular having hair 'thick as a beard', a stark contrast to Muslims, for whom this was a regular practice (Usama, 2008: 149). Usama's no doubt exaggerated tale only serves to highlight the idea that cleanliness (along with appropriate modesty and cultural sensitivity) is a foreign concept to the Franks, who are naturally filthy creatures (Hillenbrand, 1999 a: 274–82).

This idea of lack of hygiene is then extended into the spiritual sphere, in that the Franks' occupation of Muslim territory, and especially religious sites, is depicted as constituting a defilement of Muslim territory in a way that partakes of the physical pollution that the sources associate with the Franks. It is important to remember that the Muslims called the Church of the Holy Sepulchre the 'Church of Garbage'. The quotation from Ibn Jubayr, above, is striking for its juxtaposition of blasphemy, pigs, crosses and dirt. By the same token, the anonymous poet mentioned above refers to pigs' blood being used by the Christians in the mosques where they have set up their crosses [Doc. 5.i.c]. 'Imad al-Din al-Isfahani describes the purification of the sacred spaces of Jerusalem in 1187 in (no doubt embellished) detail; this apparently included the removal of structures that the Franks had added to the Aqsa Mosque and the Dome of the Rock (including carvings of pigs on a marble tabernacle over the sacred rock); and the washing of the Dome of the Rock with water, after which it was sprinkled with rose-water and perfumed with incense (al-Isfahani, 1965: 141–3). In this fashion he depicts a spiritual purification of the sacred sites of the Temple Mount from the defiling presence of the Franks that takes the form of a physical cleansing using traditional ritual tools such as rose-water and incense. Thus we see that physical and spiritual impurity and purity are intimately bound up together in the eyes of the Muslim authors (Hillenbrand, 1999 a: 282–303).

Not every reference made to Frankish Christianity is hostile. Even the *Bahr al-Fava'id* notes with apparent approval the respect with which the Frankish (and Byzantine) kings treat their clergy, though one could argue that this is only in order to suggest that Muslim rulers should follow this example (*The Sea of Precious Virtues*, 1991: 215 and 221). Usama also expresses his respect for Christian clergy, albeit in a guarded fashion; in his *Kitab al-'Asa* (Book of the Staff), an anthology of poetry and anecdotes on walking staves, he admits his admiration for a group of elderly Christian ascetics whom he saw in a church at the tomb of John the Baptist near Nablus. Usama was initially disappointed that he had never seen Muslim ascetics showing similar devotion, but at a later date his concerns were eased when he saw the pious observances of a group of Sufis in Damascus, which were 'greater than those of the priests' (Usama, 2008: 253–4). Fabricated or not, naturally Usama is aware of the message that such an anecdote sends about the relative merits of Muslim and Christian ascetics; nevertheless, it is interesting that Usama, like the anonymous author of the *Bahr al-Fava'id*, was at least willing to concede that some of the Christians demonstrated admirable piety. However, the over-arching message of this anecdote in some senses epitomizes the wider Muslim sentiment towards the Franks' religious beliefs; even those Muslims who accepted that their opponents' Christianity had some value still regarded the Franks as being, ultimately, inferior in matters of religion.

Law

Usama is our major source for Muslim views on Frankish legal procedures. Employing his typical mix of negative and (in this case seemingly) positive stories, Usama provides three anecdotes describing his experiences of Latin justice. Two of these are clearly negative; in one, he describes a case of trial by combat in which he saw two men fight to the death to determine the truth of a case, commenting, 'And that was but a taste of their jurisprudence and their legal procedure, may God curse them!' (Usama, 2008: 151–2). The second concerns a case of trial by ordeal, at which the accused's guilt or innocence was determined by whether he would, respectively, float or sink in a cask of water; the accused floated and was punished for his guilt by being blinded [**Doc. 14.i**]. Again, Usama expresses his distaste by proclaiming, 'May God curse them'. Yet Usama also notes a counter-example, in that he describes an incident when he himself sought justice from King Fulk of Jerusalem (r. 1131–43) after the lord of Banias stole some sheep from the territory of Damascus during a period of truce. Fulk turned the case over to a group of knights who, after consulting with one another, ruled in Usama's favour [**Doc. 14.i**].

In this way Usama provides evidence that seems on the surface to suggest that at times Frankish justice is arbitrary and violent, but at other times legal rulings are made through reason and consultation. Yet as Paul Cobb has shown, even the more civilized example of Frankish legal procedure would have struck Usama as strange and nonsensical, for in Muslim society there were scholars who were trained in the niceties of legal procedure, devoting their careers to exploring and applying the law as derived from the *Qur'an* and the sacred traditions of the faith. The capacity to make fair and just legal rulings was thus ascribed to those appropriately qualified, not to men who were respected for their virtues as warriors; the ability to fight on the battlefield was not seen as something that made one an expert lawyer! The examples of trial by ordeal and trial by combat noted above, in the meantime, would have struck Usama as superstitious, barbaric appeals for divine intervention followed by vicious penalties inflicted on those found guilty. As Cobb has noted, the punishments themselves would not have upset Usama; indeed, medieval Islamic legal penalties included punishments such as death and amputation. However, the nature of the legal procedures that led to their imposition struck him as unreasonable, illogical and lacking the true divine guidance that Muslims found in their own legal tradition (Cobb, 2005: 109–11).

Medicine

Usama's depiction of Frankish medicine is perhaps more genuinely balanced. Some of his depictions are indeed highly critical; in possibly his most famous anecdote, Usama describes a Frankish physician who disregarded the reasonable remedies of a Syrian Christian doctor and applied more violent treatments

that resulted in the deaths of two patients [**Doc. 14.ii**]. As Cobb has indicated, this tale is probably intended more as a critique of the Frankish physician's
haste to adopt the most drastic solution than of his methods *per se*, and
scholars have been too quick to see it as representative of a vast gap between
European and Islamic medical knowledge, when in fact both traditions based
their treatments on a mix of the medical science of the Classical world and
folk beliefs, and also enjoyed relative parity in this period (Cobb, 2005:
107–8). Usama balances this and other negative depictions with positive
ones, including a Frankish remedy for scrofula that he used himself
[**Doc. 14.ii**] and a case of a Frankish doctor washing wounds with vinegar,
leading to their being disinfected and healing (Usama, 2008: 146). Thus
his attitude towards Latin medical practices comes across as rather mixed,
possibly more so than any of his other views on the Franks.

Sexual morality

We have already seen Muslim writers expressing concern for the safety and
virtue of their womenfolk, both on an individual level and as an expression
of wider family honour. Given this concern, it is not surprising that Muslim
writers use negative depictions of Frankish attitudes towards women as a
way to cast aspersions on the Franks as a whole. Usama states that the Franks
'possess nothing in the way of regard for honour or propriety', which he
illustrates with a number of anecdotes about Frankish lack of concern for
the virtue of their women. Probably the best known of these is an incident
that Usama claims to have witnessed himself, which concerns a Frankish
wine-seller who comes home and finds another Frank in bed with his wife;
after a brief exchange, the wine-seller tells the other man, 'If you do this
again, we'll have an argument, you and I!' and Usama comments, shocked,
'And that was all the disapproval he would muster and the extent of his
sense of propriety!' [**Doc. 14.iii**]. Carole Hillenbrand has described this
as 'a cleverly constructed apocryphal tale which plays shamelessly on the
prejudices of Usama's readers', noting in particular that Usama is careful
to enhance the critique of the Franks by not only highlighting their lack
of propriety but also depicting the cuckolded husband as a wine-seller, a
morally questionable figure in the eyes of a Muslim audience (Hillenbrand,
1999 a: 348). However, if we accept that this is a constructed tale, despite
Usama's claims, we can actually gain an insight into Usama's relations with
the Franks that he may not himself have been aware of. It actually seems
likely that the tale, with its threefold questioning and punch-line, was in its
original form a joke, and the fact that at the end of this exchange the husband
still seems unaware that he has been cuckolded makes it heavily reminiscent
of the *fabliaux*, European folktales in which stupid husbands do not realize

that their wives have been unfaithful to them. The fact that the wine-seller seems to sell wine by letting people taste from the bottle that he carries, then is paid at the end of the day with that bottle, reinforces the idea that he is an idiot who can be outwitted by his wife and her lover. As we have seen, Usama claims to have had friends among the Franks, and it is thus not unrealistic to suggest that this story was told to the Shayzari emir by one of his Frankish friends, as a joke, but that Usama *did not get it*, as revealed by his final, shocked comment (Christie, 2004: 73–4).

Whatever the truth of this, Usama balances this and his other demonstrations of Frankish lack of concern for their women's honour with a tale that also acts as an effective contrast to the bath-house story mentioned above. He describes visiting a bath-house in the Frankish-held city of Tyre, where he saw a (presumably Frankish) father who had brought his daughter in to wash her hair. The daughter's mother was dead, so the father had brought her into the bath-house on a 'man day', despite this being against normal custom. Usama notes that the young woman was so well covered up that his servant had to lift the hem of her clothing to establish that she was indeed female, a marked contrast to the immodesty of the knight and his wife mentioned above, and this care for modesty, combined with the father's clear concern for his daughter's welfare, led Usama to make a comment that suggests that he himself was willing to subordinate propriety to the dictates of need: 'That's a kind thing you're doing [. . .] This will bring you heavenly reward' [**Doc. 14.iii**].

The Muslim sources show mixed attitudes towards Frankish women themselves. The poet Ibn al-Qaysarani seems to have been enraptured by some of the Frankish women, writing effusive poems praising their beauty [**Doc. 15.i**]. He was not the only Muslim to be struck by the attractions of Frankish women; Ibn Jubayr remarks on the beauty of a bride whom he saw in a wedding procession in Tyre, before commenting, 'We take refuge with God from the temptation of the sight!' (Ibn Jubayr, 1907: 305–6). Others were not as impressed; 'Imad al-Din is typically vitriolic, providing an extended pornographic passage in which he depicts women who arrived with the forces of the Third Crusade essentially as religious prostitutes who sought to support the crusade through sexual support of the crusaders. In the process he takes the opportunity to impugn both Christianity and the wider honour of the Franks in general, remarking that these women saw sexual intercourse as a form of Eucharist, and that married men, among whom he includes priests, were not criticized by the Franks for sexual activity. In this we see particular slurs cast against Christian attitudes towards the Eucharist and priestly celibacy [**Doc. 15.ii**].

Muslim attitudes towards women actually fighting in the Frankish forces, and indeed women fighters in general, seem to have been almost uniformly negative, something that resulted from an over-arching assumption that women should be restricted to the domestic sphere, while men should be the public faces of the family both in social life and on the battlefield. Indeed, Islamic religious scholars normally prohibited women from fighting in battle. The Muslim sources thus usually express amazement when they become aware of women fighting. Baha' al-Din notes that upon being brought a bow taken from a Frankish woman who fought against the Muslims at Acre in July 1191, Saladin was 'greatly surprised', and 'Imad al-Din likewise remarks on Frankish women fighting in the Crusades with a clearly critical description of their activities on the battlefield (Ibn Shaddad, 2001: 158; and **Doc. 15.ii**). Of course, it is difficult to determine how far we should take such accounts at face value; suggesting that one's enemies were unable to restrict their women to their appropriate gender roles was a way of questioning their masculinity and hence denigrating them. However, there were women who fought in the Crusades, and this seems to have surprised the Muslims who encountered them.

Usama is an important exception to the general rule that Muslim writers disapproved of women taking part in battle. In his *Kitab al-I'tibar* he highlights a number of cases of women who did so directly or indirectly. For example, his mother led the defence of Shayzar against Nizari Isma'ilis referred to above, distributing weapons to the defenders; during the same battle his aunt put on armour and shamed his male cousin into fighting; and an elderly servant named Funun veiled herself, took up a sword and plunged into the fray. Such activities prompted Usama to remark, 'No one can deny that noble women possess disdain for danger, courage for the sake of honour and sound judgment' (Usama, 2008: 135–7; Cobb, 2005: 12–14). However, we should not see in this a suggestion that Usama was a proto-feminist; these women took action in cases of need, when their home was attacked, rather than actively seeking to go on a military campaign. Usama is unlikely to have approved of women being involved in combat if the circumstances were less dire.

The cultural barrier?

We have already seen that Usama's understanding of Frankish humour was limited by his lack of familiarity with European folktales. Another of his anecdotes is similarly revealing about his flawed understanding of European society:

> In the army of King Fulk, son of Fulk, there was a respected Frankish knight who had come from their country just to go on pilgrimage and then return home. He grew to like my company and he became my constant

companion, calling me 'my brother'. Between us there were ties of amity and sociability. When he resolved to take to the sea back to his country, he said to me:

'My brother, I am leaving for my country. I want you to send your son (my son, who was with me, was fourteen years old) with me to my country, where he can observe the knights and acquire reason and chivalry. When he returns, he will be like a truly rational man.'

And so there fell upon my ears words that would never come from a truly rational head! For even if my son were taken captive, his captivity would not be as long as any voyage he might take to the land of the Franks [or: his captivity could not bring him a worse misfortune than carrying him into the lands of the Franks].

So I said, 'By your life, I was hoping for this very same thing. But the only thing that has prevented me from doing so is the fact that his grand-mother adores him and almost did not allow him to come here with me until she had exacted an oath from me that I would return him to her.'

'Your mother,' he asked, 'she is still alive?'

'Yes,' I replied.

'Then do not disobey her,' he said.

(Usama, 2008: 144, 2000: 161)

As a result of ambiguities in the Arabic the precise cause for Usama's concern, with regard to his son being taken away to Europe, is not apparent. He may have been worried that his son might be corrupted by European ways, or he may have been genuinely distressed at the thought of having to part with him for a long period of time. One could also sensibly expect that a visibly Middle Eastern boy might encounter difficulties in Europe, even though a noble patron might mitigate these somewhat, which does lead one to question whether Usama's friend seriously intended his offer to be accepted or was simply making it as a token of his esteem. In any case it is clear that Usama was not aware of the magnitude of the offer that his Frankish friend was making. In Europe at the time it was common for the sons of noble houses to be fostered out to other households, usually those of their father's lord or another prominent nobleman, in order to learn courtly etiquette and the arts of war, which paved their way for entry into knightly society. Thus having one's son accepted into such a 'training programme' was of great importance. Usama's friend was, then, offering to assist with his son's train-ing and in the process to do Usama himself an immense favour. However, Usama, lacking a deep understanding of European knightly conventions, did not understand the significance of the offer and only saw it as a bizarre sug-gestion. We are reminded again that there were limits (of which he himself was unaware) to Usama's understanding of Frankish ways.

CONCLUSION

Despite the obfuscating influences of propagandistic agendas and hostile viewpoints, it is clear from the sources that the Muslims and Franks interacted with each other on a number of levels both on and off the battlefield. Crusaders and Muslims might fight each other, but they might also form alliances against other Franks, other Muslims, or both, or they might make truces and live alongside each other in conditions of relative peace. They might visit each others' cities, trade, perform pilgrimages to sacred sites in each others' territories, or simply spend time together interacting socially, exchanging medical remedies, attending each others' festivities or attempting to swap jokes. However, there were limits to how far they could come to understand each other, limits that derived from the legacy of violence between them, a lack of shared historical and societal formation and, above all, from attitudes of religious and cultural superiority that prevented them from ever seeing each other as true equals. These insurmountable barriers would continue to poison Latin–Muslim relations and would eventually contribute to rising hostility against the Franks, leading to their ejection from the Levantine coast by the Mamluks.

FURTHER READING

For a detailed overview of the main issues addressed in this chapter, see Carole Hillenbrand, *The Crusades: Islamic Perspectives* (1999 a). Developments during the period covering the First and Second Crusades are also discussed in Niall Christie, *Levantine Attitudes towards the Franks during the Early Crusades (490/1096–564/1169)* (1999). For a study of the military aspects of the Muslim response to the Crusades, see in the first instance David Nicolle, *Crusader Warfare*, especially Volume 2, which deals directly with the Muslim and Mongol armies and strategy (2007); and ibid., *Arms and Armour of the Crusading Era, 1050–1350: Islam, Eastern Europe and Asia* (1999). Readers of French may also wish to consult Abbès Zouache, *Armées et Combats en Syrie de 491/1098 à 569/1174: Analyse Comparée des Chroniques Médiévales Latines et Arabes* (2008). On Muslim castles, see also Kate Raphael, *Muslim Fortresses in the Levant: Between Crusaders and Mongols* (2011). A good introduction to the situation of Muslims under Frankish rule is Benjamin Kedar's article, 'The Subjected Muslims of the Frankish Levant' (1990). A number of scholars have looked at peacemaking and treaties between Muslims and Franks. The standard work on Muslim legal teaching about both war and peace is Majid Khadduri's *War and Peace in the Law of Islam* (1955), but for good starting points for further enquiry about treaties specifically during the period under discussion see also Yvonne Friedman's 'Peacemaking: Perceptions and Practices in the Medieval Latin East' (2011); and Gideon Weigert's 'A Note on Hudna: Peace Making in Islam' (1997). On trade and cultural interchange, see initially Aziz S. Atiya's *Crusade, Commerce and Culture* (1962), but for qualification see also David Abulafia, 'The Role of Trade in Muslim–Christian Contact during the Middle Ages' (1994). For an excellent and extensive treatment of *funduqs*, see Olivia Remie Constable, *Housing the Stranger in the Mediterranean World: Lodging, Trade, and Travel in Late Antiquity and the Middle Ages* (2003). On Usama, see Paul M. Cobb, *Usama ibn Munqidh: Warrior Poet of the Age of the Crusades* (2005); and his translation of both the Shayzari emir's 'memoirs' and extracts from the latter's other works, *The Book of Contemplation: Islam and the Crusades* (Usama, 2008).

7

The successors of Saladin, 1193–1249

In this chapter we will discuss the period during which Saladin's successors and descendants held power in much of the Levant. After our chronological survey we will consider the later Ayyubids' conflicts with one another, which occupied much of their attention in the half-century following Saladin's death. We will then examine their approach to the Franks, including both their general reluctance to advance their illustrious forebear's conquests of Frankish territory and the diplomatic and trade relations that they enjoyed with both the Latin states of the coast and European powers across the Mediterranean. Not all Muslims approved of such dealings, naturally, so we will also discuss the activities of some of the Ayyubids' critics, considering the extent to which this was a matter of concern for their rulers.

CHRONOLOGICAL OVERVIEW

At the time of Saladin's death his territories were divided up, mostly among the various members of his family who had ruled on his behalf. The most important centres were ruled by the three sons mentioned previously: al-Afdal 'Ali held the territories in Syria, with his capital at Damascus, and was designated as the new head of the confederation (r. 1186–96); al-'Aziz 'Uthman ruled Egypt, with his capital at Cairo (r. 1193–8); and al-Zahir Ghazi controlled the vast northern principality based at Aleppo (r. 1186–1216). The remaining territories were held by other members of the family; most notably, al-'Adil Muhammad ruled a disparate range of territories to the north and east, including the important cities of Edessa and Harran in the north, and Transjordan, including the fortress of Kerak, in the south-east. This meant that these important and exposed regions were in the hands of a senior and experienced member of the family who could defend them effectively (Humphreys, 1977: 83–4).

This division of territories soon broke down, however. Al-Afdal 'Ali and al-'Aziz 'Uthman quickly became embroiled in a struggle for supremacy, in which al-'Adil Muhammad intervened, initially as a mediator and then as a skilful player. In 1196 he took control of Damascus from al-Afdal 'Ali, ruling there in the name of al-'Aziz 'Uthman, and then in 1200 he usurped power in Egypt from the young son of the now-deceased al-'Aziz 'Uthman and declared himself head of the family. Two years later he compelled the submission of al-Zahir Ghazi of Aleppo. Al-'Adil Muhammad's sons, al-Kamil Muhammad (d. 1238) and al-Mu'azzam 'Isa (d. 1227), became al-'Adil's deputies in Cairo and Damascus, respectively.

The disputes that occurred in the ten years after Saladin's death in some senses set the tone for the decades that followed, as various members of the Ayyubid family competed with each other for power. Meanwhile the Ayyubids' enemies, both Frankish and Muslim, took advantage of their disunity to stage attacks on Ayyubid territory; for example, immediately after Saladin's death the Ayyubids had to deal with an attack by the Zangids, which was fended off and successfully turned into a further expansion of Ayyubid territory, while in 1197 Beirut and Sidon were lost to a fresh wave of crusaders. This mixture of internal disputes and the periodic need to deal with external threats would characterize the remainder of the Ayyubid period.

In 1217 a new force of crusaders arrived at Acre (the Fifth Crusade). After some initial action in Syria and the Holy Land, they attacked Damietta in May 1218. In August, hearing that the Franks had stormed part of the city's defences, al-'Adil Muhammad set out for Damietta but died en route. His territories were divided between his sons al-Kamil Muhammad, al-Mu'azzam 'Isa and a third son, al-Ashraf Musa (d. 1237), who at the time held lands in northern Syria and the Jazira. In a last major show of unity by members of the Ayyubid family, al-Kamil Muhammad, al-Mu'azzam 'Isa and (eventually) al-Ashraf Musa co-operated to deal with the crusader threat. In addition to providing military support, in 1219, while the crusaders were dug in at Damietta, al-Mu'azzam 'Isa dismantled the fortifications of Jerusalem and other strongholds in his territory, to render them useless to the Franks as bases of operations should they subsequently take them. The destruction of Jerusalem's defences caused widespread panic and led many to flee the city. Al-Mu'azzam 'Isa also acquiesced to al-Kamil Muhammad's repeated attempts to persuade the crusaders to evacuate Egypt in return for most of the old Kingdom of Jerusalem, including the holy city itself, territories that at the time were under al-Mu'azzam 'Isa's control. The offer was rejected by the crusaders, who were later forced to sue for peace themselves after becoming cut off by the Nile flood opposite al-Kamil Muhammad's camp at al-Mansura, in the Nile Delta, in the summer of 1221. An eight-year truce was agreed, and the Franks were allowed to leave Egypt (Humphreys, 1977: 162–70; Riley-Smith, 1987: 149).

Relations between al-Kamil Muhammad and al-Mu'azzam 'Isa soon deteriorated, and when he heard that the Holy Roman Emperor Frederick II (r. 1220–50) was preparing a new crusade, al-Kamil Muhammad sent an embassy to the latter in 1226, offering again to surrender Jerusalem and its surroundings, but this time in an attempt to gain aid against his brother, or at least to disquiet him (Humphreys, 1977: 184; Atrache, 1996: 93). Frederick had become the king of Jerusalem a year earlier through his marriage to the heiress Isabel (Yolanda). However, by the time that he reached the Holy Land in September 1228 circumstances had changed. In 1227 al-Mu'azzam 'Isa had died, of dysentery, and Isabel had died in 1228 giving birth to a son, Conrad, for whom Frederick was now only a regent rather than being king in his own right. In addition, Frederick had delayed his departure due to problems at home, a delay to which the pope objected, excommunicating the emperor. Thus when Frederick arrived in the east he was in a much weaker political and ideological position. Meanwhile, al-Kamil Muhammad's major rival had disappeared from the scene, but the sultan faced the challenge of avoiding alienating the Muslims while also avoiding seeming to the Franks to be reneging on his offer and in the process tempting them to renew hostilities. He was also at the time embroiled in negotiations with his own family over the fate of al-Mu'azzam 'Isa's inheritance. In the end an agreement between Frederick and al-Kamil Muhammad was made in February 1229. The precise terms are unclear, but it seems that the Franks were to receive Jerusalem, along with the villages in a corridor linking the holy city to the coast. However, the other villages surrounding Jerusalem were to remain in Muslim hands, as was the Temple Mount, though the Franks would be allowed to visit the Temple area to pray. The defences of Jerusalem were not to be rebuilt by the Franks, but the Muslim inhabitants of the city were not permitted to live there any longer. Finally, a truce was made for ten years, five months and 40 days (Gottschalk, 1958: 157; Humphreys, 1977: 202–3). The agreement was greeted with vocal protests on both sides, but Frederick crowned himself in the Holy Sepulchre on 18 March, before returning to Acre the following day, where he faced further demonstrations. On 1 May he attempted to leave Acre discreetly but was spotted as he passed by the meat market and pelted with offal (Riley-Smith, 1987: 151). Frederick, the excommunicate crusader, had managed to achieve the return of Jerusalem to Christian hands, but in a way that pleased nobody.

Jerusalem did not stay in Christian hands for long. In 1239 the Ayyubid ruler of Kerak, al-Mu'azzam 'Isa's son al-Nasir Dawud (d. 1258), who had ruled Damascus for less than two years before being ousted by al-Kamil Muhammad and al-Ashraf Musa, took advantage of the weakness of the

Frankish forces and occupied the holy city. It was returned to the Franks the following year by al-Nasir Dawud and the Ayyubid ruler of Damascus, al-Salih Isma'il (r. 1237 and 1239–45), in return for aid against al-Kamil Muhammad's son al-'Adil II Abu Bakr (r. 1238–40), but in 1244 the city was taken by Muslim troops again. The troops in question, known as Khwarazmians, were Turkish warriors who had previously served the rulers of the lower Oxus region in the Muslim east but had been displaced by the Mongol advance. They had first become involved in the twisted web of Ayyubid politics as allies of al-Mu'azzam 'Isa in 1225, and had remained an active and undisciplined element in the northern Jazira thereafter. By now they were (loosely) in the service of al-Salih Ayyub (r. 1240–9), who had succeeded in Egypt in 1240 after the deposition of his brother al-'Adil II Abu Bakr by discontented troops. In the early summer of 1244 they mounted a major raid into Palestine, looting and pillaging as they went, and in July they attacked Jerusalem. After a resistance of a little over a month, the city garrison surrendered, by which time the Khwarazmians had comprehensively sacked the city. Having destroyed the Christian holy sites in Jerusalem, they joined forces with an army sent by al-Salih Ayyub and defeated a coalition of Frankish and Syrian Ayyubid forces at Harbiyya (La Forbie) in October, a victory that helped al-Salih Ayyub to take Damascus from al-Salih Isma'il the following year. However, the undisciplined Khwarazmians, who felt that they had not been adequately rewarded for their services, conducted destructive raids in the region and, in alliance with Ayyubid opponents of al-Salih Ayyub, besieged Damascus itself in March 1246, only to be attacked, defeated and scattered by troops from Homs and Aleppo (Humphreys, 1977: 274–87).

Three years later al-Salih Ayyub faced a new challenge, as on 4 June 1249 crusading forces under Louis IX of France (St Louis, r. 1226–70) attacked Damietta, taking the city after two days. Al-Salih Ayyub, like al-Kamil Muhammad before him, made his base of operations at al-Mansura, but he was by now seriously ill, and on 21 November he died. His timing could not have been worse; the sultan's son and heir al-Mu'azzam Turan-Shah was far away, governing territories in the northern Jazira, and the Frankish forces were preparing to advance on the Muslim camp. It seemed that Egypt would soon be lost to the crusaders.

FAMILY POLITICS

It is important to remember that the Ayyubid dominions were a confederation rather than a single unified entity. The major territories under their control were for the most part reigned over by members of the family who operated essentially as independent rulers. While there was normally a figure who was recognized as the head of the confederation, usually the ruler of Egypt, the extent to which he could enforce his authority over the other rulers was limited. As Humphreys has noted, this familial confederative power structure was not unusual at the time, but it was also prone to disruption through the ambitions of its members (Humphreys, 1998: 5–7). The lack of a strong central figure whose authority was continuously reinforced gave the Ayyubid princes plenty of freedom to plot against each other and their nominal overlord.

Ayyubid family politics was vicious but not normally deadly. An Ayyubid ruler who was defeated by his rivals was likely to be displaced rather than killed, often ending up in a smaller appanage. This meant that he had the opportunity to continue to participate in family disputes and might attempt to regain his lost position. An illustrative example is al-Nasir Dawud, whom Joseph Drory describes as a 'much frustrated Ayyubid prince'. Al-Nasir Dawud succeeded to the throne of his father al-Mu'azzam 'Isa in Damascus in 1228 but, as noted above, was ousted from the city by al-Kamil Muhammad and al-Ashraf Musa in 1229. He was compensated with territories in Palestine and Transjordan, making his capital at Kerak, and from there continued to be a participant in the tense family politics of the region. Al-Nasir Dawud lost further territories to al-Kamil Muhammad and al-Ashraf Musa, and when the latter died in 1237 he was not given Damascus, despite having been promised it by al-Kamil Muhammad, who was at the time the nominal head of the family. An attempt by al-Nasir Dawud to take control of Damascus in 1238 after al-Kamil Muhammad's death resulted only in a disastrous military defeat at the hands of its Ayyubid governor. As we have seen, al-Nasir Dawud did manage to take control of Jerusalem in 1239, but was forced to hand it back to the Franks the following year, and in the Syrian–Egyptian conflicts of the 1240s he sided with the Syrians and as a result lost more territory to the victorious Egyptians. In 1249 he was forced to leave Kerak, initially moving to Aleppo but then spending some years wandering Bilad al-Sham and the Jazira in search of a new state, which included two periods of imprisonment by other Ayyubids who saw him as a threat. Eventually al-Nasir Dawud was sent east to lead an army to support Baghdad against the Mongols, but he failed to reach the city before the latter took it in February 1258. Tired and worn out, he fell ill and died in the following May, aged 53 (Drory, 2003: passim). Thus in al-Nasir Dawud we see a figure who, after being displaced from his original holdings, continued to manoeuvre and scheme in an attempt to restore his fortunes. The predisposition of various members of the Ayyubid family to such machinations only exacerbated the political chaos of the time.

THE AYYUBIDS AND THE *JIHAD*

In his account of the year 628 (1230–1), Ibn al-Athir notes:

> For now we do not see among the princes of Islam one who has a desire
> to wage the Jihad or to aid the religion. On the contrary, each of them
> looks to his pleasures, his sport and the oppression of his subjects. For
> me this is more frightening than the enemy.
>
> (Ibn al-Athir, 2008: 304–5)

Ibn al-Athir's description of the situation is, naturally, exaggerated, but it
is striking that the period sees a shift in Ayyubid approaches to the Franks.
In some senses we see a return to the early years of the crusading period, in
which some rulers conducted periodic expeditions against the Franks, but at
the same time concentrated more often on conflicts with other Muslim rulers,
including employing the Franks as allies when the situation warranted it.
We will return to the medieval critics of the Ayyubids later, but it is worth
thinking in more detail about why we see a decline in attacks on the Franks
by the Ayyubids.

Certainly the death of Saladin played a part; his personal charisma and
skilful use of propaganda had enabled him to unite the Muslim rulers of
the Levant in a way that was never duplicated by his successors. However,
as we have seen, after Saladin recaptured Jerusalem in 1187 even he had
encountered difficulties in holding his coalition together. Likewise, a number
of the Ayyubid rulers must have recognized that without the draw of Jerusalem
it would be difficult to unite their fractious relatives under their command.
Jerusalem itself also seems to have been seen differently by Saladin's successors. As Donald Little and Carole Hillenbrand have noted, the Ayyubid
rulers never lost sight of the religious significance of the city, but this did not
mean that they promoted settlement in the holy city or used it as a capital,
and they were willing to allow pragmatism to trump principle if handing it
over would free them from crusader attacks (Little, 1997: 181–5; Hillenbrand,
1999 a: 211–23). In actually doing this in 1229 al-Kamil Muhammad aroused
fierce resentment among the common folk and religious classes, as we shall
see, but this did not prevent him from honouring his agreement with
Frederick II.

R. Stephen Humphreys has remarked on an additional factor that led
to reduced enthusiasm among the Ayyubids to fight the Franks: the latter's
persistence. Despite the Franks having been driven out of Jerusalem and
repeatedly defeated thereafter, there were always more of them arriving
from Europe, in a seemingly inexhaustible supply. As Humphreys puts it,
'the Ayyubids were terrified of the Franks, who, however badly mauled they

might be, just kept coming back' (Humphreys, 1998: 9–10). Thus the Ayyubids were willing to go to extraordinary lengths in making treaties and conceding territory in order to avoid provoking the arrival of fresh waves of crusaders. This does not mean that the Ayyubids allowed themselves to be passive victims of Frankish aggression, but they generally avoided conflict where they could, only engaging in military action against the Franks if severely provoked.

It is also worth considering the use of *jihad* propaganda by Saladin's successors. As Hillenbrand has noted, in official rhetoric Ayyubid rulers continued to be celebrated with titles exalting their activities as *mujahids*, even if their actions did not match up, and Laila Atrache has noted the ongoing depiction of the Franks as polytheists and infidels in the historical sources for the period, works that could also have a propagandistic function (Hillenbrand, 1999 a: 204–7; Atrache, 1996: 71). Sivan has commented that the Ayyubids even sought to justify their activities against each other with *jihad* propaganda, claiming, much as Saladin had, that they were only fighting against other Muslims for the sake of the long-term goal of defending the coast against the Franks (Sivan, 1968: 135). However, it cannot be denied that by this time the grandiose titles and pious pronouncements made by the Ayyubids had begun to ring suspiciously hollow.

Yet at the same time it is important to remember that the military *jihad* was but one aspect of the wider *jihad* doctrine in Islam. As we have seen, even greater importance was given by a number of thinkers to the struggle to promote the faith within both the individual and the state. Humphreys comments, 'In the internal *jihad*, Saladin's heirs performed splendidly', noting both the religiously educated nature of the rulers and their generosity in endowing religious buildings (Humphreys, 1998: 9). Hillenbrand remarks that even though they did not make it their capital, the Ayyubids devoted significant resources to creating and expanding religious institutions in Jerusalem (Hillenbrand, 1999 a: 211–13). In this way the Ayyubids pursued the greater, internal *jihad* with more enthusiasm than the lesser, military *jihad* through the support of the religious life of their states.

RELATIONS WITH THE FRANKS

Naturally, as before Ayyubid interactions with the Franks took on forms other than conflict on the battlefield. As we have indicated previously, the Ayyubids were content to make alliances with the Franks when it suited their purposes. Hillenbrand comments, 'The Ayyubid period witnessed the full integration of the Franks as local Levantine rulers' (Hillenbrand, 1999 a: 203). Certainly there is no denying that by now the Franks of the coast had become full participants in the conflicts of the Ayyubids and the surrounding states of the Levant, but we might in fact go one stage further and suggest that the period also witnessed a deepening of co-operative relations between states of the Levant and Europe, including and going beyond the inter-mediary territories held by the Franks on the Levantine coast. As noted in the previous chapter, trade relations had existed between the major Italian trading powers and the Levant even before the onset of the Crusades, and only expanded as the decades passed. The Ayyubid rulers continued to seek to capitalize on this relationship, allowing both Italian and other merchants to establish more *funduqs* in a number of cities in their territories in order to expand commerce between their states and Europe. Humphreys also sug-gests that the Ayyubids deliberately refrained from seeking to re-conquer coastal towns because they believed that foreign merchants would find towns under Frankish control to be more attractive trade centres, and the wealth generated in them would eventually pass to the Ayyubids' own states through trade between these towns and the Muslim hinterland (Humphreys, 1998: 9). In addition to trade, we also have records of diplomatic contacts between the Ayyubids and European rulers, which had begun as early as 1175 with negotiations between Saladin and Frederick I Barbarossa (Eddé, 2011: 244–6). We have already seen that al-Kamil Muhammad engaged in discussions with Frederick II even before the latter's departure for the east, with a view to strengthening his hand against al-Mu'azzam 'Isa. In 1248 Frederick II wrote to al-Salih Ayyub, warning him of St Louis' plans to conduct a crusade in the east, suggesting that al-Salih Ayyub hand Jerusalem over to the Franks and offering to act as a mediator between the Ayyubid sultan and the French king (Eddé, 1996: 68). We also have records of exchanges of gifts between Frederick II and al-Kamil Muhammad. Frederick sent al-Kamil Muhammad a number of horses, including his own, which bore a golden saddle encrusted with precious stones; and later a polar bear, which attracted attention because of its talents at catching fish, and a white peacock. Al-Kamil Muhammad, not to be outdone, responded with treasures from India, Yemen, Iraq, Syria, Egypt and Persia worth twice as much as the horses and saddle that Frederick had sent, as well as a golden saddle bearing jewels worth 10,000 Egyptian *dinars* (Gottschalk, 1958: 217; Atrache, 1996: 97–8 and 174). Thus the reign of the Ayyubids as a whole sees the beginning of integration of European states proper into the political affairs of the east through trans-Mediterranean diplomacy that went beyond the necessary diplomatic contacts between the Muslim rulers and their Frankish counter-parts who happened to be on crusade in the Levant.

Diplomacy during actual crusading expeditions also took on new and unusual forms. One incident, recorded in the European sources, involves a visit made to al-Kamil Muhammad by St Francis of Assisi during the Fifth

Crusade. Probably in September of 1219, during a period of truce and negotiations, St Francis visited al-Kamil Muhammad in his camp, remaining there for a few days before returning unharmed to the crusader side. What exactly took place during the encounter is unknown, and no contemporary Muslim source mentions it. St Francis was probably received politely and admitted into the presence of the sultan, who listened graciously to the friar's preaching but was otherwise unmoved. Fareed Munir suggests that St Francis and al-Kamil Muhammad may have found that they shared a similar spirituality and desire for peace, seeing them as pioneers of inter-religious dialogue, but in the absence of evidence from any contemporary eyewitnesses such claims should be considered to be no more than speculation (Munir, 2008: *passim*). Whatever the truth of the matter, the incident captured the imaginations of European writers both at the time and in the centuries that followed, but was probably seen as just another visit from what Tolan calls 'a barefoot Italian ascetic, a sort of Christian Sufi'. While non-Muslims were legally prohibited from seeking to convert Muslims, al-Kamil Muhammad was himself open to religious discussions and is likely to have tolerated St Francis' preaching, though he probably did not see it as anything remarkable (Tolan, 2009: 5–6). The very different treatments of St Francis' visit in the Frankish and Muslim sources are a salutary reminder for historians that the significance of any given event very much depends on the viewpoint of the person describing (or not describing) it.

CRITICS OF THE AYYUBIDS

As indicated previously, the Ayyubids' approach to the Franks generated a great deal of resentment among Muslim thinkers. The hand-back of Jerusalem to Frederick II, not surprisingly, was greeted with an outpouring of hostility. Ibn al-Athir comments, 'The Muslims were outraged and thought it monstrous. This caused them to feel such weakness and pain as are beyond description' (Ibn al-Athir, 2008: 294). Both common people and religious scholars railed against what had happened; the best known of the latter was the immensely popular Damascene preacher Sibt ibn al-Jawzi (d. 1257), a grandson of 'Abd al-Rahman ibn al-Jawzi, whose account of the Second Crusade we saw in Chapter 4. Sibt ibn al-Jawzi settled in Damascus in about 1204, spending most of his time there teaching and writing, when he was not travelling on preaching tours. He devoted much of his efforts to *jihad* preaching, and when the agreement was made al-Nasir Dawud, at the time the ruler of Damascus but already besieged by his uncle al-Ashraf Musa, ordered Sibt ibn al-Jawzi to preach against al-Kamil and his treacherous handover of the holy city to the infidel, a task that the Damascene preacher was happy to undertake. It is thus not surprising that when al-Ashraf Musa, reinforced by al-Kamil Muhammad, compelled al-Nasir Dawud to leave Damascus, Sibt ibn al-Jawzi was obliged to leave too (Talmon-Heller, 2007 b: 71–2). In his own chronicle, *Mir'at al-Zaman fi Ta'rikh al-A'yan* (The Mirror of Time concerning the History of Important People), when describing the reaction of the inhabitants of the region to the events, Sibt ibn al-Jawzi states, 'The news of the surrender of Jerusalem to the Franks arrived, and turmoil erupted in all the lands of Islam. The misfortunes [associated with the events] were so distressing that ceremonies of mourning were held' [**Doc. 17.ii**]. Thus his account corroborates that of Ibn al-Athir.

One might expect that the Ayyubids' dealings with the Franks, and particularly the giving of Jerusalem to them, would have shattered the alliance between the religious and political classes that we saw built up in previous chapters. However, as Sivan has shown, this was not actually the case. As we have seen, the Ayyubids continued to patronize the religious classes within their states, founding religious institutions and taking a personal interest in religious affairs, something that did much to win over the religious scholars who were keen to see Islamic orthodoxy promoted in society. However, many of these scholars continued to protest against their patrons' collaboration with the Franks and to encourage them to engage in the military *jihad* against the enemy, something that Hillenbrand has described as 'an embarrassment rather than a stimulus to these sultans' (Hillenbrand, 1999 a: 223). Yet the protest movement was never strong enough to constitute a real threat to the Ayyubids' power, which rested first and foremost upon their armies, and so while the Ayyubid rulers could not completely neglect the role of the religious classes in supporting their authority, they could for the most part proceed as they wished (Sivan, 1968: 141–55); the fact that al-Kamil Muhammad was able to commit the hugely unpopular act of handing Jerusalem over to the Franks without being deposed by a general uprising is testimony to this. The religious–political alliance was shaken but not seriously threatened.

CONCLUSION

In the wake of the death of Saladin, the Ayyubids found themselves ruling a confederation of states that were beset by enemies on several fronts. However, distrust and ambition divided them, so that rather than forming a united front to preserve their territories, they instead engaged in conflicts with one another, in which the rulers of the surrounding territories, Muslim and Frankish, became involved as allies or opponents. At times the Ayyubids were able to take advantage of relations with other states to further their own goals, while at other times their disputes weakened them, so that the other powers were able to expand their influence or territories at Ayyubid expense. The military *jihad* against the Franks, in the meantime, became largely defensive in nature, with treaties and compromises being the generally preferred option, despite the protests of religious scholars and commoners alike. At the same time, the Ayyubid rulers came to rely increasingly on their military forces as the principal basis of their power. The eventual result of this policy will become apparent in the next chapter.

FURTHER READING

Probably the best starting point for further research on the Ayyubids is R. Stephen Humphreys' *From Saladin to the Mongols* (1977), which, though centred on Damascus, provides a detailed history of the Ayyubid confederation. For a briefer overview of the structure of the Ayyubid state and its relations with the Franks, see his 'Ayyubids, Mamluks and the Latin East in the Thirteenth Century' (1998) and Carole Hillenbrand, *The Crusades: Islamic Perspectives* (1999 a). A comprehensive treatment of the Ayyubid principality of Aleppo is Anne-Marie Eddé's *La Principauté Ayyoubide d'Alep (579/1183–658/1260)* (1999). Two important biographical works on the later Ayyubids have been written by German scholars: Franz-Josef Dahlmanns's *Al-Malik al-'Adil: Ägypten und der Vordere Orient in den Jahren 589/1193 bis 615/1218* (1975) is the author's doctoral thesis on the career and reign of al-'Adil Muhammad after the death of Saladin; and Hans L. Gottschalk's *Al-Malik al-Kamil von Egypten und seine Zeit: Eine Studie zur Geschichte Vorderasiens und Egyptens in der Ersten Hälfte des 7./13. Jahrhunderts* (1958) is a study of the reign of al-Kamil Muhammad. For another, detailed, discussion of al-Kamil Muhammad's responses to the Fifth and especially Frederick II's crusades, see Laila Atrache, *Die Politik der Ayyubiden* (1996). On the encounter between St Francis and al-Kamil Muhammad see John Tolan, *Saint Francis and the Sultan: The Curious History of a Christian–Muslim Encounter* (2009); and, for a Muslim perspective, Fareed Z. Munir, 'Sultan al-Malik Muhammad al-Kamil and Saint Francis: Interreligious Dialogue and the Meeting at Damietta' (2008). On Muslim reactions to the Ayyubids' diplomatic dealings with the Franks, see Emmanuel Sivan, *L'Islam et la Croisade* (1968); and, again, Daniella Talmon-Heller, 'Islamic Preaching in Syria during the Counter-Crusade' (2007 b) and *Islamic Piety in Medieval Syria* (2007 a).

8

The Mamluks, 1249–1382

A l-Salih Ayyub had placed great reliance on *mamluk* troops, building up a large regiment of them in his armies, including an important unit known as the **Bahriyya**. In the wake of his death, the Bahriyya were instrumental in saving Egypt from St Louis' crusade. However, they then went on to depose their Ayyubid masters and set up their own state in Egypt and Syria. It is this state, and its interactions with its neighbours, that we will examine in this chapter.

Bahriyya: An important *mamluk* regiment. The Bahriyya was created by the Ayyubid sultan al-Salih Ayyub (r. 1240–9). The name derives from the fact that their original barracks was on Rawda island on the River (Arabic: *bahr*) Nile.

CHRONOLOGICAL OVERVIEW

As indicated in the last chapter, al-Salih Ayyub's heir, Turan-Shah, was absent from Egypt when his father died. However, al-Salih's widow, a former Turkish slave named Shajar al-Durr (d. 1257), acting in collusion with a senior *mamluk* emir, concealed the sultan's death, even forging his signature on official documents. Resistance to the crusaders continued, and in February 1250 the Muslims inflicted a decisive defeat on their enemies at al-Mansura, in which the Bahriyya played a prominent role. In the aftermath King Louis was taken prisoner. His wife, Queen Margaret, negotiated his release in return for Damietta, and the crusaders left Egypt. Louis himself remained in the east for four more years, strengthening the defences of the Latin Kingdom before returning home.

By the time that Louis left in 1254, a radical change had occurred in the government of Egypt. Turan-Shah had arrived at the Muslim camp at the end of February 1250 and was duly recognized as sultan. However, he soon alienated his father's senior Bahri *mamluks* by threatening them and by assigning members of his own *mamluk* retinue to the major posts in the state (Irwin, 1986: 21). Tensions soon came to a head, and on 2 May 1250 a group of Bahri *mamluks* murdered Turan-Shah. They elected Shajar al-Durr as the new *sultana* (female sultan), an act almost without precedent in Islamic history, but it soon became apparent that if the new rulers were to impose their authority on Syria, where rebellions against the new regime immediately broke out, then they would need a military leader (a man) at the helm. Less than three months later, then, Shajar al-Durr was deposed and replaced with a *mamluk* emir named Aybak al-Turkumani (r. 1250 and 1254–7). Aybak was induced to abdicate after only five days to make way for a 10-year-old member of the Ayyubid family, instead becoming the young sultan's *atabeg*, though he remained the effective ruler of the state – with the exception, as Holt puts it, that 'Shajar al-Durr ruled him' (Holt, 1986: 84). At some point during the proceedings Shajar al-Durr was married off to Aybak. In 1254, once Aybak had consolidated his own political position, he deposed his young charge and assumed the title of sultan, ruling for three years before being murdered in the bath at the orders of Shajar al-Durr, who felt threatened by his plans to take another wife. Aybak's 15-year-old son al-Mansur 'Ali (r. 1257–9) succeeded to the throne, although it was the senior *mamluk* emirs who controlled the actual positions of power in the state. In the meantime Shajar al-Durr was killed, apparently beaten to death with wooden clogs by Aybak's concubines (Irwin, 1986: 29). Thus began the Mamluk Sultanate (1250–1517), a period when Egypt and (from 1260) Syria were ruled by whichever *mamluk* emirs were able to gather the most support among the various factions of the army and (to a lesser extent) the wider elite classes of society.

Historians traditionally divide the Mamluk sultanate into the so-called **'Bahri Mamluk Sultanate'** (1250–1382) and the **'Burji Mamluk Sultanate'** (1382–1517), labels derived from the names of two prominent Mamluk units. As David Ayalon has shown, a better labelling might be the 'Turkish Mamluk Sultanate' and the 'Circassian Mamluk Sultanate', reflecting the ethnicity of the majority (though not all) of the Mamluks in each period (Ayalon, 1994: IV: 3–53). In any case, it is the first of these two periods that we will concern ourselves with here, since this was the period during which the Mamluks ejected the Franks from the Levantine coast. However, the Mamluks first had to deal with other threats. As indicated above, Turan-Shah's murder and Shajar al-Durr's accession were greeted with revolts in Syria, most of which were led by Ayyubid princes who objected to the Mamluks' usurpation of power. By 1260, these princes had mostly been eliminated or suppressed by the Mamluk forces, who in the same year also managed to break the advance of a new threat to their state: the Mongols.

In 1206, a Mongol warrior chieftain named Temujin, but better known by his title Chingiz Khan (or Genghis Khan ['Universal King'], r. 1206–27), welded together a confederation of Central Asian tribes and launched a series of campaigns intended to create a great empire. He conquered China and began expanding west into the Muslim world. After he died, his successors

Bahri (Turkish) Mamluk Sultanate: The first period of *mamluk* rule in Egypt and Syria (1250–1382), named after the Bahriyya and characterized by the fact that most of the sultans were Kipchak Turks.

Burji (Circassian) Mamluk Sultanate: The second period of *mamluk* rule in Egypt and Syria (1382–1517), during which most of the sultans were Circassians.

took up his mission and continued the Mongol expansion. A destructive expedition was launched into Russia and eastern Europe in 1236–41; the Seljuk Sultanate of *Rum* was subdued in 1243; and in 1255 Hülegü (d. 1265), the brother of the Great Khan Möngke (r. 1251–60), launched a major campaign into Persia and Iraq. In 1256 Hülegü destroyed Alamut, bringing the Persian line of the Nizari Assassins to its end. Then on 12 February 1258 he took Baghdad. The caliph, al-Musta'sim (r. 1242–58), was executed by being rolled up in a carpet and trampled to death by horses, in accordance with a Mongol custom that forbade the shedding of royal blood, and the reign of the 'Abbasid caliphate was also, temporarily, ended (but see below).

Hülegü continued his progress westwards. Aleppo fell in January 1260, Damascus in March; then, hearing of the death of his brother, Hülegü returned east to take part in the choice of the next Great Khan, leaving behind a small portion of his forces to continue the advance. The following summer a Mongol embassy arrived in Cairo, where one of Aybak's *mamluks*, Qutuz (r. 1259–60), had usurped power from al-Mansur 'Ali. Qutuz responded to the Mongols' demands for surrender by executing the ambassadors and setting out with his army. The two forces met in September at 'Ayn Jalut, to the south-west of the Sea of Galilee, and the Mamluks carried the day, putting the Mongol army to flight [**Doc. 18**]. The Mongols would make further attempts to invade Mamluk Syria in the future, but each time the Mamluks would turn them back.

On the way back from 'Ayn Jalut, Qutuz was murdered by a group of *mamluk* conspirators. Among their number was a Bahri *mamluk* named Baybars al-Bunduqdari (r. 1260–77), who had also been involved in the murder of Turan-Shah. Baybars was now chosen as the new sultan. Baybars spent most of his reign fighting wars on multiple fronts. In addition to consolidating Mamluk control of Syria, and putting down rebellions within his state, he also fought ongoing wars against the Mongols on the northern and eastern frontiers, mounted punitive expeditions into Lesser Armenia, subdued the fortresses and power of the Syrian Assassins in 1265–73 and directed almost yearly campaigns against the Franks. Baybars adopted a multi-pronged approach in his attacks on the Franks, destroying crops, pastures and livestock to damage the economic prosperity of the Latin states, while also razing coastal fortresses so that they could not be used as bridgeheads for new waves of crusaders. In May 1268 he personally oversaw the capture of Antioch, thus ending its time as a Frankish capital. These military actions were complemented by skilful diplomacy that enabled him to extract further concessions from the Franks in the form of land- and income-sharing agreements (Irwin, 1986: 47–8 and 55–7; Holt, 1986: 95–6).

Baybars died on 20 June 1277, probably accidentally poisoned by a bad batch of *qumiz* (fermented mare's milk; Irwin, 1986: 58). After brief, successive reigns by two of his sons, power was usurped, in November 1279, by another Bahri *mamluk*, Qalawun (r. 1279–90) al-Alfi ('of the thousand', so called because his first master had paid 1,000 [Arabic: *alf*] *dinars* for him). Like Baybars, Qalawun spent much of his time at war, quelling opponents within and outside the Mamluk state, including defeating the Mongols at the Battle of Hims in 1281, and pursuing the holy war against the Franks. Qalawun adopted similar tactics to those used by Baybars, destroying coastal strongholds and mixing diplomacy with force [see Doc. 19]. His crowning achievement was the capture of Tripoli in April 1289. He demolished the city and was preparing to mount an expedition against the last Frankish capital, Acre, when he fell ill, dying on 10 November 1290. Qalawun's son, al-Ashraf Khalil (r. 1290–3), sought to fulfil his father's ambition, besieging the city in March 1291. The city was taken on 18 May and was, like Tripoli, demolished [Doc. 20].

The fall of Acre did not signify the end of conflict between the Mamluks and the Franks in the Levant. There remained a handful of Frankish strongholds on the coast that had to be mopped up over the next few years, and even after that there was ongoing conflict, especially between the Mamluks and the Frankish rulers of Cyprus. For example, a particularly destructive raid on Alexandria, mounted by King Peter I (r. 1359–69) in October 1365, caused significant damage to the city and soured trade relations for several years. Nor was it only the Mamluks who were the targets of later crusades; conflicts in the Balkan Peninsula between the Hungarians and the Ottoman Turks in the early 1390s eventually led to the Crusade of Nikopolis (Nikopol) in 1396, the culmination of which was the complete rout of a coalition of European crusaders at the hands of the Ottoman armies.

Returning to the Mamluk Sultanate: al-Ashraf Khalil was assassinated in 1293, and thereafter power passed, for the most part, into the hands of the senior Mamluk officers. Often a descendant of Qalawun might occupy the sultan's throne, but real power actually lay in the hands of his theoretical subordinates. The most important exception is the third reign of Qalawun's son al-Nasir Muhammad (r. 1293–4, 1299–1309 and 1310–41), during which the sultan enjoyed firm control over a mostly peaceful realm, although as Levanoni has argued, he destroyed many of the traditional Mamluk power structures and ruined the economy of the state in order to achieve this (Levanoni, 1995: *passim*). The Qalawunid sultans thereafter were usually puppets of high-ranking Mamluk emirs, and in 1382 a Circassian *mamluk* called Barquq (r. 1382–9 and 1390–9) usurped the position of sultan. With the exception of a brief nominal restoration of a Qalawunid sultan in 1389–90, the title passed out of the hands of Turkish *mamluks* and into those of their Circassian counterparts. Circassian Mamluk sultans subsequently reigned in Egypt until 1517, when the country was conquered by the Ottomans.

THE MAMLUK EXPERIENCE

In this book we have briefly mentioned *mamluks* in the context of their involvement in the Muslim armies, but here it is appropriate to discuss in more detail the 'system' that encompassed their recruitment and employment. Muslim rulers had been making use of significant numbers of *mamluk* troops, principally Turks from Central Asia, as early as the ninth century. By the end of the Ayyubid period the majority of the *mamluks* in the sultanate's armies were Turks drawn from the Kipchak Steppe, north of the Black Sea, although other ethnic elements were also present; as we have seen, Circassians eventually rose to prominence in the Mamluk Sultanate. *Mamluks*, both male and female, were bought as slaves on the fringes of the Muslim world, while they were young children, by merchants who then imported them into the major trade centres and capitals. There they were sold to the sultan or emirs. Girls would usually be directed to domestic service or the harems (Shajar al-Durr was one such slave), while boys would be taken to barracks or other quarters in preparation for training. Indeed, the Bahriyya and **Burjiyya** units were named for the barracks where they were originally quartered: on Rawda island, on the River (*bahr* [*nahr* in modern Egyptian Arabic]) Nile, in the case of the Bahriyya, and in a *burj* (tower) of the Citadel in Cairo, in the case of the Burjiyya. *Mamluk* regiments would normally receive names derived from the titles of their owners; al-Salih Ayyub's Bahriyya were part of his wider *mamluk* regiment, known as the Salihiyya from his title of 'al-Malik al-Salih' (the Virtuous King), while Baybars' personal *mamluk* regiment was called the Zahiriyya, after his title 'al-Malik al-Zahir' (the Victorious King).

> **Burjiyya:** Another important *mamluk* regiment. The creation of the Burjiyya is usually ascribed to the Mamluk sultan Qalawun (r. 1279–90). Their name derives from the fact that they were originally quartered in a tower (Arabic: *burj*) of the Citadel in Cairo.

However, before joining such a regiment, young *mamluk* boys had to go through extensive schooling, both religious and military. Their initial scholastic training would be in Arabic, learning to speak and write the language, though how well they mastered it varied; Qalawun is said never to have learned to speak Arabic fluently (Northrup, 1998: 67). A religious scholar would then teach them the *Qur'an* and Shari'a (Islamic law). However, as soon as they were old enough the majority of their time would be spent on military training, which included horsemanship and fighting with a lance, sword and composite bow, as well as a shield and other weapons. In establishing their training system for new recruits the Mamluks drew on the Muslim tradition of *furusiyya*, military standards dating back to the eighth century that encompassed not only riding and the use of weapons, but also hunting, basic veterinary skills, sports such as wrestling and polo, and an expectation of behaviour roughly corresponding to the European concept of chivalry. *Furusiyya* literature can also be seen as including the military manuals referred to in Chapter 6 (al-Sarraf, 2004: 144–52; Nicolle, 1994: 8–9). By the time that they completed this training the best *mamluks*, then, were highly educated and skilled warriors, athletes and military tacticians. For example, it was said that they could make sword cuts to precise depths and bodily locations, depending on their leaders' instructions. A *mamluk*'s training naturally took years, so that he would be a fully grown adult by the time that he completed it. He would then graduate with his fellows in a group ceremony, being freed and normally joining the retinue of his former owner (al-Sarraf, 2004: *passim*; Rabie, 1975: *passim*; Ayalon, 1994: II: 11–13). A fully trained and armed *mamluk* was an intimidating figure, armed with a lance, sword, shield, bow and mace, wearing mail and/or lamellar armour, and riding a warhorse.

Some *mamluks*, especially those of the sultan, could rise to high ranks within the army and state. As we have seen, even before the Mamluk takeover they were senior figures in the military hierarchy and instrumental in the conduct of the resistance to Louis IX's crusade.

THE MAMLUK STATE

Naturally, the Mamluks inherited bureaucratic structures from their Fatimid and Ayyubid predecessors, but the state that they established in Egypt was much more centralized, with tighter control of its institutions by the sultan and his deputies. The state administration was divided into three parts: the Men of the Sword (the military), the Men of the Pen (the civil administration) and the Men of the Turban (the religious hierarchy). The Men of the Turban were originally led by a Shafi'i chief *qadi*, but Baybars instead instituted the practice of having a chief *qadi* from each of the four major schools of Sunni Islamic law, thus preventing the Shafi'is from monopolizing this position and making it possible for subjects to appeal to whichever chief *qadi* represented the school of law that they followed; indeed, many *mamluks* followed the Hanafi school of law and hence appreciated the appointment of a Hanafi chief *qadi* to judge their cases (Irwin, 1986: 43). The Men of the Pen consisted for the most part, as before the Mamluk takeover, of Egyptian Coptic Christians or Muslims, with the latter becoming increasingly numerous as ever more Copts converted to Islam (Little, 1983: 179–80). Of the three divisions, however, the Men of the Sword were the most influential, and offices in the other parts of the state administration were subject to inspection by Mamluk officials with appropriate expertise. Meanwhile, the major centres in Syria became the capitals of provinces, ruled by representatives of the sultan who reported directly to him in Cairo (see Plate 6).

The Men of the Sword merit further attention. At their head was the sultan, who was advised by a council of about 24 senior *mamluk* emirs, each known as *amir mi'a wa-muqaddam alf* (emir of 100 and commander of

1,000), indicating that he had a retinue of 100 cavalrymen (*mamluks* and free-born) and led 1,000 **halqa** troops (see below) in battle. Ranged below these were the emirs of 40 (each having a retinue of 40 cavalry and also known as *amir al-tablakhana*, [emir of the military band, indicating his right to maintain one]), then the emirs of 10 (with 10 cavalry). All of these senior ranks were normally reserved for *mamluks*.

The majority of the free-born soldiers in the Mamluk army formed the greater part of the body of troops known as the *halqa* (circle); this division comprised soldiers of various origins, including Kurdish and Arab troops, Mongol refugees, some *mamluks* and in particular the **awlad al-nas** (sons of the people), the sons or descendants of *mamluks* who were not normally permitted to rise to the higher ranks in the military or state, although some clearly did (Irwin, 1986: 38–40 and 50–1; Northrup, 1998: 189–200; Richards, 1998: *passim*). Of course, the major exception to this rule was the progeny of the sultan, since a number of sultans sought to establish a dynastic succession to their rule; indeed, Qalawun and his descendants reigned (in theory if not always in fact) for over a century. However, most *awlad al-nas* encountered a 'glass ceiling' that resulted from their not having gone through the *mamluk* experiences of their forebears. The Mamluks also made use of additional auxiliary troops, including in particular Turkmen, Bedouin and other free cavalry (Northrup, 1998: 199).

Of course, it is worth noting that the above list of ranks and political relations is normative, and that practice varied during the more than 250 years that the Mamluks were in power. The whole Mamluk military system was supported, as in earlier decades, by the distribution of *iqta's*. This was something that was of particular importance for higher-ranking Mamluk emirs, who were after all required to keep retinues of significant sizes.

Halqa: Arabic: 'circle'. Term used to refer to (a) a circle of students gathered around a scholar, and (b) a regiment in the armies of the Mamluk Sultanate made up of (mostly) free-born troops of various origins.

Awlad al-Nas: Arabic: 'the sons of the people'. The term used to refer to the descendants of *mamluks* in the Mamluk Sultanate. Although they might be wealthy and privileged, they were usually limited in how far they could ascend the military–political hierarchy.

LEGITIMIZING RULE

As usurpers, the Mamluks felt under particular pressure to prove the legitimacy of their rule. Baybars' supporters sought to legitimize his rule in a number of ways, arguing that divine decree had placed him in the position of sultan, that his natural abilities qualified him to rule, that he was elected to the position by his peers and that he loyally continued the pious traditions of his former master al-Salih Ayyub, including his efforts in the military *jihad* (Irwin, 1986: 42–4).

Both Baybars and his successors sought to place particular emphasis on their Islamic piety, articulating this in a number of ways. As indicated above, in 1258 the Mongols took Baghdad, putting the 'Abbasid caliph to death. In 1261 Baybars resurrected the caliphate in Cairo, placing on the throne a relative of the deceased caliph, who took the regnal title of al-Mustansir (r. 1261). The caliph in turn invested the sultan with not only Syria and Egypt, but also western Arabia, including the holy cities, the Yemen and any territory that he might conquer in the future, effectively authorizing Baybars to engage in expansion of Mamluk territory and appointing him the sultan of the Islamic world in the manner of the Great Seljuk sultans. Al-Mustansir, who seems not to have been as easy to manipulate as Baybars may have hoped, enjoyed only a brief reign; he was slain by the Mongols after being sent off to try and retake Baghdad with what may have been a deliberately inadequate force. His successors would reign, but never rule, until the Ottoman conquest of 1517, providing a veneer of caliphal approval for the Mamluk regime (Holt, 1986: 92–3; Irwin, 1986: 43–4).

In the meantime, the Mamluks capitalized on precedents set by their Ayyubid and Zangid forebears, seeking to promote their legitimacy through both official propaganda and acts of public piety, the latter including in particular endowments of religious or charitable buildings. As Robert Hillenbrand has noted, the Mamluks enthusiastically supported building projects, competing with each other to endow the most impressive mosques, *madrasas* and other buildings. The Mamluks' efforts were supported by an influx of skilled craftsmen and architects from the eastern Islamic world, who came as refugees from the Mongol conquests. Cairo soon became crowded with buildings, forcing architects to design vertically rather than horizontally, and the city became home to awe-inspiring structures that towered over the common folk, emphasizing the conspicuous amount of wealth that Mamluk patrons had spent on their construction, and with it their piety and power. Naturally, such buildings bore inscriptions naming and exalting their patrons with titles that emphasized their pious support of the faith. Jerusalem also benefited greatly from Mamluk attention during this period. While it was no longer seen as being at risk from the Franks, its holiness attracted the patronage of Mamluk sultans and emirs keen to demonstrate their piety through the restoration or construction of religious buildings within its walls, especially on the Temple Mount (Hillenbrand, 1999 b: 140–50; Little, 1997: 186–93).

Mamluk emirs also richly supplemented their endowments of buildings with salaries for their staffs, furnishings and equipment, including ornate *Qur'an* manuscripts, lamps and bookstands. The Mamluks also made widespread use of blazons, circular emblems bearing devices that identified particular emirs in a way similar to western heraldry. Such devices were used in both architectural decoration and, where possible, the minor arts, in this way publicly proclaiming the piety and influence of the patrons in question; thus the blazon of a Mamluk emir might, for example, appear on the stucco work of a building or on a glass lamp donated to a particular mosque (Hillenbrand, 1999 b: 150–66). Baybars made particularly widespread use of the lion or panther found on his blazon, using this device even on objects as small as coins (see, for example, Plate 7). A particularly striking example of Baybars' use of this device is on the Jisr Jindas, a bridge built by the sultan at Lydda (Lod) in 1273 and bearing on each side an inscription comme-morating the date of its construction (Plate 8). Each inscription is flanked on either side by a depiction of a lion toying with a rat, probably intended to exalt the sultan in his superiority over his puny enemies; it has been suggested that the rat was a visual parody of the lion rampant heraldry of the Lusignan kings, or possibly an Arabic linguistic pun on the words *far* (rat) and *kuffar* (blasphemers or infidels), and was intended to refer specifically to the Franks (Clermont-Ganneau, 1896: 110–18).

Baybars' particular use of the lion device at the Jisr Jindas reminds us that there was, of course, one more way in which the Mamluks could assert their pious credentials: the military *jihad* against the Franks and other enemies, which, as we have seen, a number of sultans pursued with considerable enthusiasm. We will consider this in more detail in the next section, but it is worth noting for the moment that a heightened atmosphere of hostility to non-Muslim external enemies may have had a collateral effect within Mamluk territory, in that religious minorities within the state, especially Christians, suffered increasingly harsh discriminatory measures at the time. The extent to which the two phenomena were actually linked is still debated, however (Hillenbrand, 1999 a: 414–19).

As with Nur al-Din and Saladin, it is important to avoid being too cynical about the Mamluks' religious activities, as it can be tempting to write them off merely as attempts to make use of religious ideas for political gain. While it is more than likely that there were some sultans who sought to use Islam in this fashion, a number of sultans do seem to have been genuinely engaged with their faith in a real and personal way. Baybars, for example, is known to have been devoted to a Sufi **shaykh** named Khadir al-Mihrani (d. 1277), consulting him constantly, allowing him to persecute Christians and Jews, and sharing state secrets with him despite the opposition of his senior emirs (Thorau, 1992: 225–9). This suggests that on some level Baybars' piety was genuine, even if it does not prove that all his activities were undertaken for the good of Islam. It is likely that for many of the Mamluk sultans and their followers the line between religious devotion and political ambition was extremely blurred.

Shaykh: A term used to refer to (1) a highly regarded scholar or teacher and (2) the master of a Sufi order.

THE MAMLUK *JIHAD*

As indicated above, the Mamluks were enthusiastic proponents of the *jihad*, both in propaganda and in action. As with their predecessors, the buildings

that they endowed bore inscriptions loudly attesting to their participation in
the military *jihad*, and their panegyrists numbered their enthusiasm for the
holy war among their virtues (Hillenbrand, 1999 a: 227–37). However, the
Mamluk period sees two major shifts in the way that the *jihad* was approached
by the rulers of Egypt and Greater Syria. First, as Humphreys has noted, the
Mamluks placed a much greater emphasis on the military aspect of the *jihad*,
something that is reflected in the sources from the time; as he states of one
biography of Baybars, 'a reader [. . .] almost gets a headache from the throbbing drums and the glare of sunlight on armor' (Humphreys, 1998: 11–12).
Second, the Mamluks fought a military *jihad* that was multi-faceted, having
to deal with several enemies both outside and within their state, including
the Franks, the Mongols, the Armenians and the Assassins. Of these it was
the Mongols who most occupied the Mamluks' attention, since they, unlike the
others, posed a clear and present danger to the survival of the Mamluk
regime, and it was the Mongol threat that dictated the course of Mamluk
military activity, with expeditions against other enemies normally only undertaken when the frontier with the Mongols was secure (Amitai-Preiss, 1995:
114; Northrup, 1998: 100).

Thinking about the Franks in particular, we should not take this as
an indication that the Mamluks saw them as a trivial concern. There were
a number of reasons for the swift elimination of the Frankish states on the
coast by the end of the thirteenth century. As we have seen, early Mamluk
propaganda sought to draw attention to the Mamluks' links with the previous regime, including their claims to be continuing the holy war against the
Franks undertaken by such exalted figures as Saladin and al-Salih Ayyub,
and so fighting the military *jihad* was an important means for the sultans
and their followers to emphasize these links in a way that also attested to
their pious support of the faith. Showing contentedness with the presence
of the Franks on the coast would have belied the Mamluks' claims to be
defenders of the Muslim lands and alienated the religious classes upon whom
the Mamluks relied for support. Instead, as Carole Hillenbrand has noted,
the Mamluk sultans forged close links with the religious elite (Hillenbrand,
1999 a: 238).

One of the most important religious scholars of the Mamluk era was Ahmad
ibn Taymiyya (d. 1328). Ibn Taymiyya was born into a family of Hanbali
religious scholars in Harran in modern-day Turkey. His family fled the
Mongols in 1268–9, moving to Damascus, where Ibn Taymiyya received an
education in – and by the age of 19 mastered – the religious sciences, becoming a high-profile teacher and public scholar. As Donald Little has put it, 'It
is Ibn Taymiyya's distinction that he opposed by word and deed almost every
aspect of religion practiced in the Mamluk Empire'; he objected to both
popular practices and Mamluk policies and was imprisoned six times over

the course of his career for his outspokenness (Little, 1983: 180–1). Yet at the same time he was an influential figure who periodically served the Mamluks as a *jihad* propagandist. Ibn Taymiyya was an enthusiastic advocate for a vigorous *jihad* within the Muslim world, in terms of both personal engagement in the greater *jihad* and state-level correction of the errors of Muslim society, to the point that rulers who did not behave correctly could legitimately be rebelled against, since they were evidently heretics and hypocrites. At the same time, Ibn Taymiyya saw the external, military *jihad* as a defensive obligation, incumbent on all Muslims when their security was threatened. Ibn Taymiyya's ideas were influential in his own time and have also had a great impact in the modern day. In particular, aspects of his teachings have been selectively quoted – and distorted – by modern violent extremists to justify acts of terrorism (Bonney, 2004: 111–26); for more on this topic, see Chapter 9.

Returning more directly to the Mamluk military *jihad* against the Franks, it is clear that there were also serious strategic gains to be made through the liquidation of the Frankish states. When the Mongols had invaded Syria in the mid-thirteenth century, they had received the submission and support of both the Principality of Antioch and the Kingdom of Lesser Armenia (Amitai-Preiss, 1995: 24–5 and 54), an alliance that even briefly persisted after the Battle of 'Ayn Jalut. The Mamluks remained concerned that the Franks might form a grand alliance with the Mongols; history tells us that while there were embassies exchanged between various European, Levantine Frankish and Mongol rulers, no such alliance materialized, but the Mamluks of course did not know that this was how such discussions would turn out (Amitai-Preiss, 1995: 94–105). Thus they took action to remove the Franks from the equation, systematically destroying the coastal cities and fortresses that they captured in order to make it more difficult for the European powers to re-establish a presence in the region.

Yet at the same time, practicalities dictated that the Mamluks could not pursue a uniformly hostile policy towards the Franks. It was important to come to terms with them from time to time, at least temporarily, especially when the Mongols threatened to launch new expeditions into the Mamluk state and the Mamluks had to direct their military resources elsewhere. Consequently, we see Mamluk sultans making peace agreements with the Franks (both of the east and of Europe) whenever it proved necessary or convenient (Humphreys, 1998: 14–15). One particularly important set of treaties was that made with the intention of guaranteeing ongoing supplies of slaves from the Kipchak Steppe, a vital resource for the Mamluks who, after all, based their power primarily on slaves from this region during this period. The securing of this supply required peace agreements not only with the rulers of the Golden Horde (the part of the former Mongol Empire north of the Black and Caspian Seas), the Byzantine Empire and Lesser Armenia, through which the trade routes ran, but also with the Genoese, who controlled trade across the Black Sea (Northrup, 1998: 284–5). Fortunately for the Mamluks, the Genoese, along with the other Italians, do not seem to have had strong objections to the destruction of the Latin states on the coast (Amitai-Preiss, 1995: 103), which did not impede them from continuing to pursue immensely profitable trade through Alexandria and other ports on the Egyptian coast.

CONCLUSION

In this chapter we have seen the Mamluks transform the Ayyubid confederation of Muslim Egypt and Greater Syria into a centralized polity geared first and foremost to military activity. It is understandable that the Mamluks, themselves military men, sought to organize their state in this way, and given that they faced major threats to their territory's integrity from the start, it is not surprising that this conditioned the structure of the sultanate. There is, however, a striking tension between the old and the new that can be seen in how the Mamluk sultanate evolved; this was a state where those most qualified to rule rose to the top (sometimes in a brutal fashion), yet the Mamluks themselves seem to have felt that this was not enough. It is notable that the Mamluks also sought to emphasize their links to pre-existent precedents, in particular previous regimes and Islamic tradition; witness the number of sultans who claimed to be ruling as successors to, on behalf of, or as representatives of earlier sultans and caliphs. Such rationales were widely disseminated through official propaganda, public buildings and examples set by the Mamluks themselves in their conduct. The Mamluk sultans also looked forwards, seeking themselves to establish dynasties on the sultan's throne and thus still showing a preference for hereditary rather than merit-based transmission of power.

Where did this leave the Franks? Arguably the destruction of the Latin states in the Levant was more a collateral result of other concerns than something that had been seen as a major goal by the Mamluks. After the defeat of Louis IX's crusade the Franks posed no direct threat to the existence of the Mamluk state; instead, their extirpation resulted principally from the potential danger posed by a Frankish–Mongol alliance, and the Mamluks' own need to legitimize their rule through visible engagement in the military *jihad*. It is testimony to the secondary nature of the Frankish menace, in Mamluk eyes, that it took almost a half-century after the Mamluk takeover for the sultans to destroy the last of the Latin strongholds on the coast, and they were content both to make treaties with and to conduct commerce with the Franks in the meantime.

FURTHER READING

An excellent overview of the Bahri Mamluk Sultanate is Robert Irwin's *The Middle East in the Middle Ages* (1986). P.M. Holt's *The Age of the Crusades* (1986) also provides an account of the complex political developments that took place in the period. On a *mamluk*'s education, see in the first instance Shihab al-Sarraf, 'Mamluk *Furusiyah* Literature and Its Antecedents' (2004); and Hassanein Rabie, 'The Training of the Mamluk Faris' (1975). The structure of the Mamluk army is the subject of a number of articles by David Ayalon; see his *Studies on the Mamluks of Egypt* (1977). Some of his conclusions have been questioned by other scholars; see, for example, Donald S. Richards, 'Mamluk Amirs and Their Families and Households' (1998). A number of Mamluk sultans have been the subject of scholarly biographies. On Baybars, see Peter Thorau, *The Lion of Egypt: Sultan Baybars I and the Near East in the Thirteenth Century* (1992); and Abdul-Aziz Khowaiter, *Baibars the First: His Endeavours and Achievements* (1978). Qalawun is the subject of an important study by Linda S. Northrup: *From Slave to Sultan: The Career of al-Mansur Qalawun and the Consolidation of Mamluk Rule in Egypt and Syria (678–689 A.H./1279–1290 A.D.)* (1998). On al-Nasir Muhammad, see Amalia Levanoni, *A Turning Point in Mamluk History: The Third Reign of al-Nasir Muhammad Ibn Qalawun (1310–1341)* (1995). For an excellent discussion of the last years of the Qalawunid sultans see Jo van Steenbergen, *Order out of Chaos: Patronage, Conflict and Mamluk Socio-Political Culture, 1341–1382* (2006). The conflict between the Mamluks and the Mongols is addressed in Reuven Amitai-Preiss, *Mongols and Mamluks: The Mamluk–Ilkhanid War, 1260–1281* (1995), while the multiple challenges faced by the Mamluks are succinctly discussed in R. Stephen Humphreys, 'Ayyubids, Mamluks and the Latin East in the Thirteenth Century' (1998). On Mamluk practice of Islam, see Donald P. Little, 'Religion under the Mamluks' (1983). On Ibn Taymiyya, his teachings on *jihad* and their impact, including in the modern day, see in the first instance Richard Bonney, *Jihad: From Qur'an to bin Laden* (2004).

9

Conclusion

I n our Introduction (Chapter 1) we noted that the Crusades had an immense impact on Europe, both on those who left their homes to come east and those who stayed behind, and it cannot be denied that they continue to loom large in popular memory today. Yet what was their legacy in the Middle East? As we conclude our exploration of Muslim responses to the Crusades, we will consider their impact both at the time and in modern Muslim perceptions of the past.

THE IMPACT OF THE CRUSADES ON THE MEDIEVAL MIDDLE EAST

As we have noted previously, the Muslims of the Levant felt the effects of the activities of the Franks in the region both on and off the battlefield. There were, of course, the battles themselves, traumatic affairs involving the death and injury of people on both sides of the religious divide. Then there were the events that came in their aftermath, including the looting and plundering of territory, the uncertain fates of prisoners, the sufferings of those who had lost loved ones in the fighting and the negotiation of the terms of truces. Yet the impact of the Crusades on the inhabitants of the region went further than this. On the political level there were the diplomatic dealings that took place between rulers. As we have seen, the Franks were quickly drawn into the realpolitik of the region, becoming participants in the web of alliances, rivalries and manoeuvrings for power that continued throughout the period, and their presence in the Levant also gave rulers such as Nur al-Din and Saladin new justifications for their own political and territorial ambitions; the subjugation of Muslim rivals could now be justified on the grounds of the need for Muslim unity in the face of the Latin threat. We have also seen that there was an expansion in the diplomacy that took place between rulers in Europe and the Levant, bringing them more closely into contact with one another. Meanwhile, on a more personal level, Muslims and Franks in the Levant attended each other's festivals, visited each other's homes and formed friendships, albeit ones that were restricted by limited inter-cultural understanding.

It was not only diplomacy that underwent an expansion; as we have noted, trade flourished as a result of the greater presence of European merchants in the east, despite condemnation by angry popes, and military conflict led to only limited hiatuses in the exchange of goods and money. We have also seen the transfer of technological and practical innovations, though – with the possible exception of some aspects of military technology and maybe some medical knowledge – this seems largely to have been a one-way transfer from the Levant to Europe. Of course, there were also the physical remains that the Franks left behind, especially the fortresses that had not been demolished during the counter-crusade and were now re-occupied, modified and repurposed. Meanwhile, for the Muslim peasants little on the whole seems to have changed. They continued to work their lands and pay their taxes, even though they might be paying them to different overlords. Only in a limited number of cases do they seem to have suffered at the hands of new masters, or even chosen to flee their homes.

It is important to remind ourselves of the highly localized impact of the Frankish campaigns in the Levant. The Muslim world, after all, was vast, extending at this time from Spain and North Africa in the west to Central Asia, northern India and Indonesia in the east. While in the west the Muslims of Spain and North Africa were also dealing with European aggression, their interactions with their Levantine co-religionists were limited. Meanwhile, the effects of the Crusades in the Levant were little felt in the eastern Muslim world; as we have noted in our Introduction (Chapter 1), a Muslim merchant in Samarkand, for example, probably neither knew nor cared about the activities of Europeans in lands further west, unless they disrupted his supplies of goods from that direction. Thus the impact of the Levantine Crusades, while significant for the inhabitants of the region itself, made relatively little impression on the Muslim world as a whole.

This does not mean, however, that once the crusaders had been driven from the area they were then simply forgotten. This was until recently indeed the assumption of a number of scholars, who stated that the majority of Muslims essentially forgot about the Crusades, and their interest in them was only re-awakened in the nineteenth century, as a result of increasing encounters with the European colonial powers (Abouali, 2011: 176–8). According to this narrative, two figures from the period did remain prominent after the demise of the crusader states: Nur al-Din and al-Zahir Baybars; Nur al-Din was remembered by the religious classes as the *mujahid* par excellence, while Baybars became the hero of a hugely popular folk epic. Notably absent was Saladin, who was regarded by modern scholars as having been forgotten in the Middle East until he was re-introduced into the Muslim world as a result of the renown that he had achieved in the West, especially in the eyes of politicians such as Kaiser Wilhelm II (r. 1888–1918), who visited the sultan's tomb in 1898 and publicly described how famous the sultan was in Europe (Hillenbrand, 1999 a: 592–4). However, in an important article Diana Abouali has recently demonstrated that this narrative is seriously mistaken, and both the Crusades and Saladin continued to have a significant presence in the consciousness of Muslims of the Levant for centuries after the Franks had been expelled from the region. This did not, however, mean that the Muslims felt insecure and that they needed to be constantly prepared for another attack from Europe, but the events remained part of their collective historical memory, and figures like Saladin became seen as models of ideal behaviour for others to follow (Abouali, 2011: 179–85). Meanwhile, the inhabitants of the region carried on with their lives, with their rulers continuing to pursue their military and political conflicts, their merchants continuing to engage in their commercial endeavours, their scholars continuing to expand and pass on their knowledge and their peasants continuing to till their fields.

THE IMPACT OF THE CRUSADES ON THE MODERN-DAY MUSLIM CONSCIOUSNESS

On 16 September 2001 the US president George W. Bush declared, as he promised to pursue the perpetrators of the terrorist attacks of 11 September, 'This crusade, this war on terrorism is going to take a while' (Bush, 2001). Both Muslims and scholars of the Muslim world were aghast, for his choice of wording showed an utter lack of sensitivity and cultural awareness. The word 'crusade', used so often in English simply to refer to a sustained effort to achieve something, has long been associated in the Muslim historical memory with European colonialism, interference in the Muslim world and violent military action by Christians against Muslims, so in using the term Bush raised a spectre of Christian–Muslim hostility that most had hoped to have left in the past (Esposito, 2003: 74–5). In response to the outcry that followed, Bush apologized for his remark, but the damage was done, and he had by then played directly into the hands of his enemies, as we shall see.

As Carole Hillenbrand has noted, the Arabic equivalent of the term 'crusade', al-hurub al-salibiyya (the cross wars) began to be used to refer to the crusading period in Muslim political discourse and historical writing in the nineteenth century. The Ottoman sultan Abdülhamid II (r. 1876–1909) repeatedly described European colonial efforts in the Middle East as a 'crusade', and his use of this concept was widely taken up and circulated in the pan-Islamic press of the region. The Egyptian historian Sayyid 'Ali al-Hariri, in his pioneering Arabic history of the Crusades, *al-Akhbar al-Saniyya fi'l-Hurub al-Salibiyya* (the Splendid Accounts in the Crusading Wars, published in 1899) also reiterated the sultan's comments, stating, 'Our most glorious sultan, Abdülhamid II has rightly remarked that Europe is now carrying out a Crusade against us in the form of a political campaign' (Hillenbrand, 1999 a: 591–3).

The twentieth century saw the Crusades and the Muslim heroes who fought in them frequently invoked in Muslim political discourse. The Crusades have been presented by some as precursors to modern colonial activity and intervention in the Muslim world, with Israel being seen as a modern crusader state, planted by western powers and used as a bridgehead for their activities in the region. Meanwhile, figures such as Saladin and Baybars have become seen as models for modern leaders to imitate, or at least to associate themselves with to boost their legitimacy. A few examples will suffice to illustrate this.

An influential figure in the development of many of the ideas and rhetoric of modern Muslim radicals was the Egyptian Sayyid Qutb (1906–66), a member of the Muslim Brotherhood who was hanged for treason by the Egyptian authorities, and whom Esposito describes as 'a godfather to Muslim extremist movements around the globe' (Esposito, 2003: 56). Qutb saw the Crusades as part of a wider sequence of conflicts between Muslims and non-Muslims that had begun with the Muslim conquests of the seventh and eighth centuries. He asserted that the term 'crusade' should be understood to mean all Christian attacks on Muslims, even including Christian resistance to the early Muslim expansion. However, Qutb also expanded his view of what constituted crusading to encompass both Zionism and western imperialism. Thus in modern times it was acceptable to talk about Jewish crusading as well as Christian crusading, and he saw these as manifestations of an ongoing desire by Christians and Jews to exterminate Islam, a doctrinal aim that was disguised as conflicts over land or military or economic resources (Hillenbrand, 1999 a: 600–1). Drawing selectively on the works of Ibn Taymiyya, Qutb divided the world into two sides, the good and the evil, arguing that since governments had failed to promote good, it was up to individuals to do so, through armed struggle (military *jihad*) if necessary, and any Muslims who refused to take up this duty were themselves apostates who also deserved to die (Esposito, 2003: 58–61). Qutb's writings were extremely influential in the development of later movements like **al-Qa'ida** (al-Qaeda) and **Hamas** (Bonney, 2004: 215–23).

The charter of Hamas ('fervour', and also an acronym for *Harakat al-Muqawama al-Islamiyya* [Islamic Resistance Movement]), which currently runs the Gaza Strip, adopts a position that very much follows that laid out

Al-Qa'ida (al-Qaeda): Arabic: 'the base'. A multinational terrorist network that conducts operations against targets across the world, founded by Usama ibn Ladin (Osama bin Laden, d. 2011) in about 1988.

Hamas: (*Harakat al-Muqawama al-Islamiyya* [Islamic Resistance Movement]). Politico-military organization dedicated to the Palestinian struggle against Israel.

by Qutb. It sees Palestine as being occupied by the 'Zionist enemy', essentially meaning the Jews of Israel, and the movement was therefore originally dedicated to the destruction of that state. From the charter's perspective, the Jewish occupation is the latest episode in a sequence of western attacks on the Holy Land that include the Crusades and, again like the Crusades, will only be successfully repulsed through fighting for the cause of God in the military *jihad*. The charter also expresses a desire to establish an Islamic state in the area; militant sentiment and piety are seen as going hand in hand, and the religious impulse manifests in particular in the extensive social welfare programmes that the movement runs and the calls for increased piety among Muslims that it issues (Hillenbrand, 1999 a: 602; Esposito, 2003: 94–7). After winning the Palestinian Authority elections in 2006 Hamas refused to sign peace agreements previously made by the Palestinian Authority with Israel and to renounce violence, though it did offer a ten-year truce in exchange for the withdrawal of Israeli troops from the West Bank, Gaza Strip and East Jerusalem. This is one indication of how recently more moderate figures have begun to attain prominence in the movement, though whether they or the more hard-line figures will dominate in the future remains to be seen.

Al-Qa'ida (the Base) was founded in the late 1980s by Usama ibn Ladin (Osama bin Laden, 1957–2011) with the initial objective of co-ordinating resistance to the Soviet occupation of Afghanistan, but has since become dedicated to the removal of foreign presence and interference from the Muslim world as a whole. It is now a multinational network that uses terrorist operations as a means to achieve its aims. The USA became Ibn Ladin's primary target because, he maintained, it supported both Israel and other un-Islamic regimes in the Middle East and thus was propping up the first barriers to the establishment of true Islamic regimes (Bonney, 2004: 357–60). Like Hamas, al-Qa'ida uses counter-crusading rhetoric. Statements issued by Usama ibn Ladin and his associates in 1998, seven years after the Gulf War undertaken to eject Iraqi forces from Kuwait in 1990–1, assert that the continuing American presence in the Middle East is evidence of an ongoing crusade intended to enable it to exploit the region's resources, attack Islam and support Zionist efforts both to maintain their occupation of Palestine and to expand their holdings in the region [**Doc. 21**]. Thus one can see why it was so unfortunate that President Bush used the word 'crusade' to refer to his planned war on terrorism; in doing so he essentially confirmed the description that his enemies had themselves been using to describe US activities in the Muslim world.

We have mentioned that medieval Muslim religious scholars imposed a number of restrictions on the military *jihad*, including the forbidding of the killing of non-combatants and of deliberately killing oneself on the battlefield (see Chapter 2). Usama ibn Ladin and those who follow his views sidestep

these restrictions by adopting a distorted view of how they should be understood: suicide bombings are recast as 'martyrdom operations', a term also
used by Hamas and others, while all the people in democracies such as the
USA are seen as being combatants because they participated in the elections
that put their governments in place (Bonney, 2004: 314–17; Esposito, 2003:
23). Regarding the latter, in one of his statements issued in 1998 Ibn Ladin
comments, 'If their people do not wish to be harmed inside their very own
countries, they should seek to elect governments that are truly representative
of them and that can protect their interests'. Yet at the same time he contradicts
himself, for elsewhere in the same statement he comments, 'We, however,
differentiate between the Western government and the people of the West. If
the people have elected these governments in the latest elections, it is because
they have fallen prey to the Western media, which portrays things contrary
to what they really are' [Doc. 21.i]. Thus Ibn Ladin seems on the one hand
to have wanted to make the people of the West valid targets of al-Qaʻida's
operations through their being responsible for the actions of their governments, but on the other hand he also seems to have seen them as sheep
who elect whichever governments the media tells them to. This internally
inconsistent perspective defied logic for the sake of rhetoric.

As mentioned previously, modern political leaders in the Muslim world
have also taken the Muslim heroes of the crusading period as models, or at
least as figures with whom to associate themselves in propaganda. Since the
nineteenth century the most frequently recalled of these heroes is Saladin,
and a number of modern political leaders have sought to emphasize links
with the famous sultan. Perhaps the most striking example is the former Iraqi
president Saddam Husayn (r. 1979–2003), who had himself portrayed as
a latter-day Saladin, a Sunni leader opposing both the Shiʻites of Iran and
the interference of the non-Muslim western powers (see Plate 9). Children's
books and newspaper articles depicted Husayn as the new Saladin; his birth-
place was noted as being Tikrit, the same as that of the sultan, though it
is actually more likely that he was born in nearby ʻAwja; and his official
biographies listed his date of birth as 1937, exactly 800 years after Saladin's
birth in 1137, rather than the 1939 listed in the population register of the
ministry of the interior (Bengio, 1998: 82–4). An awful irony, of course, is that
Saladin was a Kurd, and Saddam Husayn wiped out hundreds of thousands
of Kurds during his presidency (Hillenbrand, 1999 a: 595).

FINAL WORDS

As we have noted, a number of modern Muslim individuals and organizations
have drawn on the memory of the Crusades to support their own political

and religious agendas. Yet it is important, of course, to highlight the fact that most Muslims see the Crusades as events that happened long ago, which do not have immediate bearing on the present, and they see the rhetorical twisting of history by figures like Usama ibn Ladin and Saddam Husayn for what it is. However, the memory of the Crusades in the Muslim world is one that still carries more negative connotations than it does in the West, something that is reinforced by such rhetoric, especially in countries where there is strict government control of the media and official state hostility to western governments. Even Muslims living in the West are nervous of the term 'crusade', particularly in political discourse; as we have mentioned above, it conjures up negative images of Christian hostility against Muslims. In the wake of the terrible events of 9/11, Muslims living in western countries feared a backlash against them. In some cases, their fears were well founded, since they, as well as some non-Muslims who were mistaken for Muslims because of their skin colour, were hurt or killed in revenge attacks. They were also subject to racial or religious profiling that threatened their rights and liberties. Even now some Muslims are nervous each time the anniversary of the 9/11 attacks comes around, fearing further retribution. As Sumbul Ali-Karamili has noted, what is missed is that the majority of Muslims are as frightened of figures like Usama ibn Ladin as non-Muslims are, since most Muslims do not adhere to extremist, militant positions and thus in the eyes of the violent extremists are also potential targets. This is worse for Muslims living in the Middle East, as they must also live with the danger of their governments being subverted by such extremists (Ali-Karamili, 2008: 215).

In conclusion, it is worth emphasizing two major points. First, the period of the Crusades was one that, while we must acknowledge the bitter warfare and bloodshed that took place, also saw Muslims and Franks living in neighbouring states and interacting on a tolerant, and sometimes even friendly, basis for extended periods of time. Second, the counter-crusading rhetoric that receives so much attention from some western media channels today, with its representation of the Crusades as a phase in an ongoing war of Judaism and Christianity against Islam, is a modern fabrication used by some figures for primarily political reasons, and does not represent the views of the majority of Muslims living in the world today. Indeed, as we have seen, the modern rhetoric also ignores half the story; it focuses only on the wars that took place between the Muslims and the crusaders, and it completely neglects the periods of peaceful interaction that we have examined. The mixed nature of interactions between the Muslims and the Franks in the crusading period, then, has something important to teach in the modern day. Even in a world where there was overwhelming pressure to see only the divisions between Christians and Muslims, people on both sides enjoyed amicable and collaborative relations in the spaces between the battles. We must acknowledge that they saw each other as religious inferiors, and that their understanding of each other was limited, but this did not prevent them from meeting, trading and enjoying each other's company. In the modern world there are far more opportunities for Muslims and non-Muslims to interact on a friendly basis, people have far better access to information than did their forebears in the Middle Ages and discriminating against someone on the basis of religion is forbidden by UN declaration. There is, then, no excuse for Muslims and non-Muslims not to create deep, meaningful relationships at home and abroad, despite the barriers that they encounter in the rhetoric of extremists and the distortions of some media outlets.

FURTHER READING

For useful discussions of the impact of the Crusades on both the medieval and modern Muslim world, see Carole Hillenbrand, *The Crusades: Islamic Perspectives* (1999 a); Emmanuel Sivan, *Modern Arab Historiography of the Crusades* (1973); and John M. Chamberlin V, *Imagining Defeat: An Arabic Historiography of the Crusades* (2007). These works should, however, be read in tandem with Diana Abouali's recent valuable article, 'Saladin's Legacy in the Middle East before the Nineteenth Century' (2011). An excellent, if now slightly dated, introduction to the topic of modern terrorism conducted in the name of Islam is John L. Esposito's *Unholy War: Terror in the Name of Islam* (2003). For a more detailed discussion of modern use of *jihad* ideology see Richard Bonney, *Jihad: From Qur'an to bin Laden* (2004). For an American Muslim's response to modern Muslim terrorism in general and 9/11 in particular, see Sumbul Ali-Karamili, *The Muslim Next Door: The Qur'an, the Media and that Veil Thing* (2008).

Plate 1 The Dome of the Rock, Jerusalem. Completed in 691 and repeatedly restored since, the Dome of the Rock marks the place from which, according to Muslim belief, the Prophet Muhammad ascended when he visited the heavens and met God.

Plate 2 Nur al-Din's *minbar* (pulpit) in the Aqsa Mosque, Jerusalem. Nur
al-Din commissioned this around 1168, probably intending to place it
in the Aqsa Mosque once he had conquered Jerusalem. It was placed
there by Saladin after the conquest of 1187, and remained there until
it was destroyed by a Christian fanatic in 1969. Courtesy of the
Creswell Archive, Ashmolean Museum, Oxford, neg. EA.CA.5005

Plate 3 Bab al-Futuh (the Gate of Conquests) in Cairo, Egypt. Completed in 1087, this is one of a set of gates built into the walls of the Fatimid city of Cairo by Armenian architects. It bears striking similarities to fortifications constructed at about the same time in Greater Armenia.

© Vivek Agrawal and Sonit Bafna, 1992. Courtesy of the MIT Libraries, Aga Khan Visual Libraries.

Plate 4 The Castle of Ajlun, Jordan. Overlooking the Jordan valley, this castle was built on the orders of Saladin near the crusader castle of Belvoir in 1184–85. It was enlarged during the reign of al-'Adil Muhammad and used at times as a link in communications using beacons and pigeons and as a store for weapons and supplies.

Plate 5 The Citadel of Cairo, Egypt. Saladin ordered the construction of the citadel in 1176. Work was continued by al-ʿAdil Muhammad and later rulers. Now the Mosque of Muhammad ʿAli Pasha (bt. 1828–48) dominates the skyline.

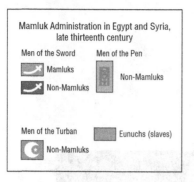

Mamluk Administration in Egypt and Syria,
late thirteenth century

Men of the Sword

⚔ Mamluks

⚔ Non-Mamluks

Men of the Pen

Non-Mamluks

Men of the Turban

☾ Non-Mamluks

Eunuchs (slaves)

MEN OF THE PEN

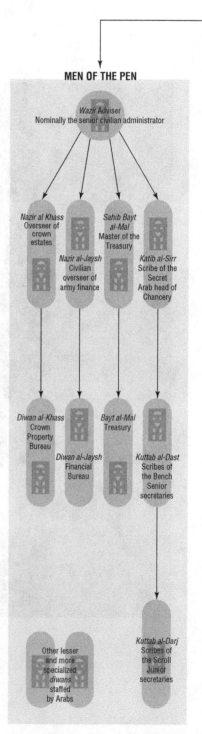

Wazir Adviser
Nominally the senior civilian administrator

Nazir al Khass
Overseer of crown estates

Sahib Bayt al-Mal
Master of the Treasury

Nazir al-Jaysh
Civilian overseer of army finance

Katib al-Sirr
Scribe of the Secret
Arab head of Chancery

Diwan al-Khass
Crown Property Bureau

Bayt al-Mal
Treasury

Diwan al-Jaysh
Financial Bureau

Kuttab al-Dast
Scribes of the Bench
Senior secretaries

Other lesser and more specialized *diwans* staffed by Arabs

Kuttab al-Darj
Scribes of the Scroll
Junior secretaries

PROVINCIAL GOVERNMENT OF SYRIA

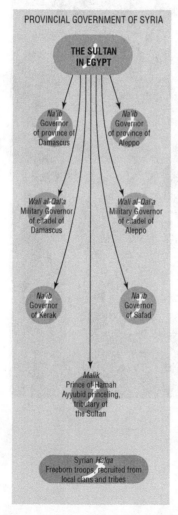

**THE SULTAN
IN EGYPT**

Na'ib
Governor
of province of
Damascus

Na'ib
Governor
of province of
Aleppo

Wali al-Qal'a
Military Governor
of citadel of
Damascus

Wali al-Qal'a
Military Governor
of citadel of
Aleppo

Na'ib
Governor
of Kerak

Na'ib
Governor
of Safad

Malik
Prince of Hamah
Ayyubid princeling,
tributary of
the Sultan

Syrian *Halqa*
Freeborn troops, recruited from
local clans and tribes

Plate 6 Source: Jonathan Riley-Smith (ed.), *The Atlas of the Crusades* (New York, 1991), pp. 110–111. Courtesy of Swanston Publishing.

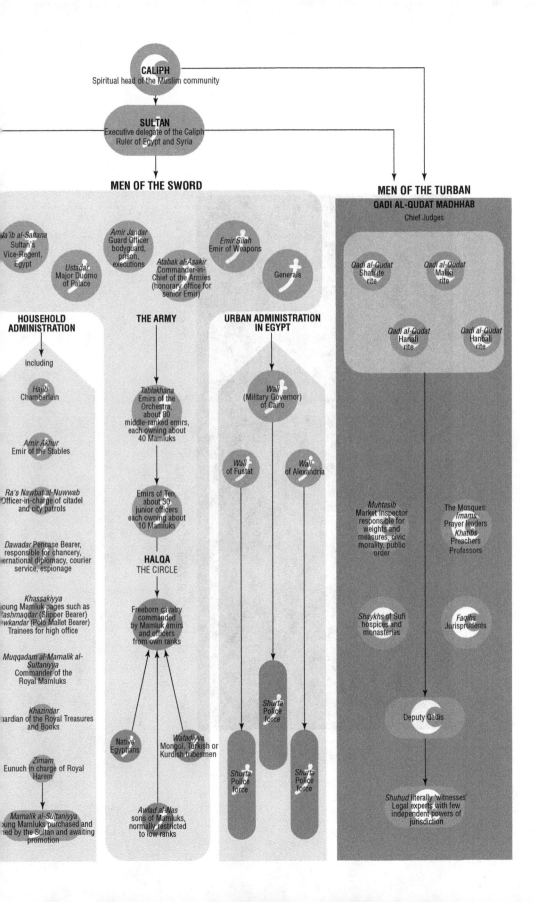

CALIPH
Spiritual head of the Muslim community

SULTAN
Executive delegate of the Caliph
Ruler of Egypt and Syria

MEN OF THE SWORD

MEN OF THE TURBAN

QADI AL-QUDAT MADHHAB
Chief Judges

Na'ib al-Saltana
Sultan's Vice-Regent, Egypt

Ustadar
Major Duomo of Palace

Amir Jandar
Guard Officer bodyguard, prison, executions

Atabak al-Asakir
Commander-in-Chief of the Armies (honorary office for senior Emir)

Amir Silah
Emir of Weapons

Generals

Qadi al-Qudat
Shafi'ite rite

Qadi al-Qudat
Maliki rite

Qadi al-Qudat
Hanafi rite

Qadi al-Qudat
Hanbali rite

HOUSEHOLD ADMINISTRATION

THE ARMY

URBAN ADMINISTRATION IN EGYPT

including

Hajib
Chamberlain

Amir Akhur
Emir of the Stables

Ra's Nawbat al-Nuwwab
Officer-in-charge of citadel and city patrols

Dawadar Pencase Bearer, responsible for chancery, international diplomacy, courier service, espionage

Khassakiyya
young Mamluk pages such as *Tashmaqdar* (Slipper Bearer) *Jawkandar* (Polo Mallet Bearer) Trainees for high office

Muqqadam al-Mamalik al-Sultaniyya
Commander of the Royal Mamluks

Khazindar
Guardian of the Royal Treasures and Books

Zimam
Eunuch in charge of Royal Harem

Mamalik al-Sultaniyya
young Mamluks purchased and owned by the Sultan and awaiting promotion

Tablakhana
Emirs of the Orchestra, about 80 middle-ranked emirs, each owning about 40 Mamluks

Emirs of Ten
about 30 junior officers each owning about 10 Mamluks

HALQA
THE CIRCLE

Freeborn cavalry commanded by Mamluk emirs and officers from own ranks

Native Egyptians

Wafadiyya
Mongol, Turkish or Kurdish tribesmen

Awlad al-Nas
sons of Mamluks, normally restricted to low ranks

Wali
(Military Governor) of Cairo

Wali
of Fustat

Wali
of Alexandria

Shurta
Police force

Shurta
Police force

Shurta
Police force

Muhtasib
Market Inspector responsible for weights and measures, civic morality, public order

The Mosques:
Imams
Prayer leaders
Khatibs
Preachers
Professors

Shaykhs of Sufi hospices and monasteries

Faqihs
Jurisprudents

Deputy Qadis

Shuhud literally 'witnesses' Legal experts with few independent powers of jurisdiction

Plate 7 *Dinar* of al-Malik al-Zahir Baybars. This gold *dinar* was struck in 1268. Note the use of Baybars' lion/panther blazon.

Plate 8 Jisr Jindas, Lydda (Lod), Israel. Built by Baybars in 1273, panels flanking the inscription on this bridge bear his lion/panther blazon. On each panel the lion plays with a rat, possibly intended specifically to symbolize the sultan's Frankish enemies. Used with kind permission of Uri Zackhem

Plate 9 Propaganda picture of Saddam Husayn as the heir of Saladin. This image was probably commissioned in the 1980s during the Iran-Iraq war, and hence aims to depict Husayn as the defender of Sunni Islam against what he would have regarded as the Shi'ite heresy of the Iranians.

DOCUMENTS

Unless otherwise noted, all translations are by the author of this book.

Document 1   EXTRACTS FROM THE *QUR'AN* AND *HADITH*

The following extracts from the Qur'an *and* hadith *demonstrate the at times mixed attitudes towards warfare and other faiths that are found in their pages.*

(i) Qur'an

The Muslim holy book, the Qur'an, is believed by Muslims to have been revealed to the Prophet Muhammad by God. Its arrangement seems somewhat haphazard, but a number of early Muslim scholars wrote works establishing a chronology for the revelation of its verses. The verses below, however, are presented in the order in which they appear in the received text.

(a) 2: 62. Those who believe (in the *Qur'an*), and those who follow the Jewish (scriptures), and the Christians and the Sabians – any who believe in Allah and the Last Day, and work righteousness, shall have their reward with their Lord; on them shall be no fear, nor shall they grieve.

(b) 2: 190. Fight in the cause of Allah those who fight you, but do not transgress limits, for Allah loveth not transgressors.

(c) 2: 256. Let there be no compulsion in religion: Truth stands out clear from Error: whoever rejects Evil and believes in Allah hath grasped the most trustworthy handhold, that never breaks. And Allah heareth and knoweth all things.

(d) 5: 32. On that account: We ordained for the Children of Israel that if anyone slew a person – unless it be for murder or spreading mischief in the land – it would be as if he slew the whole people. And if anyone saved a life, it would be as if he saved the life of the whole people. Then although there came to them Our Messengers with Clear Signs, yet, even after that, many of them continued to commit excesses in the land.

(e) 5: 65–6. If only the People of the Book had believed and been righteous, we should indeed have blotted out their iniquities and admitted them to Gardens of Bliss. If only they had stood fast by the Law, the Gospel, and all the revelation that was sent to them from their Lord, they would have enjoyed happiness from every side. There is from among them a party on the right course: but many of them follow a course that is evil.

(f) 9: 5. But when the forbidden months are past, then fight and slay the Pagans wherever ye find them, and seize them, beleaguer them, and lie in wait for them in every stratagem (of war); but if they repent, and establish regular prayers, and practise regular charity, then open the way for them: for Allah is Oft-Forgiving, Most Merciful.

(g) 9: 29. Fight those who believe not in Allah nor in the Last Day, nor hold that forbidden which hath been forbidden by Allah and his Messenger, nor acknowledge the Religion of Truth, from among the People of the Book, until they pay the *jizya* with willing submission, and feel themselves subdued.

(h) 15: 94–5. Therefore expound openly what thou art commanded, and turn away from those who join false Gods with Allah. For sufficient are We unto thee against those who scoff.

(i) 16: 125. Invite (all) to the Way of thy Lord with wisdom and beautiful preaching; and argue with them in ways that are best and most gracious: for thy Lord knoweth best, who have strayed from His Path, and who receive guidance.

(j) 22: 39–40. To those against whom war is made, permission is given (to fight), because they are wronged – and verily, Allah is Most Powerful for their aid – (They are) those who have been expelled from their homes in defiance of right – (for no cause) except that they say, 'Our Lord is Allah'. Had not Allah checked one set of people by means of another there would surely have been pulled down monasteries, churches, synagogues, and mosques, in which the name of Allah is commemorated in abundant measure. Allah will certainly aid those who aid His (cause) – for verily Allah is Full of Strength, Exalted in Might, (Able to enforce His Will).

Source: The Meaning of the Holy Qur'an. (2004) Ed. and trans. 'Abdullah Y. 'Ali. 11th Ed. Beltsville, MD: Amana Publications, pp. 33–4, 76, 106–7, 257, 269, 438, 445, 635, 669 and 832–3.

(ii) Hadith

Used by Muslims to assist with their interpretation of the Qur'an, the hadith are accounts of the sayings and actions of the Prophet and his Companions. The hadith presented below are drawn from the Sahih of Muhammad ibn Isma'il al-Bukhari (d. 870), widely regarded among Muslims as one of the foremost compilers of reliable accounts. Each hadith begins with an isnad (chain of transmitters); we have retained the isnad of the first hadith presented here, to demonstrate how it works, but have omitted the isnads of the subsequent hadiths for reasons of space.

(a) Al-Hasan ibn Sabbah reported to us [that] Muhammad ibn Sabiq reported to us [that] Malik ibn Mighwal reported to us, saying [that he] heard al-Walid ibn al-'Ayzaz speak on the authority of Abu 'Amr al-Shaybani, who said [that] 'Abd Allah ibn Mas'ud, may God be pleased with him, narrated: 'I asked the Messenger of Allah, Allah's blessing and peace be upon him: "O Allah's Apostle! What is the best deed?" He replied: "To offer the prayers at their early stated fixed times." I asked: "What is next in goodness?" He replied, "To be good and dutiful to your parents." I further asked: "What is next in goodness?" He replied: "To take part in *jihad* in Allah's Cause." I did not ask the Messenger of Allah, Allah's blessing and peace be upon him, any more, and if I had asked him more, he would have told me more.'

(b) 'A'isha bint Talha narrated that 'A'isha [the wife of the Prophet], Allah be pleased with her, had said: 'O Allah's Apostle! We consider *jihad* as the best deed. Should we not fight in Allah's Cause?' He said: 'The best *jihad* (for women) is *hajj* which is accepted by Allah.'

(c) Abu Hurayra, Allah be pleased with him, narrated: 'I heard Allah's Apostle, Allah's blessing and peace be upon him, saying: "The example of a militant in Allah's Cause, and Allah knows better who really strives in His Cause, is like a person who fasts and prays continuously. Allah guarantees that He will admit the militant in His Cause into Paradise if he is killed, otherwise He will return him to his home safely with rewards and war booty."'

(d) Anas, Allah be pleased with him, narrated: 'The Prophet, Allah's blessing and peace be upon him, said: "A single endeavour (of fighting) in Allah's Cause in the afternoon or forenoon is better than the entire world and its contents. A place in Paradise (even though) as small as a bow or a lash of one of you is better than all of the world with its contents. If a woman with beautiful, big and lustrous eyes from Paradise appeared to the people of the earth, she would fill the space between Heaven and the Earth with light and pleasant scent; and her head cover is better than the world and whatever it contains."'

(e) Nafi' narrated from 'Abd Allah ibn 'Umar, Allah be pleased with both: 'During some of the holy battles of the Prophet, Allah's blessing and peace be upon him, a woman was found killed. Allah's Apostle, Allah's blessing and peace be upon him, forbade killing women and children.'

(f) 'Amr ibn Maymun narrated: 'Umar [caliph, 634–44] (after he was stabbed [by a Persian slave]) instructed (his would-be successor) saying: "I urge him (the new caliph) to take care of those non-Muslims who are under the protection of Allah and His Apostle. That is to observe the convention agreed upon with them, and fight on their behalf (to secure their safety). He also should not overtax them beyond their capability."'

Source: Muhammad ibn Isma'il al-Bukhari. (2003) *Sahih al-Bukhari*. Ed. and trans. Muhammad M. al-Sharif. Beirut: Dar al-Kutub al-'Ilmiyya, Vol. 2, pp. 217–18, 220, 275 and 285. At some points we have edited al-Sharif's translation for clarity.

A DEPICTION OF THE FATIMID CALIPH AL-HAKIM BI-AMR ALLAH   **Document 2**
(R. 996–1021)

The Fatimid caliph al-Hakim bi-Amr Allah gained notoriety in western Europe after he ordered the destruction of the Church of the Holy Sepulchre in 1009. This event is described by the Egyptian historian and teacher Taqi al-Din Ahmad ibn 'Ali al-Maqrizi (1364–1442) in his Itti'az al-Hunafa' bi-Akhbar al-A'imma al-Fatimiyyin al-Khulafa' *(Lesson for True Believers in the Stories of the Fatimid Imam-Caliphs).*

In [the year 1009] the Christians went out from Egypt to Jerusalem to celebrate Easter at the Church of Garbage [the Church of the Holy Sepulchre], as was their yearly custom, setting out in a great crowd just as the Muslims set out to perform the *hajj*. Al-Hakim questioned [. . .] one of his leaders about that, asking what he knew about what happened at the church, and he said, 'This is a place of worship of which the Christians are proud, and to which they perform pilgrimage from all over the country. Kings donate to it, and much money is brought to it, along with clothes, drapes, soft furnishings, lamps, crosses made of gold and silver, and other such things, so that there are large amounts of these things there. On Easter Day, when the Christians gather at the Church of Garbage, the crosses are set up, and the lamps are hung around the altar, they use an artifice to make fire appear on the altar, daubing it with black elder and quicksilver, which makes the altar glow with a bright light so that whoever sees it thinks that the light is fire that has descended from heaven.' Al-Hakim forbade that [. . .] and wrote to Ahmad ibn Ya'qub, the missionary, telling him to head for Jerusalem, destroy the Church of Garbage and let the people plunder it until all traces of it were obliterated, and that was done. Then he ordered the destruction of the synagogues and churches that were in the districts of his kingdom, but he became frightened that the Christians would destroy the Muslim mosques that were in their lands, so he stopped that.

Source: Ahmad ibn 'Ali al-Maqrizi. (1967–73) *Itti'az al-Hunafa' bi-Akhbar al-A'imma al-Fatimiyyin al-Khulafa'.* Ed. Jamal al-Din al-Shayyal and Muhammad H.M. Ahmad. Cairo: Lajnat Ihya' al-Turath al-Islami, Vol. 2, pp. 74–5.

AL-MAS'UDI ON THE FRANKS   **Document 3**

'Ali ibn al-Husayn al-Mas'udi (d. 956) was a Muslim traveller and geographer. He has left us two rather different depictions of the Franks in two different geographical works.

(i) *From* Muruj al-Dhahab wa-Ma'adin al-Jawhar (*Meadows of Gold and Mines of Gemstone*)

The Franks are the strongest of [the] races, the most fearsome and the most numerous. They have the most widespread power and the most numerous cities. They are the best-organised, the most obedient to their kings and the most compliant, except that the Galicians [who are a type of Frank] are stronger and more harmful than the [other] Franks. One Galician is a match for several Franks.

All of Ifranja [the land of the Franks] is unified in one kingdom. There is no competition between them about that, nor is there any factionalism. The name of the capital of their kingdom at this time is Paris. It is a great city.

Al-Mas'udi then draws the reader's attention to a book that he came upon in Fustat (now part of greater Cairo), which was originally presented to the Muslim ruler of Spain by the Bishop of Gerona. The book included this partial list of the Frankish kings:

The first of the kings of Ifranja was Clovis [r. 481–511]. He was a Zoroastrian, but his wife converted him to Christianity. Her name was Clotild. Then his son Theuderic [r. 511–24] ruled after him. Then Theuderic's son Dagobert ruled after him. Then Dagobert's son Theuderic ruled after him, then after him ruled his brother Carloman. Then his son Charles [probably Charles Martel, *major domo* of the Merovingian kings 714–41] ruled after him. Then his son Pippin [III, *major domo* 741–51, King of the Franks 751–68] ruled after him. Then after him ruled his son Charles [Charlemagne, r. 768–814], who ruled for 26 years, and he was in the days of al-Hakam, the ruler of **al-Andalus** [r. 796–822]. After him his children fought each other and fell into disputes until Ifranja was ruined because of them. Then Louis, the son of Charles [Louis the Pious, r. 814–40] became the ruler of their kingdom, and he ruled for 28 years and six months, and he was the one who advanced on Tortosa and besieged it.

Al-Andalus: The Arabic term used to refer to the Iberian Peninsula and the Muslim states therein. The modern Spanish word 'Andalucia' derives from this.

Al-Mas'udi goes on to comment on the reigns of subsequent Carolingian kings up to the time that he read the book, the Muslim year 336 (CE 947–8).

Source: 'Ali ibn al-Husayn al-Mas'udi. (1965–79) *Muruj al-Dhahab wa-Ma'adin al-Jawhar.* Ed. Charles Pellat. Beirut: Manshurat al-Jami'a al-Lubnaniyya, Vol. 2, pp. 145–8.

(ii) *From* Kitab al-Tanbih wa-l-Ishraf (*The Book of Instruction and Supervision*)

As for the peoples of the northern region [. . .] like the Slavs, the Franks and those nations next to them, the sun shines weakly upon them because of their distance from it, cold and damp have overcome their region, and snow and ice come upon them in uninterrupted succession. They have little warm temperament in them; their bodies have become enormous, their humour dry, their morals crude, their intellect stupid and their tongues sluggish. Their colour has become excessively white, to the point of becoming blue, their skins thin, their flesh coarse, their eyes blue in accordance with their colouring, and their hair lank and reddish-brown because of the excess of steam and damp. Their beliefs have no solidity, and this is because of the nature of the cold and the lack of warmth. The ones who are from further north have become overcome with ignorance, dryness of humour and brutishness. This increases in them the further north that they go.

Source: 'Ali ibn al-Husayn al-Mas'udi. (1894) *Kitâb at-Tanbîh wa'l-Ischrâf*. Ed. M.J. de Goeje. Bibliotheca Geographorum Arabicorum, Vol. 8. Leiden, Netherlands: E.J. Brill, pp. 23–4.

THE FALL OF JERUSALEM TO THE CRUSADERS: TWO ACCOUNTS   **Document 4**

(i) Ibn al-Qalanisi

Hamza ibn Asad ibn al-Qalanisi (d. 1160) was born into an important family in Damascus and occasionally held prominent positions in the city's administration. His best-known work, Dhayl Ta'rikh Dimashq (The Continuation of the History of Damascus), is a continuation of an older chronicle and focuses on the history of Damascus, covering the years 1056–1160; as such it forms part of the genre of so-called 'city chronicles'. Ibn al-Qalanisi's work was a major source for other historians who came after him, including Ibn al-Athir, below.

The Franks went to Jerusalem and fought its people and besieged them. They set up a siege tower and leaned it against the city wall. The news reached them that al-Afdal had set out from Egypt with an overwhelming army to pursue the *jihad* against them, engage them in combat, aid the city against them and protect it from them, so they pressed their attack, persevering until the end of that day. Then they withdrew from the city, promising to renew their attack the next day, and the people descended from the walls at the time of the sunset prayer. Then the Franks returned to the attack, going up the tower and climbing onto the city wall. The people were put to flight, and they stormed the city and took control of it. Some of the people fled to the Tower of David, and many people were killed. The Jews gathered in the synagogue, and the Franks burned it down on their heads. The people in the Tower of David surrendered it in return for safe-conduct on 22 Sha'ban of that year [492, 14 July 1099]. Then the Franks destroyed the shrines and tomb of Abraham, may peace be upon him.

Source: Hamza ibn Asad ibn al-Qalanisi. (1983) *Ta'rikh Dimashq*. Ed. Suhayl Zakkar. Damascus: Dar Hassan li-l-Tiba'a wa-l-Nashr, p. 222.

(ii) Ibn al-Athir

'Izz al-Din 'Ali ibn Muhammad ibn al-Athir (1160–1233) spent most of his life in Mosul working as a historian, though he also sometimes served as a diplomatic envoy of the rulers of the city. He is best known for his universal history, al-Kamil fi'l-Ta'rikh (The Complete History), from which the following extract is drawn. Ibn al-Athir's work is regarded by historians as being fairly reliable, though it is permeated with a bias towards the family of Zangi. This is more evident in another of his works, as we will see later.

The Egyptians appointed as deputy in Jerusalem a man called Iftikhar al-Dawla, who remained there until this present time, when the Franks attacked after they had besieged Acre but with no success. After their arrival they erected forty trebuchets or more and they constructed two towers, one on Mount Zion side but the Muslims burnt that one and killed all inside. After they had completely destroyed it by fire, their help was then called for, as the city defences had been overwhelmed on the other side. The Franks did indeed take the city from the north in the forenoon of Friday, seven days remaining of Sha'ban [492, 15 July 1099]. The inhabitants became prey for the sword. For a week the Franks continued to slaughter the Muslims. A group of Muslims took refuge in the Tower of David and defended themselves there. They resisted for three days and then the Franks offered them safe-conduct, so they surrendered the place. The Franks kept faith with them and they departed at night for Ascalon, where they remained.

In the Aqsa Mosque the Franks killed more than 70,000, a large number of them being imams, ulema, righteous men and ascetics, Muslims who had left their native lands and come to live a holy life in this august spot. The Franks took forty or more silver candlesticks from the Dome of the Rock, each of which weighed 3,600 dirhams, and also a silver candelabrum weighing forty Syrian rotls. They removed 150 small candlesticks of silver and twenty or so of gold. The booty they took was beyond counting.

Source: 'Izz al-Din ibn al-Athir. (2006) *The Chronicle of Ibn al-Athir for the Crusading Period from al-Kamil fi'l-Ta'rikh: Part 1: The Years 491–541/1097–1146: The Coming of the Franks and the Muslim Response*. Trans. D.S. Richards. Crusade Texts in Translation 13. Aldershot, UK: Ashgate, pp. 21–2.

MUSLIM VIEWS OF THE CRUSADERS AND THEIR MOTIVES   **Document 5**

(i) *A number of Muslim poets wrote emotionally charged works about
the impact of the First Crusade, calling on their patrons to take up arms
against the Franks. These include the Khurasani poet al-Abiwardi (d. 1113),
whose call is quoted in the work of Ibn al-Athir [see Doc. 4.ii]; the Syrian
Ibn al-Khayyat (d. 1120s); and an anonymous poet quoted by the Egyptian
historian Ibn Taghri Birdi (c. 1410–70).*

(a) *Al-Abiwardi. Note that the Muslims frequently confused the* ifranj *(Franks)
and* rum *(Byzantines) in this period.*

We have mixed blood with flowing tears, and there are none of us
    left worth pitying.
The tears that a man sheds are the worst of weapons when sharp
    blades stir up the fires of war.
O sons of Islam, behind you are battles in which sons [of your
    enemies] fell at your feet.
Are you drowsing in the shade of safety, bliss and life, carefree like
    a flower in a luxuriant grove?
How can your eye sleep, filling its lids, in the face of sinful acts that
    wake every sleeper,
While the resting-places of your brothers in *al-Sham* become the
    backs of their warhorses or the bellies of lions?
The *rum* inflict humiliation upon them, while you drag behind you
    the coat-tail of a life of ease, acting like a peaceful man.
How much blood has been shed, and how many fair ladies have
    concealed, in shame, their beauty behind their hands,
When white swords have points that are stained red, and brown iron
    spearheads have become bloodied tips?
Between the seizing of an opportunity to stab and the impact itself
    is a blow, [for fear of] which children's hair turns as white as that
    of old men.
This is war, and whoever stays away from its adversities to keep
    himself safe will afterwards grind his teeth in regret.
Sharp swords are unsheathed in the hands of the polytheists, and will
    be sheathed again in necks and skulls.
In the face of them, the one who is veiled in goodness [the Prophet]
    all but calls at the top of his voice, 'O family of Hashim [the
    Prophet's clan],
'I see my community not pointing their spears at the enemy, and the
    faith on weak pillars!

'[The Muslims] avoid the fire [of war] for fear of destruction, not real-
   ising that disgrace is the inevitable consequence.
'Must the brave Arabs be content with the harm [that they suffer],
   while the valiant Persians close their eyes to their dishonour?'

Source: 'Izz al-Din ibn al-Athir. (1966) Al-Kamil fi'l-Ta'rikh. Ed. C.J. Tornberg. Beirut:
Dar Sadir, Vol. 10, pp. 284–5.

(b) Ibn al-Khayyat

How long [will this go on]? For the polytheists have swollen in a
   flood, of which the torrent [of the sea] is frightened by the extent.
Armies like mountains have stormed out of the land of *Ifranja*, to
   bring about our destruction.
They treat well whoever gives way to adversity, and they buy off
   whoever prepares for war.

The tribe of polytheism does not disapprove of evil-doing, and does
   not know any economy with injustice.
They do not prevent anyone from [taking part in] the killing, and do
   not spare any effort in destruction.
How many young women have started to beat their throats and
   cheeks in fear of them,
And mothers of young girls who never before knew the heat [of day]
   nor suffered cold at night?
They are almost wasting away from fear, and dying of sadness and
   painful agitation.
So protect your religion and your harem, defending them like
   someone who does not see death as a loss.

The heads of the polytheists have ripened. Do not neglect them as
   a vintage and a harvest.
Their [sword] edge must be notched, and their cornerstone
   demolished.
For Alp-Arslan, in similar circumstances, went out [to fight], and he
   was sharper than the sword.

Source: Ahmad ibn Muhammad ibn al-Khayyat. (1994) Diwan ibn al-Khayyat. Ed. Kh.
Mardam Bey. Beirut: Dar Sadir, pp. 184–6.

(c) Anonymous poet

Unbelief has made harm to Islam lawful, about which lamentation for
   the religion is prolonged.
What is right perishes and what is forbidden is permitted. The sword
   cuts and blood is shed.

How many Muslims have become spoils of war? [How many] Muslim
  women have [had] that which is forbidden stolen away?
How many a mosque have they made into a church, a cross set up in
  its *mihrab*?
Pig's blood in it is suitable for them, and the burning of *Qur'ans* in it
  as incense.
Do God and Islam not have a right whereby young men and old
  should be defended?
So say to those with insight, wherever they are, 'Respond to God and
  [what] He obliges [you to], respond!'

Source: Jamal al-Din ibn Taghri Birdi. (1963) *Al-Nujum al-Zahira fi Muluk Misr wa-l-Qahira*. Ed. M.'A. al-Q. Hatim. Cairo: Dar al-Kutub al-Misriyya, Vol. 5, pp. 151–2.

**(ii) Muhammad ibn 'Ali al-'Azimi (d. after 1161) wrote a city chronicle
about his hometown of Aleppo, Ta'rikh Halab (The History of Aleppo). In
it he ascribed motives of revenge to the crusaders. Note that the reference
to the pilgrims 'who escaped', below, is intended to convey that some of
them were killed.**

The people of the coastal ports prevented Frankish and Byzantine pilgrims
from crossing to Jerusalem. News of what happened spread from those
who escaped to their countries, and [the Franks] prepared to invade [the
Levant].

Source: Muhammad ibn 'Ali al-'Azimi. (1984) *Ta'rikh Halab*. Ed. Ibrahim Za'rur.
Damascus: n.p., p. 356.

**(iii) Usama ibn Munqidh (1095–1188) was a Syrian emir who travelled
widely, often as a result of tactful departures after becoming embroiled in
political conflicts. He is well known to modern historians for his 'memoirs',
which contain entertaining tales of Frankish behaviour [see Doc. 14].
However, in his own time he was actually more highly regarded for his
poetic talents. The following is drawn from Lubab al-Adab (The Kernels
of Refinement), an anthology on cultured behaviour that also includes
historical anecdotes.**

When the Franks (God forsake them) came out in the year 490 [1096–7],
conquered Antioch and defeated the people of Syria, greed insinuated itself
into them, and their innermost feelings told them of the riches of Baghdad
[or 'taking control of Baghdad'] and the country of the east. So they mobilised,
gathered and set out, aiming for the country.

Source: Usama ibn Munqidh. (1987) *Lubab al-Adab*. Ed. Ahmad M. Shakir. Cairo: Dar
al-Kutub al-Salafiyya, p. 132.

(iv) Ibn al-Athir [see Doc. 4.ii] suggests two possible causes for the First Crusade.

When it was the year 490 [1096–7] they invaded Syria. The reason for their invasion was that their ruler, Baldwin, a relative of Roger the Frank who had conquered Sicily, gathered a great host of Franks and sent to Roger, saying, 'I have gathered a great host and I am coming to you. I shall proceed to Ifriqiya [the eastern Maghrib] to take it and I shall be a neighbour of yours.' Roger assembled his men and consulted them about this. They said, 'By the truth of the Gospel, this is excellent for us and them. The lands will become Christian lands.' Roger raised his leg and gave a loud fart. 'By the truth of my religion,' he said, 'there is more use in that than in what you have to say!' 'How so?' they asked. 'If they come to me,' he replied, 'I shall require vast expenditure and ships to convey them to Ifriqiya and troops of mine also. If they take the territory it will be theirs and resources from Sicily will go to them. I shall be deprived of the money that comes in every year from agricultural revenues. If they do not succeed, they will return to my lands and I shall suffer from them. Tamim [the ruler of Ifriqiya] will say, "You have betrayed me and broken the agreement I have [with you]." Our mutual contacts and visits will be interrupted. The land of Ifriqiya will be waiting for us. Whenever we find the strength we will take it.'

He summoned Baldwin's envoy and said to him, 'If you are determined to wage holy war [jihad] on the Muslims, then the best way is to conquer Jerusalem. You will free it from their hands and have glory. Between me and the people of Ifriqiya, however, are oaths and treaties.' They therefore made their preparations and marched forth to Syria.

It has been said that the Alid rulers of Egypt [the Fatimids] became fearful when they saw the strength and power of the **Saljuq** state, that it had gained control of Syrian lands as far as Gaza, leaving no buffer state between the Saljuqs and Egypt to protect them, and that Aqsis [Atsiz, a Turkmen chieftain] had entered Egypt and blockaded it [in 1077]. They therefore sent to the Franks to invite them to invade Syria, to conquer it and separate them and the [other] Muslims, but God knows best.

Saljuqs: See *Seljuks*.

Source: Ibn al-Athir. (2006) *The Chronicle of Ibn al-Athir for the Crusading Period*, pp. 13–14. Richards' translation has been slightly modified.

EXTRACTS FROM THE *BOOK OF THE* JIHAD *OF 'ALI IBN TAHIR*   **Document 6**
AL-SULAMI (D. 1106)

'Ali ibn Tahir al-Sulami (1039 or 1040–1106) was a religious scholar who taught grammar in the Umayyad Great Mosque in Damascus. In 1105, over the course of several months, he publicly composed **Kitab al-Jihad** *(The Book of the* **Jihad**), *a treatise on the* jihad *that was intended to serve as a call to the inhabitants of the region, and especially to its political leaders, exhorting them to respond to the Frankish offensive.*

A number of the enemy pounced on the island of Sicily while the Muslims disputed and competed, and they conquered in the same way one city after another in *al-Andalus* [Muslim Iberia]. When the reports confirmed for them that this country suffered from the disagreement of its masters and its rulers' meddling, with its consequent disorder and disarray, they confirmed their resolution to set out for it, and Jerusalem was their dearest wish.

They looked out from *al-Sham* on separated kingdoms, disunited hearts and differing views laced with hidden resentment, and with that their desires became stronger and extended to whatever their outstretched arms could desire. They did not stop, tireless in fighting the *jihad* against the Muslims. The Muslims were sluggish, avoiding fighting them and reluctant to engage in combat until the enemy had conquered more than their greatest hopes had conceived of the country and destroyed and humiliated many times the number of people that they had wished. Still now they are spreading further in their efforts, assiduous in seeking an increase in their achievements. Their desires are multiplying all the time because of what appears to them of the Muslims' abstinence from opposing them, and their hopes are invigorated by virtue of what they see of their enemies' contentedness with being unharmed by them, until they have become convinced that the whole country will become theirs and all its people will be prisoners in their hands. May God in His generosity frustrate their ideas by the bringing together of everyone and the setting in order of the unity of the Muslim community. He is near and answers prayers.

The most astonishment is [what one feels] at a sultan who takes pleasure in life or remains where he is despite the appearance of this calamity, of which the outcome is conquest by these infidels, expulsion from the country by force and subjugation, or staying with them in degradation and servility, with the killing, capture, torture and torment by night and day that this involves. By God! By God, you community of sultans of this country, and those aides, soldiers and others from the local militia, stalwart auxiliaries and lords recently acquired with wealth and passed as inheritance among yourselves, families and close friends, who follow them [meaning *mamluks*], go out, lightly or heavily armed, and fight the *jihad* with your wealth and your selves [*Qur'an* 9: 41]. O you who believe, if you aid God, he will aid you and make your footsteps firm [*Qur'an* 47: 7]. Do not fight one another or you will fail and expire [*Qur'an* 8: 46]. [. . .] Know that God, be He praised, only sent this enemy to you as a trial, to test your steadfastness with it. He, be He blessed and exalted, said, 'We will test you so that We will know those of you who fight hard and are steadfast, and We will test your experiences' [*Qur'an* 47: 31].

Put the *jihad* against your souls ahead of the *jihad* against your enemies, for truly your souls are greater enemies to you than your human enemies. So prevent your souls from being disobedient to their Creator, be He praised. You may [hence] succeed in your hopes of victory over your human enemies. Make right what is between you and your Creator, and what is wrong with your current state of being will be made right for you, and your enmity [in your relationship with God] will be reconciled. Tear out your disobedience to God, be He praised, and follow your tearing it out with doing what is right in what you start afresh. It may be that your Lord will destroy your enemy and make you rulers over the world. He may observe how you act and how you conduct that which God, be He praised, ordered your Prophet, may God bless him, and his Companions regarding giving Him priority by carrying out the *jihad*, and they were endowed with seriousness in obedience to Him and being sincere in fighting hard in the *jihad*. Among His words, be He exalted, are: 'O you who believe! Bow and prostrate yourselves in prayer, worship your Lord and do good. Perhaps you will prosper' [*Qur'an* 22: 77].

In this way it is obligatory on our sultans and whomever God, be He praised, has appointed to rule us, may God make good their peace-making and guidance, that they emulate those like them who preceded them, according to what was said about that in their religion and what their Prophet, may God bless him, entrusted them with, about which his words, may God bless him, are approximately: 'Do not snub each other, oppose each other or envy each other. Be worshippers of God in a brotherhood as God, be He exalted, ordered you,' and other such words of instruction. Helping them and aiding them all that they can, applying their hands and abilities to the cause, and taking on all this burden and toil in targeting this group [of enemies], is obligatory on all the people, be they soldiers, citizens, peasants or all the rest of the people. Even the smallest contribution will be appreciated. They will perform in their *jihad* many times what people did in their military expeditions to their lands and the lands of the *rum*, to drive them from there and efface their traces. That is because there are associated with the duties of fighting hard against the enemy many requirements that make insignificant the great number of deeds involved and defy with them the greatness of the terrors that must be faced. Among them is defence of the country of the coast and support of its peoples, who are besieged and fighting with great efforts because they are currently keeping the enemy distracted from these countries, what is near them, Egypt and its environs. From them come our hopes of hastening a victory over the enemy because of what is true concerning [the enemy's] weakness, the paucity of their horses and equipment and the far distance of their reinforcements and support. That has happened with the help of God, be He praised, along with the calming of concerns about them by the removal of their devouring of worldly riches from what they have taken as booty, the deferred requital accompanying suitable behaviour towards them and liberation in this world from the shame of delaying in opposing them and from the disgrace of fearing them.

Source: 'Ali ibn Tahir al-Sulami. (in press) *The Book of the* Jihad *of 'Ali ibn Tahir al-Sulami (d. 1106): Text, Translation and Commentary*. Ed. and trans. Niall Christie. Crusade Texts in Translation. Aldershot, UK: Ashgate, pp. 200–1, 205, 212–13 and 228–9.

THE FAILURE OF THE SECOND CRUSADE AT DAMASCUS: **Document 7**
TWO ACCOUNTS

(i) Ibn al-Qalanisi

Ibn al-Qalanisi, in his Dhayl Ta'rikh Dimashq, **gives the following description of the attack on Damascus made by the forces of the Second Crusade.**

In the first days [of the year] successive reports came from various directions about the arrival of ships of the aforementioned Franks on the coast of the Mediterranean Sea, and their coming to the coastal ports of Tyre and Acre, where [the newly arrived Franks] joined with the Franks who were there. [. . . Some subsequently returned home, but] Alman, the greatest of their kings [Conrad III of Germany, r. 1138–52], and others of lesser rank, remained, and their views differed regarding which of the lands of Islam and the cities of Syria they should seek to attack, until they settled on attacking Damascus. Their wicked souls reassured them of their conquest of it, so that they agreed on the division of its estates and districts. A series of reports arrived about that, and the governor of the city, the emir Mu'in al-Din Unur, began to make preparations to fight them. [. . . The Franks] headed for Damascus [. . .] in a host estimated, according to what was said, at 50,000 cavalry and infantry. [. . .] The infidels overcame the Muslims with their superior numbers and equipment. They took control of the water-sources, spread throughout the orchards and camped in them. They approached the city and took over a part of it that no army had been able to hold in ancient or recent times.

[Three days later, after further fighting, the Muslims] made an early attack on them [. . .] like hawks attacking mountain quail, and falcons descending on the nests of partridges. They surrounded them in their tents, encompassing their dwellings, where the Franks had fortified themselves among the olive trees. They destroyed them with volleys of arrows and showers of rocks. The Franks had refrained from coming out [to fight the Muslims]. They were fearful and faint of heart, and not one of them showed themselves.

Reports reached [the Franks] about the Muslim armies [from elsewhere] that were hastening to wage the *jihad* against them and rushing to exterminate them, and they became convinced that they would be destroyed and perish, and that ruin would overtake them. They consulted each other and did not find any deliverance for themselves from the net into which they had fallen and the abyss into which they had thrown themselves, except to depart in fright at dawn of the [. . .] following day, and to run away forsaken and thwarted.

Source: Ibn al-Qalanisi. (1983) *Ta'rikh Dimashq*, pp. 462–6.

(ii) *Ibn al-Athir*

Ibn al-Athir gives this account of the siege in al-Kamil fi'l-Ta'rikh.

This year the king of the Germans came from his lands with a great host and large following of Franks, aiming to attack Islamic territory and not doubting that he would conquer it with the easiest of fighting because of the great multitude of his following and the abundance of his money and equipment. On his arrival in Syria, the Franks there sought him out and waited upon him, obeying his every command and prohibition. He ordered them to march with him to besiege and take Damascus, as he asserted. They duly set out with him, came to the city and put it under siege. [. . .] The people were convinced that he would conquer the city. Mu'in al-Din sent to Sayf al-Din Ghazi, son of Atabeg Zanki [Zangi], calling on him to come to the aid of the Muslims and to drive the enemy from them. Accordingly he gathered his troops and set out for Syria, taking with him his brother, Nur al-Din Mahmud, from Aleppo. [. . .] Mu'in al-Din wrote to the newly arrived Franks, 'The ruler of the East has come. If you do not withdraw, I shall surrender the city to him and then you will be sorry.' On the other hand, he sent to the Franks of Syria, to say to them, 'By what reasoning do you aid these men against us? You know that, if they take Damascus, they will seize the coastal lands that you have in your hands. For myself, if I see that I am too weak to hold the city, I shall surrender it to Sayf al-Din, and you know that, if he controls Damascus, he will not allow you to retain any foothold in Syria.' They agreed with him to withdraw cooperation with the German emperor and Mu'in al-Din offered to hand over to them the castle of Banyas.

The Levantine Franks met with the German emperor and warned him against Sayf al-Din, his large forces and his constant supply of reinforcements. 'Possibly he would take Damascus and you will be too weak to resist him.' They continued to press him until he withdrew from the city. They then received the surrender of Banyas and the Germans returned to their own lands beyond Constantinople. Thus God saved the believers from their evil.

Source: 'Izz al-Din ibn al-Athir. (2007) *The Chronicle of Ibn al-Athir for the Crusading Period from* al-Kamil fi'l-Ta'rikh: *Part 2: The Years 541–589/1146–1193: The Age of Nur al-Din and Saladin.* Trans. D.S. Richards. Crusade Texts in Translation 15. Aldershot, UK: Ashgate, pp. 21–2.

MUHAMMAD IBN AHMAD AL-WASITI (FL. 1019): EXTRACTS FROM   **Document 8**
THE MERITS OF JERUSALEM

Although written nearly 80 years before the arrival of the First Crusade in the Levant, al-Wasiti's Fada'il al-Bayt al-Muqaddas (Merits of Jerusalem) was a popular text among Muslim proponents of the jihad propaganda campaigns of the late twelfth century. Both Ibn 'Asakir (1105–76) and Ibn al-Jawzi (1126–1200) made use of this work in their preaching and writings.

The Messenger of God, may God bless him and grant him salvation, said, 'You are only compelled to travel to three mosques: the Mosque of the Haram [in Mecca], my mosque here [the Mosque of the Prophet in Medina] and the Aqsa Mosque [in Jerusalem].'

Maymuna asked the Messenger of God, may God bless him and grant him salvation, about Jerusalem. He said, 'How happy is the one who dwells in Jerusalem! Whoever performs one ritual prayer there performs the equivalent of 1,000 prayers elsewhere.' She asked, 'What about the person who is not able to do that?' He replied, 'Let him make a donation of oil to it [for the mosque lamps].'

The Messenger of God, may God bless him and grant him salvation, said, 'When I was taken by night to Jerusalem, Gabriel led me [first] to the tomb of Abraham [in Hebron], may God bless him and grant him salvation.

Gabriel said, "Dismount [from al-Buraq, the Prophet's supernal steed] and pray two prayer-cycles here, for this is the tomb of your father Abraham." Then he led me to Bethlehem and said, "Dismount and pray two prayer-cycles here, for this is where your brother Jesus, may God bless him, was born." Then he brought me to the Rock [in Jerusalem] and said, "From here your Lord ascended to the heavens [after the creation]," and God, be He glorified and exalted, inspired me to say, "We are at the place from which my Lord ascended to the heavens." So I prayed with the prophets and then Gabriel took me up to the heavens.'

'Abdiyya reported to us on the authority of her father, who said, 'On the Day of Resurrection the Ka'ba will be brought to Jerusalem, in procession like a bride, with those who were performing the *hajj* there clinging to it. The Rock will say, "Welcome to the guest and the one who is visited [by pilgrims]."'

Source: Muhammad ibn Ahmad al-Wasiti. (1979) *Fada'il al-Bayt al-Muqaddas*. Ed. Isaac Hasson. Max Schloessinger Memorial Series 3. Jerusalem: The Hebrew University, pp. 4, 24–5, 72 and 93.

Document 9   IBN AL-ATHIR ON NUR AL-DIN AND SALADIN

In addition to his universal history, Ibn al-Athir also wrote a rather more partisan dynastic history of the Zangids, al-Ta'rikh al-Bahir fi'l-Dawla al-Atabakiyya (The Dazzling History of the Atabeg State). The following extracts from this work give some sense of the tensions that arose between Nur al-Din and Saladin after the destruction of the Fatimid caliphate of Egypt.

Nur al-Din sent to Saladin, ordering him to gather the armies of Egypt and take them to the land of the Franks, and to descend upon Kerak and besiege it, so that Nur al-Din could also gather his armies and travel there, and they could join together to fight the Franks and take possession of their territory. So Saladin set out from Cairo on 20 Muharram [AH 567 (22 September 1171)], and he wrote to Nur al-Din to inform him that his departure had not been delayed. Nur al-Din had gathered his armies and got them ready, and was awaiting the arrival of the news from Saladin that the latter had set out, so that he himself could [also] depart. When the news of that came to him, he set out from Damascus, resolved to make for Kerak. He arrived there and waited for the arrival of Saladin [who had forced the surrender of Shawbak and then withdrawn]. A letter from Saladin came to him, in which the former excused himself from coming to Nur al-Din because there were disturbances in the country [of Egypt], and he was afraid for the country because he was far from it. Saladin returned to Egypt, but Nur al-Din did not accept his excuse.

The reason for Saladin's reticence was that his companions and leading officials had made him afraid of joining with Nur al-Din, and when Saladin did not follow the order of Nur al-Din the latter found that troubling and resolved to go down to Egypt and expel Saladin from it.

Ibn al-Athir goes on to describe how on this occasion Nur al-Din was mollified when Saladin, acting on the advice of his father Najm al-Din Ayyub, who was one of Nur al-Din's most trusted lieutenants, wrote to Nur al-Din re-affirming his loyalty to him. Later, Ibn al-Athir gives the following assessment of the reasons behind Saladin's reserve.

The thing that prevented Saladin from mounting an expedition [to fight the Franks] was fear of Nur al-Din, for he was convinced that when Nur al-Din had swept the Franks out of his way he would take the country [of Egypt] from him, so he was protecting himself with them and not undertaking their extermination. Nur al-Din was only interested in being serious about conducting an expedition against them with his [utmost] effort and capability, and when he saw Saladin failing to fulfil his obligations in the expedition and learned his [true] objective, he prepared to set out against him, but the order of God that cannot be resisted came to him [and he died].

Source: Ibn al-Athir. (1963) *Al-Ta'rikh al-Bahir fi'l-Dawla al-Atabakiyya*. Ed. 'Abd al-Qadir A. Tulaymat. Cairo: Dar al-Kutub al-Haditha, pp. 158 and 161.

'IMAD AL-DIN AL-ISFAHANI ON THE BATTLE OF HATTIN AND SALADIN'S CONQUEST OF JERUSALEM

Document 10

Originally from Persia, 'Imad al-Din Muhammad ibn Muhammad al-Isfahani (1125–1201) studied jurisprudence in Baghdad, then held a variety of positions before eventually passing into the service of Nur al-Din. Soon after the latter died he became the personal secretary of Saladin, a position that he occupied until the death of his master. The following selections are drawn from al-Fath al-Qussi fi'l-Fath al-Qudsi (Qussian Eloquence on the Conquest of Jerusalem), a chronicle covering the period from 1187 to 1193.

On 2 July 1187 Saladin attacked Tiberias. The following day the Franks marched out from Sepphoris, aiming to rescue the town. Saladin surrounded the Frankish army at the Horns of Hattin, cutting them off from sources of water. The following day, 4 July, battle was joined.

When morning broke and daylight shone, when dawn cast streaks of daylight and the sound of trumpets startled the crow from the dust, when sharp swords awoke in their sheaths and slender horses became enflamed with fiery eagerness, when bowstrings were alert and fire wrathful, when weapons were drawn and stillness snatched away, the vanguard went out to burn with their arrows the people of Hellfire, bows twanged and bowstrings hummed, foot-soldiers' supple lances danced to unveil the executioner's brides [swords], whose whiteness appeared from their sheaths, naked before the crowd, while the brown [spears] feasted on their flourishing pasture of [the enemies'] kidneys.

The Franks hoped for a respite, and their troops sought a way out of their predicament, but whenever they set out they were injured, and the heat of war set out with them, so that they did not get away. They attacked, afflicted with thirst, for the only water that they had was the water of the swords in their hands. The fire of the arrows roasted them and injured their limbs, and the hard hearts of the bows seized on them and deafened them. They were paralysed and alarmed, hard-pressed and driven off. Whenever they attacked they were turned back and destroyed, and whenever they struck out and launched an assault, they were captured and bound. Not even an ant got away, and none of their attacks protected them. They were burned and agitated, lamenting and afire with thirst. Arrows struck them so that their lions returned as hedgehogs, and harassed them so that great holes appeared in their ranks. They sought refuge on the mountain of Hattin to defend them from the deluge of ruin, and shining destruction surrounded Hattin. Blades sucked away [their lives] and scattered them on the heights. Bows shot them, fates flayed them, misfortunes ground them up and calamities afflicted them. They became known to ruin and targeted by fate. [. . .] Satan and his armies were captured, and the king [Guy of Lusignan] and his counts were taken.

The sultan sat to review the most important prisoners [. . .] and when [Reynald of Châtillon] came before him, he made him sit beside the king, with the king next to him. He upbraided him for his treachery and reminded him of his sins, saying, 'How many times have you sworn oaths and violated them, agreed to treaties and infringed on them, made agreements and broken them, accepted covenants and rejected them?' He answered through the translator, saying 'I have followed the custom of kings in that, and I have only acted according to the usual practices.'

Meanwhile the king was dying of thirst, bent over by the greatness of his intoxicating terror. So the sultan treated him pleasantly and spoke to him, soothing the intensity of the dread that was besetting him, calming his fear and reassuring his heart. He gave him iced water to quench his thirst and drive away the lack of water that was distressing him. [The king] passed it to the prince so that he might also quench his thirst, and he took it from his hand and drank it, but the sultan said to the king, 'You did not take it from me with my permission to give him a drink, so that does not oblige me to give him a guarantee of safety.' Then he got on his horse and left them alone. [. . .] When he went into his tent, he had the prince brought there. He went up to him, took up his sword and cut through his shoulder. When [Reynald] fell down, he ordered him to be beheaded, and it was done. When [Reynald] was taken out he was dragged by the feet before the king, who became frightened and alarmed. The sultan realized that terror had overcome him, dismay had beset him, and anxiety had afflicted him, so he summoned him and made him come close, reassuring and soothing him, strengthening him with his presence and calming him by saying, 'This one's wickedness destroyed him, and his treachery betrayed him, as you see. He has perished from his sins and injustice.'

In the wake of the battle, Saladin and his generals conquered a number of important Frankish towns and cities, including Acre, Jaffa, Beirut and Ascalon. Then in September he besieged Jerusalem, which was commanded by Balian of Ibelin. After some days of fighting the Muslims broke through the city wall, and Balian asked for terms.

Ibn Barzan [Balian of Ibelin] came out, seeking safety through an agreement from the sultan, and asking for a guarantee of security for his people, but the sultan refused and asserted a higher obligation, saying, 'No safety for you, and no guarantee of security! Our only desire is that degradation will be your constant companion. Tomorrow we will master you by force and spread death and imprisonment among you. We will spill the blood of your men and take your women and children prisoner.' [. . .] They replied, 'If we despair of your guarantee of safety, fear your power, are disappointed in our hopes for your favour [. . .] we shall seek death, fighting to the last drop of blood. We shall face existence with annihilation, and we shall demonstrate the boldness of those who persist in evil. We shall hurl ourselves forward like those who rush to get away from harm, and we shall commit ourselves to the fire, but we shall not give ourselves up to ruin and dishonour. None of us shall be wounded until he has wounded ten [of your men], and the hand of death shall not encompass us until our hands are seen spreading death [among you]. We shall burn the houses, demolish the Dome [of the Rock], and leave to you the shame of taking us prisoner. We shall uproot the Rock and make you grieve for it. We shall kill all the Muslim prisoners that we hold, and there are thousands of them, for it has become known that each of us is averse to ignominy and devoted to honour. As for the riches [that we hold], we shall destroy them and not hand them over, and as for the children, we shall hasten to kill them and not be found slow to do so. What do you gain from this niggardliness, when this gain will mean the loss of everything for you?' [. . .] The sultan summoned a council meeting [. . .] and said, 'In truth, the opportunity has presented itself, and we should aim to take advantage of it. Our share has fallen to us, and we should seek God's right guidance in taking it. If it passes, it will not return, and if it slips away, we will not be able to seize it.' They said, 'God has destined you for success, and dedicated you for this act of devotion. Your view is rightly guided.' [. . .] After goings back and forth, negotiations and delegations, entreaties from the people and intercessions, they settled on a fee that would satisfy [the Muslim conquerors] and act as a precautionary payment. With it they ransomed themselves and their possessions from us, liberating their men, women and children.

The ransoms were collected, and 'Imad al-Din notes that Saladin excused a large number of people from making the payments. 'Imad al-Din gives this portrait of his master in victory.

The date of the conquest of Jerusalem coincided with that of the night of the *mi'raj* [the Prophet's ascension to heaven], and the road to victory that had become apparent ended in rejoicing. Tongues multiplied their prayers, humble supplications and praises. The sultan sat to receive congratulations, meeting with the senior officers and *amirs*, Sufis and *'ulama'*. He sat with a bearing of humility and an appearance of dignity, among the jurisprudents and the savants, his devoted courtiers. His face shone with obvious joy, and his hope for the glory of success was abundant and victorious. His gate was open, his support given, his curtain raised, his speech heard, his power accepted, and his carpet kissed. His face was glowing and his perfume pleasant. His affection delighted and his dignity awakened admiration. His territory shone and his character exhaled a sweet fragrance. His hand overflowed with the waters of liberality and unsealed the lips of generosity; its back was the *qibla* [direction of prayer] of acceptance and its palm was the *Ka'ba* of hope.

'Ulama' (Ulema): The class of Muslim scholars educated in religion, theology and law. Muslim rulers would often patronize the *'ulama'* as a means to prove their devotion to Islam.

Source: 'Imad al-Din al-Isfahani. (1965) *Al-Fath al-Qussi fi'l-Fath al-Qudsi*. Ed. Muhammad M. Subh. Cairo: al-Dar al-Qawmiyya li-l-Tiba'a wa-l-Nashr, pp. 78–81, 126–7 and 130.

Document 11   BAHA' AL-DIN IBN SHADDAD ON SALADIN'S VIRTUES

Baha' al-Din Yusuf ibn Shaddad (1145–1234) was born and educated in Mosul. He worked as a teacher, and was also employed by the Zangid rulers of Mosul as an ambassador. Then in 1188 he was appointed qadi *(judge) of the army by Saladin, in whose service he remained until Saladin's death. He continued to work as an ambassador for the Ayyubids until two years before his own death. The extracts below are taken from his biography of Saladin, al-Nawadir al-Sultaniyya wa-l-Mahasin al-Yusufiyya (The Rare Qualities of the Sultan and the Merits of Yusuf [Saladin's given name, which Baha' al-Din shared]), coming from an opening section on Saladin's virtues.*

His creed was good and he was much mindful of God Almighty. He took his creed from proof by means of study with the leading men of religious learning and eminent jurisconsults. He understood of that what one needs to understand, such that, when disputation occurred in his presence, he could contribute excellent comments, even if they were not in the language of learned specialists. Consequently he gained a creed free from the defilement of anthropomorphism but his studies did not dig too deep to the extent of denying the divine attributes or misrepresentation. His creed followed the straight path, agreed with the canon of true discernment and was approved by the greatest of the ulema.

Saladin was just, gentle and merciful, a supporter of the weak against the strong. Every Monday and Thursday he used to sit to dispense justice in public session, attended by the jurisconsults, the Qadis and the doctors of religion. The door would be opened to litigants so that everyone, great and small, senile women and old men, might have access to him. That was his practice both at home and abroad. However, at all times he would accept petitions presented to him, to discover what injustices were reported to him. Every day he collected the petitions, and then used to sit with his clerk for a while, either at night or during the daytime, and minute each petition with whatever God put into his heart.

Saladin's generosity was too public to need to be recorded and too famous to need to be recounted, and yet we will give an indication of it in general terms. He ruled all that he ruled and, when he died, in his treasure chest were found only forty-seven Nasiri dirhams of silver and a single Tyrian gold coin, the weight of which was unknown to me. He would give away whole provinces. [. . .] In times of shortage he would be generous, just as he would in easy circumstances. The officials of the Royal Chest used to hide a certain amount of money from him, as a precaution in case some crisis surprised them, because they knew that, if he learnt of it, he would spend it.

Saladin was one of the great heroes, mighty in spirit, strong in courage and of great firmness, terrified of nothing [. . .] I have never at all seen him consider the enemy too numerous nor exaggerate their strength. However, he was sometimes deep in thought and forward planning, dealing with all departments and arranging what was required for each without any onset of bad temper or anger.

Saladin was very diligent in and zealous for the Jihad. If anyone were to swear that, since his embarking on the Jihad, he had not expended a single dinar or dirham on anything but the Jihad or his support for it, he would be telling the truth and true in his oath. The Jihad, his love and passion for it, had taken a mighty hold on his heart and all his being, so much so that he talked of nothing else, thought of nothing but the means to pursue it, was concerned only with its manpower and had a fondness only for those who spoke of it and encouraged it. In his love for the Jihad on the path of God he shunned his womenfolk, his children, his homeland, his home and all his pleasures, and for this world he was content to dwell in the shade of his tent with the winds blowing through it left and right. [. . .] We travelled in his service along the coast, making for Acre. [. . .] He turned to me and said, 'Shall I tell you something?' 'Of course,' I said. He went on, 'I have it in mind that, when God Almighty has enabled me to conquer the rest of the coast, I shall divide up my lands, make my testament, take my leave and set sail on this sea to [the Franks'] islands to pursue them there until there no longer remain on the face of the earth any who deny God – or die [in the attempt].'

On the plain of Acre I saw Saladin overcome by an extremely poor state of health on account of numerous boils which had appeared on his body from his waist to his knees, so that he was unable to sit down. [. . .] Despite all, he rode from early morning till the noonday prayer, going the rounds of his battalions, and also from late afternoon until the sunset prayer, enduring the intense pain and the throbbing of the boils, while I expressed my amazement at that. He would say, 'When I ride, the pain goes away, until I dismount.' This is divine solicitude.

He was forbearing, forgiving and rarely angry. I was in attendance on him at Marj 'Uyun before the Franks marched on Acre (may God facilitate its conquest). It was his custom to be out on horseback at the normal time for that, later to dismount for food to be served. He would eat with his staff, and then go to a personal tent to sleep. Later, when he awoke, he would pray and then relax in private, with me in attendance, when we would read a little Hadith or a little canon law.

One day I was on horseback in attendance on him face to face with the Franks when one of the forward pickets arrived with a woman in great distress, bitterly weeping and continually beating her breast. The man said, 'This woman has come out from the Frankish lines and asked to be brought to you, so we have done so.' The sultan ordered the dragoman to question her about her business. She said, 'Muslim thieves entered my tent yesterday and stole my daughter. I spent all night until this morning pleading for help. I was told, "Their prince is a merciful man. We shall send you out to him to ask him for your daughter." So they sent me to you, and only from you will I learn of my daughter.' The sultan took pity on her. His tears flowed out and, prompted by his chivalry, he ordered someone to go to the army market to ask who had bought the little girl, to repay what had been given for her and bring her back, having heard something about her early that day. Hardly an hour had passed before the horseman arrived with the little girl over his shoulder. The moment the woman's eye lighted upon her, she fell to the ground, besmirching her face with earth, while all around wept for what she had suffered. She was lifting her eyes to heaven, although we did not know what she was saying. Her daughter was handed to her, then she was taken off and restored to their camp.

These are some random remarks on the excellencies of his character and his noble qualities which I have limited myself to for fear of prolixity and wearying [the reader]. I have only recorded what I witnessed or what trust-worthy sources told me which I have checked. [. . .] However, this amount will suffice an intelligent person as evidence of the purity of these morals and qualities of his.

Source: Baha' al-Din ibn Shaddad. (2001) *The Rare and Excellent History of Saladin*. Trans. D.S. Richards. Crusade Texts in Translation 7. Aldershot, UK: Ashgate, pp. 18, 22–3, 25–30, 33 and 37–8.

AN EXCHANGE OF LETTERS DURING THE THIRD CRUSADE   **Document 12**

Baha' al-Din's work includes the following letters, exchanged between Saladin and Richard in October 1191. They provide a succinct summary of the issues at stake.

Richard to Saladin

The Muslims and the Franks are done for. The land is ruined, utterly ruined at the hands of both sides. Property and lives on both sides are destroyed. This matter has received its due. All we have to talk about is Jerusalem, the Holy Cross and these lands. Now Jerusalem is the centre of our worship which we shall never renounce, even if there were only one of us left. As for these lands, let there be restored to us what is this side of the Jordan. The Holy Cross, that is a piece of wood that has no value for you, but is important for us. Let the sultan bestow it upon us. Then we can make peace and have rest from this constant hardship.

Saladin's reply

Jerusalem is ours just as much as it is yours. Indeed, for us it is greater than it is for you, for it is where our Prophet came on his Night Journey and the gathering place of the angels. Let not the king imagine that we shall give it up, for we are unable to breathe a word of that amongst the Muslims. As for the land, it is also ours originally. Your conquest of it was an unexpected accident due to the weakness of the Muslims there at that time. While the war continues God has not enabled you to build up one stone there. From the lands in our hands we, thanks be to God, feed on the produce and draw our benefit. The destruction of the Holy Cross would in our eyes be a great offering to God, but the only reason we are not permitted to go that far is that some more useful benefit might accrue to Islam.

Source: Baha' al-Din ibn Shaddad. (2001) *The Rare and Excellent History of Saladin*, p. 186.

Document 13   EXTRACT FROM AL-HARAWI'S TREATISE ON MUSLIM MILITARY TACTICS

Abu'l-Hasan 'Ali al-Harawi (d. 1215) was a wandering ascetic and Sufi. He was the author of both a guide to pilgrimage sites and the work from which the following extract is drawn, al-Tadhkira al-Harawiyya fi'l-Hiyal al-Harbiyya *(The Memoir of al-Harawi on Stratagems of War). This second treatise, both a 'mirror for princes' and a guide to military tactics, was composed between 1192 and the author's death in 1215, probably for the Ayyubid prince al-Zahir Ghazi (d. 1216).*

If [an emir] desires an encounter with the enemy and to arrange his army for battle, let him strive to ensure that the sun is in the eyes of his enemy and the wind against them. If the enemy has done that to him, and it is not possible for him to shift them from their position or dislodge them from where they have set up [their forces], let him march with his army to one side so that the situation will be to his advantage and to their detriment. [. . .] Let him make his companions afraid of [enemy] stratagems and warn them about ruses, so that they will not occupy themselves with taking plunder, so that profit will mislead them, for it may be that the enemy will turn back upon them, or concealed forces may come out at them, master them, take them prisoner and kill them.

Let [the emir] terrify the hearts of the enemy by displaying banners, beating *kusat* (small drums), and sounding *buqat* (trumpets), along with the noise of *tubul* (large drums) and *naqqarat* (kettle-drums). He [himself] should not fear the numbers of the [enemy] army, nor the foot-soldiers gathered together, nor the useless mass of common people (irregular volunteers), for they are easy to defeat, and it is rare that an army of this sort is victorious.

Let him allocate each unit himself, not depending on anyone else, and let him place his trust first of all in God, be He exalted. Let him build up the centre [of the army], placing many men there and picking elite troops, for it is possible that it will be targeted [by the enemy]. Let him place in the right wing those upon whom he can depend and rely, and treat likewise the left wing. Let him arrange both sides and set up both wings, and let him put in reserve, from his army, a contingent of troops and a unit of elites from those who have seen stratagems of war and tasted the sweetness of stabbing and striking.

Let him observe in which direction the attack from the enemy side is sent and which segment of the army it targets, and if the attack comes from the right wing, let him reinforce his left wing, and if it comes from the left wing, let him strengthen his right wing [. . .] Let the infantry, slingers, archers, javelineers and sappers go in front of the cavalry, and let [the emir] observe the vanguard of the enemy army and place opposite it excellent foot-soldiers and outstanding *fursan* (knights), each sufficient to face their match and like to oppose like. Let him know that the troops are depending upon them and are looking to them [for reassurance]. If they break, the rest of the army will not resist, but rather will do ill and be of no use.

Source: Abu'l-Hasan 'Ali al-Harawi. (1962) 'Les Conseils du Sayh al-Harawi à un Prince Ayyubide'. Ed. Janine Sourdel-Thomine. *Bulletin d'Études Orientales* 17, pp. 250–49 (17–18).

USAMA IBN MUNQIDH ON FRANKISH CULTURE   **Document 14**

As indicated previously [Doc. 5.iii], Usama ibn Munqidh is best known to historians for his Kitab al-I'tibar (Book of Contemplation), a lively work posing as a memoir but in reality a text on good conduct, the human condition and the inevitability of divine decree, probably written for Saladin. The following extracts address aspects of Frankish culture and behaviour. Note the balance of good and bad examples that Usama uses.

(i) Frankish justice

The Franks (may God confound them) have none of the human virtues except for courage. They have neither precedence nor high rank except that of the knights, and have no men worthy of the name except the knights – it is they who are the masters of legal reasoning, judgment and sentencing. I once brought a case before them concerning some flocks of sheep that the lord of Banias had seized from the woods while there existed a truce between us. At the time, I was based in Damascus.

I said to the king, Fulk, son of Fulk, 'This man has encroached upon our rights and seized our flocks right at the time of lambing. But they gave birth and the lambs died, so he returned them to us after so many lambs were lost.'

Then the king turned to six or seven knights: 'Arise and render a judgment for him.'

So they left his audience-chamber, sequestering themselves and deliberating until their minds were all agreed upon one decision, and then they returned to the king's audience-chamber.

'We have passed judgment,' they said, 'to the effect that the lord of Banias should pay compensation equal to the value of the lambs that were lost from their flock of sheep.'

And so the king ordered him to pay compensation.

On one occasion, I went with the amir Mu'in al-Din [Unur] (may God have mercy upon him) to Jerusalem, and we stopped at Nablus. While there, a blind man – a young man wearing fine clothes, a Muslim – came out to the amir with some fruit and asked him for permission to be admitted into his service in Damascus. The amir did so. I asked about him and I was told that his mother had been married to a Frank, whom she had killed. Her son used to attempt various ruses on their pilgrims, and he and his mother used to work together to kill them. They finally brought charges against him for that and made him subject to the legal procedure of the Franks, to wit:

They set up a huge cask and filled it with water and stretched a plank of wood across it. Then they bound the arms of the accused, tied a rope around his shoulders and threw him into the cask. If he were innocent, then he would sink in the water and they would then pull him up by that rope so he wouldn't die in the water; if he were guilty, then he would not sink in the water. That man tried eagerly to sink into the water when they threw him in, but he couldn't do it. So he had to submit to their judgment – may God curse them – and they did some work on his eyes [blinding him].

(ii) Frankish medicine

The first of these two accounts was related to Usama by a Syrian Christian physician from Shayzar who had visited a Frankish court:

They brought before me a knight in whose leg an abscess had formed and a woman who was stricken with a dryness of the humours. So I made a small poultice for the knight and the abscess opened up and he was healed. For the woman, I prescribed a special diet and increased the wetness of her humours. Then a Frankish physician came to them and said, 'This fellow don't know how to treat them.' He then said to the knight, 'Which would you like better: living with one leg or dying with both?' 'Living with one leg,' replied the knight. The physician then said, 'Bring me a strong knight and a sharp axe.' A knight appeared with an axe – indeed, I was just there – and the physician laid the leg of the patient on a block of wood and said to the knight with the axe, 'Strike his leg with the axe and cut it off with one blow.' So he struck him – I'm telling you I watched him do it – with one blow, but it didn't chop the leg all the way off. So he struck him a second time, but the marrow flowed out of the leg, and he died instantly.

He then examined the woman and said, 'This woman, there is a demon inside her head that has possessed her. Shave off her hair.' So they shaved her head. The woman then returned to eating their usual diet – garlic and mustard. As a result, her dryness of humours increased. So the physician said, 'That demon has entered further into her head.' So he took a razor and made a cut in her head in the shape of a cross. He then peeled back the skin so that the skull was exposed and rubbed it with salt. The woman died instantaneously. So I asked them, 'Do you need anything else from me?' 'No,' they said. And so I left, having learned about their medicine things I had never known before.

Here is another wondrous example of their medicine. We had at Shayzar an artisan called Abu al-Fath, who had a son on whose neck scrofula sores had formed. Every time one would close in one place, another would open up in another place. Once Abu al-Fath went to Antioch on an errand and his son accompanied him. A Frankish man noticed him and asked him about the boy. 'He is my son,' Abu al-Fath said.

The Frank said to him, 'Do you swear to me by your religion that, if I prescribe for you some medicine that will cure your boy, you will not charge money from anyone else whom you yourself treat with it?'

Our man swore to that effect. The Frank then said, 'Take him some uncrushed leaves of glasswort, burn them, then soak the ashes in olive oil and strong vinegar. Treat him with this until it eats up the pustules in the affected area. Then take some fire-softened lead and soak it in butter. Then treat the boy with this and he will get well.

So our man treated the boy as he was told and the boy got well. The wounds closed up and he returned to his previous state of health. I have myself treated people afflicted by this ailment with this remedy, and it was beneficial and removed all of their complaints.

(iii) Frankish sexual morality

The Franks possess nothing in the way of regard for honour or propriety [. . .] Here is an example that I myself witnessed. Whenever I went to Nablus, I used to stay at the home of a man called Mu'izz, whose home was a lodging house for Muslims. The house had windows that opened onto the road and, across from it on the other side of the road, there was a house belonging to a Frankish man who sold wine for the merchants. He would take some wine in a bottle and go around advertising it, saying, 'So-and-So the merchant has just opened a cask of this wine. Whoever wishes to buy some can find it at such-and-such a place.' And the fee he charged for making that announcement was the wine in the bottle. So one day, he came back home and discovered a man in bed with his wife. The Frank said to the man, 'What business brings you here to my wife?'

'I got tired,' the man replied, 'so I came in to rest.'

'But how did you get into my bed?' asked the Frank.

'I found a bed that was all made up, so I went to sleep in it,' he replied.

'While my wife was sleeping there with you?' the Frank pursued.

'Well, it's her bed,' the man offered, 'Who am I to keep her out of it?'

'By the truth of my religion,' the Frank said, 'if you do this again, we'll have an argument, you and I!'

And that was all the disapproval he would muster and the extent of his sense of propriety!

I once went to the baths in the city of Tyre and took a seat in a secluded room there. While I was there, one of my attendants in the bath said to me, 'There are women in here with us!' When I went outside, I sat down on the benches and, sure enough, the woman who was in the bath had come out and was standing with her father directly across from me, having put her garments on again. But I couldn't be sure if she was a woman. So I said to one of my companions, 'By God, go have a look at this one – is she a woman?' What I meant was for him to go and ask about her. But instead he went – as I watched – and lifted her hem and pulled it up. At this, her father turned to me and explained, 'This is my daughter. Her mother died, and so she has no one who will wash her hair. I brought her into the bath with me so that I might wash her hair.'

'That's a kind thing you're doing,' I assured him. 'This will bring you heavenly reward.'

Source: Usama ibn Munqidh. (2008) *The Book of Contemplation: Islam and the Crusades*. Trans. Paul M. Cobb. Penguin Classics. London: Penguin Books, pp. 76–7, 152, 145–6 and 148–50.

IBN AL-QAYSARANI AND 'IMAD AL-DIN AL-ISFAHANI ON   **Document 15**
FRANKISH WOMEN

(i) Ibn al-Qaysarani

When he was not writing poems lauding the virtues of Zangi and Nur al-Din, the court poet Ibn al-Qaysarani (1085–1154) wrote a number of poems on the beauty of Frankish women. Here are two examples.

By your religion, O priest of [the church of] Barbara, and that which
    you continued to recite in the dark night,
Protect me from the eloquent figures whenever they stand around
    you in the church.
When they draw near at the time of prayer, in every colour of satin,
With girdles encircling their waists, and vestments of silk brocade
    burdening them,
And the burdensomeness of their chaperones makes them sit (and
    the gathering [for Mass] protects them from that).
Were it not for refraining from sin against the requirements of my
    religion, I would go up to them in a chasuble,
And stand up to chant their Mass, without stupidity or muteness.
Their knights did not engage [anyone] braver or more perceptive
    than me in battle.
Truly, how lovely is that which passion stirs up in the coverts* of
    these retiring antelopes.
You see every charming woman, her face bare of a veil in the
    morning sun,
Because of the beauty of [the sight], the icons almost boil over with
    eloquence of the soul.
A Frankish woman, her necklace silent, but her girdle restless in its
    place,
When she kisses an image, draws near to it with her imperious eye.
Oh if only I were an effigy to her, she would see me, and there is no
    doubt that some part of me would be touched.
I swear, if I was able I would be changed into an image of Saint George.

*A pun on the Arabic root k-n-s, which includes both a church and a covert for animals. Women are often likened to gazelles or antelopes in Arabic poetry from the period.

> A gentle Frankish woman has charmed me. The fragrance of her lingers.
> In her garment are soft limbs, and in her crown is a radiant moon.
> If there is blueness in her eye, then truly the head of a spear is blue.

Source: Muhammad ibn Nasr ibn al-Qaysarani. (1991) Shi'r Ibn al-Qaysarani. Ed. 'Adil J.S. Muhammad. Al-Zarqa', Jordan: al-Wakalat al-'Arabiyya li-l-Nashr wa-l-Tawzi', pp. 254–5 and 310.

(ii) 'Imad al-Din al-Isfahani

Meanwhile, Saladin's secretary, 'Imad al-Din al-Isfahani [see Doc. 10], took a radically different view. Here he describes the arrival of Frankish women at Acre in 1189.

There arrived in a ship 300 Frankish women who were considered attractive, endowed with youth and adorned with beauty. They had gathered from the islands and devoted themselves to sin. They had emigrated to provide assistance to the foreigners, dedicated themselves to cheering the wretched, sustained themselves to provide help and support, and were burning for fornication and sex. [. . .] Each trailed her head cloth on the ground behind her and bewitched her observer with her gracefulness. She swayed like a tree branch, revealed herself like a castle [waiting to be stormed], swung her hips like a switch and counterfeited her religion with a cross on her breast. [. . .] They said that they intended by their coming out [to the east] to dedicate their privates [to the cause], that they would not refrain from any unmarried man, and that they were of the opinion that they would not receive a better Eucharist than this.

Al-Isfahani then provides an extended and lurid description of the activities that the women apparently engaged in, ending with the following:

According to the Franks there is no sin imputed to an unmarried man if a woman gives herself to him, and what enhances her in the eyes of the priests is if she offers her privates as a relief for those who are suffering as a result of their celibacy.

There also arrived by sea a woman who had great power and abundant wealth. In her country she was a woman of great influence. In her entourage were 500 knights with their horses, followers, servants and adherents, to whom she gave all the provisions that they needed, exceeding the necessary level of support in what she spent on them. They rode at her side, attacking when she attacked, rushing [into battle] when she did, and standing firm as long as she did.

Among the Franks were women knights, with armour and helmets, dressed like men, who distinguished themselves in the thick of battle and did acts of intelligent men while being gentlewomen. They considered these all to be acts of worship, and they believed that they would gain happiness through them and made them their customary practice. Praise be to the One who led them astray and made them slip off the path of restraint! [. . .] They wore no clothing except a loose-fitting garment, and they were not known [to be women] until they were stripped of their arms and undressed. A number of them were found out and sold [as slaves], and as for the old women, the town centres were full of them! At times they were a reinforcement and at others a source of weakness. They goaded and incited [others to action], saying that the cross would only be satisfied by scorn [of the enemy], that there would be no immortality through it except through [fighting to the] death, and that the tomb of their god was under enemy occupation. Observe the agreement in error of their men and women!

Source: 'Imad al-Din al-Isfahani. (1965) *Al-Fath al-Qussi fi'l-Fath al-Qudsi*, pp. 347–9.

AL-KAMIL MUHAMMAD AND THE FIFTH CRUSADE   **Document 16**

Ahmad ibn Muhammad ibn Khallikan (d. 1282) was an Iraqi jurist. He worked as a qadi in both Cairo and Damascus, in the second of which he twice attained the rank of chief justice (1261–71 and 1278–82). He is best known for his biographical dictionary, **Wafayat al-A'yan wa-Anba' Abna' al-Zaman** *(The Deaths of Notables and Information on the Sons of the Age). The following extracts are from his entry in this work on al-Malik al-Kamil.*

Abu'l-Ma'ali Muhammad, the son of al-Malik al-'Adil, mentioned above, called by the titles al-Malik al-Kamil [and] Nasir al-Din (The Perfect King, Supporter of the Faith): some information about him has already been given in the biography of his father. When the Franks arrived at Damietta, as we have mentioned above, al-Malik al-Kamil had just begun to rule independently as sultan.

Ibn Khallikan then gives a detailed account of a failed attempt by one of al-Kamil's brothers and a senior emir to depose the sultan. His account of the Fifth Crusade, on the other hand, is somewhat briefer:

The well-known incident at Damietta took place, and there is no need to elaborate on it here. After the Franks took control of Damietta, and it fell into their hands, they set out from there aiming for the new and old cities of Cairo. They encamped on the tip of the island on which Damietta lies, with the Muslims opposite them in the village known as al-Mansura and the river, which was the River Ushmum, forming a barrier between them. God, be He exalted, through His grace and the beauty of His benevolence, gave victory over them to the Muslims, as is well known, and the Franks departed from their position on the eve of Friday 7 Rajab 618 (26 August 1221). Peace was concluded between them and the Muslims on the 11th of the month mentioned (30 August 1221), and the Franks departed from the country in Sha'ban (September–October) of the same year. They had spent 40 months and 17 days in the lands of Islam, partly in *al-Sham* and partly in Egypt, but God protected [us from] their evil. Praise be to God for that! That [event] has been set forth in detail in the biography of Yahya ibn Jarrah, and may be examined there *(in fact, the biography referred to provides little more detail)*.

When al-Malik al-Kamil's mind was eased with regard to this enemy, he occupied himself with the emirs who had taken sides against him, and he banished them from the country, dispersed their unity and drove them out. He entered Cairo, where he made arrangements to restore the prosperity of the country and to gather the taxes from its various districts. He was a sultan mighty in power and fine in reputation, having affection for the ulema and holding closely to the Prophetic sunna, correct in his belief, on intimate terms with eminent men and judicious in his affairs, never resolving any matter in a way that was either extravagant or stingy. Every Thursday night a group of learned men would spend the evening with him, and he would take part in their discussions, asking them about difficult topics of all sorts, behaving with them as if he were [merely] one of them.

The author goes on to describe al-Kamil's campaigns to extend his territory, including those against his relatives, up to the sultan's death, and then gives a brief synopsis of the reigns of the other major Ayyubids up to the Mamluk takeover. It is striking that Ibn Khallikan completely omits any mention of Frederick II's crusade and the handover to him of Jerusalem by al-Kamil.

Source: Ahmad ibn Muhammad ibn Khallikan. (1968–94) *Wafayat al-A'yan wa-Anba' Abna' al-Zaman.* Ed. Ihsan 'Abbas. Beirut: Dar Sadir, Vol. 5, pp. 79–81.

TWO SOURCES ON THE HANDOVER OF JERUSALEM TO FREDERICK II   **Document 17**

(i) Ibn Wasil

Al-Kamil's handover of Jerusalem to Frederick II, and the latter's subsequent visit to the Temple Mount, are described in the Mufarrij al-Kurub fi Akhbar Bani Ayyub (The Remover of Worries about Reports of the Scions of Ayyub) of the qadi and historian Jamal al-Din Muhammad ibn Wasil (d. 1298).

Al-Malik al-Kamil was of the opinion that if he broke [his agreement] with the emperor and did not satisfy him with everything [that had been promised], he would open up an episode of war with the Franks, disruption would spread and everything that vanishes because of it would thus slip away. He believed that he should satisfy the Franks with the city of Jerusalem in ruins, and make peace with them for a time, and then he would be able to seize it from them whenever he wished. The emir Fakhr al-Din ibn al-Shaykh carried the messages between him and the king-emperor, and between them there were discussions on various topics. During these the emperor sent al-Malik al-Kamil difficult philosophical, geometrical and mathematical questions, in order to put the learned men who were with him to the test. Al-Malik al-Kamil showed the mathematical questions that had come to him to the *shaykh* 'Alam al-Din Qaysar ibn Abi'l-Qasim, who was a leader in the field, and showed the remainder to a group of learned men, and they answered the lot. Then the sultan al-Malik al-Kamil swore to abide by what they had agreed on, as did the emperor, and they concluded a peace agreement for a fixed term. The matter was arranged between them, and each side felt secure with the other. It reached me that the emperor said to Fakhr al-Din, 'Had I not feared that my reputation among the Franks would collapse, I would not have imposed any of this on him. I have no desire to take Jerusalem or anywhere else, and only really want to preserve my honour among them.'

When it was proclaimed in Jerusalem that the Muslims were to leave, and [the city] was to be surrendered to the Franks, tumult and weeping broke out among the people of Jerusalem. It was distressing for the Muslims. They grieved for Jerusalem's passing out of their possession and disapproved of al-Malik al-Kamil for this act [. . .] but al-Malik al-Kamil, may God have mercy on him, knew that it would be impossible for the Franks to restrain themselves from [attacking] Jerusalem, since its walls had been destroyed, and that if he achieved his objective and the situation stabilised for him, he would be able [later] to purify it of the Franks and expel them from it.

When the matter of the truce was concluded, the emperor asked the sultan for permission to visit Jerusalem, and he gave it to him. The sultan commissioned the *qadi* Shams al-Din, the *qadi* of Nablus, may God have mercy on him, who was revered in the state and given precedence by the rulers of the Ayyubid family, that he provide service to the emperor until he had visited Jerusalem and returned to Acre. Shams al-Din, may God have mercy on him, related to me, 'When the emperor came to Jerusalem, I accompanied him as the sultan al-Malik al-Kamil commanded me. I entered the Noble Sanctuary with him, and he looked at the shrines in it. Then I entered the Aqsa Mosque with him, and the building amazed him, as did that of the sanctified Dome of the Rock. When he reached the *mihrab* of the Aqsa [Mosque] its beauty, and the beauty of the *minbar*, astounded him, and he went up the steps [of the *minbar*] to its top. Then he descended and took my hand, and we went out of the Aqsa [Mosque]. He saw a priest, with the Gospel in his hand, who was intending to enter the Aqsa [Mosque], and he shouted an objection at him, saying, "What has brought you here? By God! If any of you comes in here again without my permission, I shall certainly pluck his eyes out! We are the slaves and servants of this sultan al-Malik al-Kamil, and he has donated this church to me and you as a way of granting favour, so let not one of you exceed his limits." The priest went away, trembling with fear of him, and the emperor passed on to the house that had been assigned for him to dwell in, and stayed there.'

The *qadi* Shams al-Din, the *qadi* of Nablus, said, 'I ordered the muezzins not to give the call to prayer that night, out of esteem for him, and when we got up in the morning and I went in to see him, he asked me, "O *qadi*, why did the muezzins not utter the call to prayer from the *minbars* according to their custom?" I answered him, "This slave forbade it to them out of respect for the king and esteem for him." He said, "You committed an error in what you did. By God, the greatest of my aims in staying overnight in Jerusalem was to hear the muezzins making the call to prayer and glorifying God in the night." Then he departed for Acre.'

Source: Jamal al-Din Muhammad ibn Wasil. (1953–75) *Mufarrij al-Kurub fi Akhbar Bani Ayyub*. Ed. Jamal al-Din al-Shayyal *et al*. Cairo: Al-Matba'a al-Amiriyya, Vol. 4, pp. 242–5.

(ii) Sibt ibn al-Jawzi

The famous religious scholar Yusuf ibn Qizughli, known as Sibt ibn al-Jawzi (d. 1257) was initially brought up by his equally famous grandfather, 'Abd al-Rahman ibn al-Jawzi, then moved to Damascus in about 1204 after the latter's death. There he taught and preached, as well as serving a number of the Ayyubid rulers including al-Mu'azzam 'Isa and al-Nasir

Dawud. The following account of the same events is drawn from his universal history, Mir'at al-Zaman fi Ta'rikh al-A'yan (*The Mirror of Time concerning the History of Important People*).

In [the year AH 626/CE 1229] al-Kamil gave the emperor Jerusalem [. . .] This grieved [al-Ashraf], and he reproached al-Kamil, who said, 'I only did this because I was obliged to by al-Mu'azzam' and stated that al-Mu'azzam had given the emperor [the lands] from the Jordan to the [Mediterranean] Sea, and the estates from the gate of Jerusalem to Jaffa, and others. When al-Ashraf and al-Kamil joined together they agreed to besiege Damascus. The news of the surrender of Jerusalem to the Franks arrived, and turmoil erupted in all the lands of Islam. The misfortunes [associated with the events] were so distressing that ceremonies of mourning were held. Al-Malik al-Nasir Dawud asked me to host a meeting in the [Umayyad] Great Mosque of Damascus and speak about what had happened to Jerusalem. I could not refuse him, seeing conformity with his desires as part of the religious duties that defend Islam. So I sat in the Great Mosque of Damascus, in the presence of al-Nasir Dawud, at the Gate of the Mashhad of 'Ali. It was a day witnessed by many, with not one of the people of Damascus being absent. Among the words [that I spoke] were: 'Parties of pilgrims have been cut off from Jerusalem! O, for the desolation of those who live around it! How many prayer-cycles have they performed in those places? How many tears have they shed in those dwellings? By God, if their eyes became springs, they would not shed sufficient tears [for such a calamity], and if their hearts were rent by sorrow, they would not ease it. May God grant consolation to the believers. Shame upon the rulers of the Muslims! At such events tears are poured out. At such [events] hearts break from sighs. At such [events] sorrows increase.'

The emperor entered Jerusalem, while Damascus was being besieged, and remarkable things happened [during his visit]. Among them was that when he entered the [Dome of the] Rock he saw a priest sitting at the Foot[print of the Prophet Muhammad], taking pieces of paper from the Franks. He came up as if he wanted a blessing from [the priest], but [the emperor] struck him and threw him to the ground, saying, 'You pig! The sultan has honoured us with a visit to this place, and you do such deeds here? If any of you comes back and starts behaving in such a way again, I will surely kill him!'

The custodians of the [Dome of the] Rock described this situation, and they said, '[The emperor] looked at the inscription in the Dome, which said, "Salah al-Din has purified Jerusalem of the polytheists," and asked, "Who are the polytheists?" He asked the custodians, "What is the purpose of these nets on the doors of the [Dome of the] Rock?" They answered, "So that little birds do not come in." He responded, "God has brought you giants."'

They added, 'When it was time for the midday prayer, and the muezzin uttered the call to prayer, all those who were with him got up, his attendants and pages, and his teacher, who was from Sicily and with whom he was reading [Aristotle's] *Logic* chapter-by-chapter, and performed the *salat*, for they were Muslims.' [The custodians] said, 'The emperor was light-skinned, with weak eyes. If he was a slave he would not be worth 200 dirhams,' and they added, 'What was apparent from his words was that he was a materialist, and that he was only play-acting at being a Christian.'

Sibt ibn al-Jawzi follows this passage with an account, similar to that of Ibn Wasil, in which Frederick II demonstrates great respect for the muezzins of Jerusalem.

Source: Sibt ibn al-Jawzi. (1951–2) *Mir'at al-Zaman fi Ta'rikh al-A'yan*. Hyderabad-Deccan, India: Dairatu'l-Maarifil-Osmania, Vol. 2, pp. 653–6.

Document 18   IBN AL-DAWADARI ON THE BATTLE OF 'AYN JALUT

Abu Bakr ibn al-Dawadari was the son of a Mamluk military and adminis-trative official and himself served in the military, although as a member of the awlad al-nas *he is unlikely to have risen to a high rank. He also wrote several historical works. The following account of the Battle of 'Ayn Jalut is drawn from his abridged universal chronicle,* Kanz al-Durar wa-Jami' al-Ghurar *(The Treasure of Pearls and the Collector of the Best Parts), which he wrote between 1309 and 1336. Ibn al-Dawadari's claim that Baybars lured the Mongols to 'Ayn Jalut is probably a fabrication (Amitai-Preiss, 1995: 40–1).*

The departure of the sultan al-Malik al-Muzaffar [Qutuz] with his army from the lands of Egypt to face the Tatars [Mongols] took place on Monday 15 Sha'ban (658, 26 July 1260). Hülegü had prepared the armies of the Mongols, who were led by Ket-Buqa Noyan. The latter descended on Homs, and when it reached him that the sultan al-Muzaffar had arrived at Marj 'Akka he rode away from Homs and turned so that he would come to the Jordan Valley. Al-Muzaffar sent the emir Rukn al-Din Baybars al-Bunduqdari with a number of seasoned cavalry as an advance guard to stab and strike [at the enemy]. When [Baybars'] eyes fell upon [the Mongols] he sent word to the sultan. Then he seized the opportunity to engage in a skirmish with them, so that he could be credited with good deeds by God (be He exalted) and Islam, and so that the impact [of the enemy] might be reduced in the eyes of the troops coming upon them. He met them anew and lured them to destruction, he turned to attack them and advanced ahead of them, until they reached 'Ayn Jalut. On Friday 25 Ramadan the Sublime (3 September) the two armies met in battle, and swords and spearheads engaged in striking and stabbing. The brave stood firm and the cowardly fled, the misfortune of calamity came upon the blaspheming idol-worshippers, and God gave victory to the bearers of the *Qur'an*. The infidel Tatars were put to flight, sharp blades severed their necks, and they were scattered throughout the land. The Muslims rode in hot pursuit, capturing and killing, until that satisfied [the carrion-eating appetites of] the wild beasts of the waterless deserts. Their cursed leader, Ket-Buqa Noyan, was killed, and the evil-doing people were eradicated. Praise be to God, Lord of the Worlds!

Source: Abu Bakr ibn 'Abd Allah ibn al-Dawadari. (1971) *Kanz al-Durar wa-Jami' al-Ghurar*. Vol. 8. Ed. Ulrich Haarmann. Cairo: al-Ma'had al-Almani li-l-Athar, pp. 49–50.

QALAWUN'S TREATY WITH THE LADY OF TYRE, 1285   **Document 19**

As indicated previously, despite their vigorous prosecution of the military jihad against the Franks, the Mamluks also made periodic treaties and peace agreements with them as circumstances dictated. The following extracts are drawn from a treaty made by Qalawun with Margaret, the Lady of Tyre, in 1285. The text of the treaty is found in a biography of Qalawun written by the head of his royal chancery, Ibn 'Abd al-Zahir (d. 1293), entitled **Tashrif al-Ayyam wa-l-'Usur fi Sirat al-Malik al-Mansur** *(The Honouring of Days and Ages concerning the Biography of al-Malik al-Mansur [Qalawun's regnal title: the King Aided by God]). For a fuller discussion of this treaty, including a translation of the complete text, see P.M. Holt,* **Early Mamluk Diplomacy** *(1995), pp. 106–17.*

In the Name of God, the Merciful, the Compassionate: The blessed peace agreement has been established between our lord, the sultan al-Malik al-Mansur [Qalawun], Sayf al-Dunya wa-l-Din (Sword of the World and the Faith), sultan of Islam and the Muslims, partner of the Commander of the Faithful [the caliph], [two of Qalawun's sons are then specified], and the sublime ruler, Dame Margaret, daughter of Sir Henry, son of Prince Bohemond, ruler of Tyre during the period of the establishment of this truce [Lady Margaret's representative is also named], for a period of ten years, complete, uninterrupted and consecutive, of which the start is Thursday, 14 Jumada I 684 (18 July 1285) [. . .] and the end is 14 Jumada I 694 (1 April 1295).

Regarding all the Islamic lands within the sovereignty of the lands of our lord the sultan, al-Malik al-Mansur [the precise geographical areas are then specified]: their fortresses, citadels, ports, cities, villages, coasts, harbours and inland areas, both close and distant, plains and mountains, cultivated and abandoned, lowlands and highlands, east and west, Yemen and Hijaz, *Bilad al-Sham* and Egypt, and the villages, cultivated lands, rivers, mills, towers and gardens included therein, and those people included in these territories, including troops, soldiers and civilians [. . .], staying in them, resident or travelling to, from or within them, merchants and travellers, shall be safe and secure, [in the case of the people] with respect to their selves, goods and livestock.

With regard to the territory of the ruler, Dame Margaret, daughter of Sir Henry, son of Prince Bohemond, specified as being hers in particular and shared in this peace agreement, which is the city of Tyre and the walls and suburbs that surround it as its property [. . .] these suburbs mentioned shall be the property of Tyre [. . .] on the condition that Rashmun, Ma'shuqa and the garden of al-'Awja remain lands in the suburbs of Tyre without dwellings or villages.

The treaty then goes on to specify at length which lands around Tyre shall belong to Qalawun, which shall belong to Lady Margaret, and which shall have their incomes shared between them. The treaty then indicates the obligations of each ruler to both the other and their subjects, including the following clauses.

This territory belonging to the ruler of Tyre shall be safe and secure, along with those [living] within it, be they troops, cavalry, infantry, civilians or merchants, with respect to their selves, goods, children and livestock.

When someone from either side is killed, and the killer is found, if the killer is Muslim, the representatives of our lord, the sultan al-Malik al-Mansur (may God aid him), shall judge him according to the requirements of the noble, pure usages of the sultanate, and if he is a Christian from the people of Tyre, the ruler, Dame Margaret, the ruler of Tyre, shall judge him. Each party shall carry out the judgement, in the presence of a representative from the other side, according to what the laws of both sides require.

And on the condition that the ruler, Dame Margaret, the ruler of Tyre, does not begin anew the construction of the citadel, nor the restoration of the wall, nor the digging of a moat, nor anything that will fortify [Tyre], protecting or defending [it]:

And on the condition that our lord the sultan does not give leeway for any of his troops or soldiers, or any of the people of his lands, to seek to gain access into the territory of Tyre specified in this peace agreement to cause injury, damage, theft, hostile action, or treachery on land or sea, nor that any of the troops, soldiers or allies of our lord the sultan undertakes action against the ruler, Dame Margaret, the ruler of Tyre, either against herself, her cavalry or her associates, with the exception of the Isma'ilis who are under the jurisdiction of our lord the sultan; the sultan has the right to send whom-ever of them that he wishes to the ruler of Tyre to carry out evil and damage whenever he wishes (*this refers to the remnants of the Nizari Assassins, who had come under Mamluk control; as Holt notes, Qalawun backs up the agreement with a threat [Holt, 1995: 116]*):

And on the condition that the ruler, Dame Margaret, the ruler of Tyre, shall take on the duty of defending the territory of our lord the sultan, from her side, from any criminal, troublemaker, foreign intruder and the rest of the Franks who seek to gain access from her territory into the lands of our lord the sultan to carry out injury, attack, wickedness or hostile action:

And on the condition that the ruler, Dame Margaret, the ruler of Tyre, does not agree with any of the rest of the Franks on any matter that might cause harm to the territory of our lord the sultan, or damage his territories, people or whomever or whatever is therein, nor aids anyone in that with any sign, written word, advice or message, until the time of the termination of this truce:

She shall have the right to similar treatment from our lord the sultan.

The treaty closes with an indication that it will remain in force for the ten-year period specified even if one of the two parties dies or is deposed.

Source: Muhyi'l-Din ibn 'Abd al-Zahir. (1961) *Tashrif al-Ayyam wa-l-'Usur fi Sirat al-Malik al-Mansur*. Ed. Murad Kamil and Muhammad 'A. al-Najjar. Cairo: al-Sharika al-'Arabiyya li-l-Tiba'a wa-l-Nashr, pp. 103–10.

ABU'L-FIDA' ON THE FALL OF ACRE, 1291   **Document 20**

'Imad al-Din Isma'il, best known by his kunya of Abu'l-Fida' (1273–1331) was a descendant of Saladin's nephew Taqi al-Din 'Umar and one of the last Ayyubid rulers to be tolerated by the Mamluk sultans. In 1310 he was appointed governor of his ancestral home of Hamah by the sultan al-Nasir Muhammad; in 1320 he was granted the title of Sultan of Hamah, and he continued to rule there until his death. The following account is from his Mukhtasar fi Akhbar al-Bashar (Short Account of Human Affairs), a universal history starting with Adam and continuing to his own time.

Here he describes the fall of Acre in 1291, which he witnessed himself, aged 17, as an emir of 10 in the halqa.

The descent of the Islamic armies upon [Acre] occurred in the first days of Jumada I of this year (AH 690, May 1291). The fighting became fierce; the Franks had not closed most of their gates, but rather they were open, with [the Franks] fighting in them. The location of the troops from Hamah was at the head of the right wing, according to their custom. We were beside the sea, with the sea on our right as we faced Acre. Ships bearing wooden vaulting covered with ox hides would come at us, shooting at us with arrows and [crossbow] bolts, so that there was fighting [coming] from in front of us, from the direction of the city, and from our right, from the sea. They brought up a ship upon which was a mangonel that shot at us and our tents from the direction of the sea, and we suffered hardship until one night strong gale-force winds arose, the ship was caught up and sank because of the waves, and the mangonel that was in it was broken in such a way that it was shattered and was not set up [again] after that.

During the time of the siege, the Franks came out by night and took the army by surprise. They routed the sentries and reached the tents, getting entangled in the guy-ropes. One of their knights fell into the latrine of one of the emirs and was killed there. The [Muslim] troops came to outnumber them, and the Franks fled, defeated, to the city. The troops of Hamah killed a number of them, and when morning came al-Malik al-Muzaffar, the lord of Hamah, hung a number of the Franks' heads on the necks of the horses that the soldiers had taken from them and took them to the sultan al-Malik al-Ashraf [Khalil].

The [Muslim] troops' attack on Acre became more aggressive until God, be He exalted, gave them its conquest by the sword on Friday, 17 Jumada II (17 June). When the Muslims stormed into [the city], some of its people fled in ships. Within the city were a number of towers that were resisting like citadels, which a large number of Franks entered and fortified themselves within. The Muslims killed [many people] and took in Acre a quantity of plunder greater than can be reckoned. Then the sultan called for the surrender of all who were resisting in the towers, and not one person hesitated. Then he issued orders regarding them, and they were beheaded, to the last man, around Acre. Then he gave orders regarding the city of Acre, and it was torn down to the ground and completely demolished.

A wondrous thing is the coincidence that the Franks took control of Acre, taking it from Salah al-Din (Saladin) at noon on Friday, 17 Jumada II 587 (12 July 1191), capturing the Muslims who were in it and then killing them, and God, be He glorified and exalted, with His advance knowledge decreed that it should be conquered in this year (690/1291) on Friday, 17 Jumada II, at the hand of the sultan al-Malik al-Ashraf Salah al-Din; its conquest was similar to the day that the Franks took possession of it, and likewise the *laqabs* of the sultans.

Source: 'Imad al-Din Isma'il ibn 'Ali, known as Abu'l-Fida'. (1998–9) *Al-Mukhtasar fi Akhbar al-Bashar*. Ed. Muhammad Z.M. 'Azab *et al*. Cairo: Dar al-Ma'arif, Vol. 4, pp. 34–5.

STATEMENTS OF USAMA IBN LADIN (OSAMA BIN LADEN,   **Document 21**
1957–2011), 1998

Usama ibn Ladin was born into an extremely wealthy family in Saudi Arabia and enjoyed a privileged upbringing. At university he met the Islamist thinker 'Abd Allah Azzam (1941–89), under whose influence he became convinced of the need to liberate the Muslim world from foreign intervention. Ibn Ladin participated in the Afghan resistance to the occupation of the country by Soviet forces, during which period he founded al-Qa'ida (al-Qaeda, 'the Base'), an organization that initially operated in Afghanistan but later expanded its operations to other venues. When the Americans were invited to station troops in Saudi Arabia in the wake of the Iraqi invasion of Kuwait in 1990, Ibn Ladin was outraged and publicly denounced the move. Disowned by his family and banished from Saudi Arabia, he began orchestrating attacks on American targets, issuing a public declaration of war against America itself in 1996. The following statements, made in 1998 and thus before the events of 11 September 2001, outline his views.

(i) From an interview with his followers:

The call to wage war against America was made because America has spear-headed the crusade against the Islamic nation, sending tens of thousands of its troops to the land of the two Holy Mosques [Saudi Arabia], over and above its meddling in its affairs and its politics and its support of the oppressive, corrupt, and tyrannical regime that is in control [the Saudi monarchy]. These are the reasons behind the singling out of America as a target. And not exempt from responsibility are those Western regimes whose presence in the region offers support to the American troops there. We know at least one reason behind the symbolic participation of the Western forces and that is to support the Jewish and Zionist plans for expansion of what is called the Great Israel. Surely, their presence is not out of concern over their interests in the region [. . .] Their presence has no meaning save one and that is to offer support to the Jews in Palestine who are in need of their Christian brothers to achieve full control over the Arab Peninsula, which they intend to make an important part of the so-called Great Israel.

The terrorism we practice is of the commendable kind, for it is directed at the tyrants and the aggressors and the enemies of Allah, the tyrants, the traitors who commit acts of treason against their own countries and their own faith and their own prophet and their own nation. Terrorizing those and punishing them are necessary measures to straighten things and to make them right. Tyrants and oppressors who subject the Arab nation to aggression ought to be punished. The wrongs and the crimes committed against the Muslim nation are far greater than can be covered by this interview. America heads the list of aggressors against the Muslims. The recurrence of aggression against Muslims everywhere is proof enough. For over half a century, Muslims in Palestine have been slaughtered and assaulted and robbed of their honor and of their property. Their houses have been blasted, their crops destroyed. And the strange thing is that any act by them to avenge themselves or to lift the injustice befalling them causes great agitation in the United Nations, which hastens to call for an emergency meeting only to convict the victims and to censure the wronged and the tyrannized whose children have been killed and whose crops have been destroyed and whose farms have been pulverized. [...] In today's wars, there are no morals, and it is clear that mankind has descended to the lowest degrees of decadence and oppression. They rip us of our wealth and of our resources and of our oil. Our religion is under attack. They kill and murder our brothers. They compromise our honor and our dignity and if we dare to utter a single word of protest against their injustice, we are called terrorists.

What prompted us to address the American government in particular is the fact that it is on the head of the Western and crusading forces in their fight against Islam and the Muslims. [...] We, however, differentiate between the Western government and the people of the West. If the people have elected these governments in the latest elections, it is because they have fallen prey to the Western media, which portrays things contrary to what they really are. And while the slogans raised by these regimes call for humanity, justice and peace, the behavior of their governments is completely the opposite. It is not enough for their people to show pain when they see our children being killed in Israeli raids launched by American planes, nor does this serve the purpose. What they ought to do is change their governments that attack our countries. The hostility that America continues to express against the Muslim people has given rise to feelings of animosity on the part of Muslims against America and against the West in general. Those feelings of animosity have produced a change in the behavior of some crushed and subdued groups, who, instead of fighting the Americans inside the Muslim countries, went on to fight them inside the United States of America itself.

The Western regimes and the government of the United States of America bear the blame for what might happen. If their people do not wish to be harmed inside their very own countries, they should seek to elect governments that are truly representative of them and that can protect their interests.

Source: 'Interview with Usama bin Laden by His Followers, 1998'. (2004) Trans. Akram Fouad Khater, in Akram Fouad Khater (ed.), *Sources in the History of the Modern Middle East*. Boston, MA: Houghton Mifflin Company, pp. 360–2.

(ii) Comments on the jihad *against Jews and crusaders*:

No-one argues today about three facts that are known to everyone; we will list them, in order to remind everyone:

First, over seven years the United States has been occupying the lands of Islam in the holiest of places, the Arabian Peninsula, plundering its riches, dictating to its rulers, humiliating its people, terrorizing its neighbors, and turning its bases in the peninsula into a spearhead through which to fight the neighboring Muslim peoples.

If some people have in the past argued about the fact of the occupation, all the people of the peninsula have now acknowledged it. The best proof of this is the Americans' continuing aggression against the Iraqi people using the peninsula as a staging post, even though all its rulers are against their territories being used to that end, but they are helpless.

Second, despite the great devastation inflicted on the Iraqi people by the crusader–Zionist alliance, and despite the huge number of those killed, which has exceeded 1 million [. . .] despite all this, the Americans are once again trying to repeat the horrific massacres, as though they are not content with the protracted blockade imposed after the ferocious war or the fragmentation and devastation.

So here they come to annihilate what is left of its people and to humiliate their Muslim neighbors.

Third, if the Americans' aims behind these wars are religious and economic, the aim is also to serve the Jews' petty state and divert attention from its occupation of Jerusalem and murder of Muslims there. The best proof of this is their eagerness to destroy Iraq, the strongest neighboring Arab state, and their endeavor to fragment all the states of the region – such as Iraq, Saudi Arabia, Egypt and Sudan – into paper statelets and through their disunion and weakness to guarantee Israel's survival and the continuation of the brutal crusade occupation of the peninsula.

All these crimes and sins committed by the Americans are a clear declaration of war on God, His Messenger, and Muslims.

The ruling to kill the Americans and their allies – civilians and military – is an individual duty for every Muslim who can do it in any country in which it is possible to do it, in order to liberate the al-Aqsa Mosque and the holy mosque [Mecca] from their grip, and in order for their armies to move out of all the lands of Islam, defeated and unable to threaten any Muslim. This is in accordance with the words of Almighty God, 'and fight the pagans all together as they fight you all together' [Qur'an 9: 36], and 'fight them until there is no more tumult or oppression, and there prevail justice and faith in God' [Qur'an 8: 39].

Source: 'Jihad against Jews and Crusaders: World Islamic Front Statement'. (2004) Trans. Akram Fouad Khater, in Akram Fouad Khater (ed.), *Sources in the History of the Modern Middle East*, pp. 364–5.

Select bibliography

PRIMARY SOURCES

This list includes both primary sources cited in this book and, where judged appropriate, additional primary texts, either in Arabic or in translation, that may be of interest to readers or have been helpful in the preparation of this work.

Abu'l-Fida', 'Imad al-Din Isma'il. (1983) *The Memoirs of a Syrian Prince: Abu'l-Fida', Sultan of Hamah (672–732/1273–1331)*. Trans. P.M. Holt. Freiburger Islamstudien 9. Wiesbaden, Germany: Franz Steiner Verlag GMBH.

———. (1998–9) *Al-Mukhtasar fi Akhbar al-Bashar*. Ed. Muhammad Z.M. 'Azab, Yahya S. Husayn and Muhammad F. Wasif. 4 vols. Cairo: Dar al-Ma'arif.

Arab Historians of the Crusades. (1984) Ed. Francesco Gabrieli. Trans. Francesco Gabrieli and E.J. Costello. Berkeley, CA: University of California Press.

Al-'Azimi, Muhammad ibn 'Ali. (1984) *Ta'rikh Halab*. Ed. Ibrahim Za'rur. Damascus: n.p.

Al-Bukhari, Muhammad ibn Isma'il. (2003) *Sahih al-Bukhari*. Ed. and trans. Muhammad M. al-Sharif. 4 vols. Beirut: Dar al-Kutub al-'Ilmiyya.

Chronicles of the Crusades: Eyewitness Accounts of the Wars between Christianity and Islam. (2000) Ed. Elizabeth Hallam. Trans. Michael Parkison. New York: Welcome Rain.

Al-Harawi, Abu'l-Hasan 'Ali. (1962) 'Les Conseils du Sayh al-Harawi à un Prince Ayyubide'. Ed. and trans. Janine Sourdel-Thomine. *Bulletin d'Études Orientales* 17, pp. 205–68.

Ibn 'Abd al-Zahir, Muhyi'l-Din. (1961) *Tashrif al-Ayyam wa-l-'Usur fi Sirat al-Malik al-Mansur*. Ed. Murad Kamil and Muhammad 'A. al-Najjar. Cairo: al-Sharika al-'Arabiyya li-l-Tiba'a wa-l-Nashr.

Ibn al-'Adim, Kamal al-Din. (1951–68) *Zubdat al-Halab min Ta'rikh Halab*. Ed. Sami Dahan. 3 vols. Damascus: al-Ma'had al-Firansi.

Ibn al-Athir, 'Izz al-Din. (1963) *Al-Ta'rikh al-Bahir fi'l-Dawla al-Atabakiyya*. Ed. 'Abd al-Qadir A. Tulaymat. Cairo: Dar al-Kutub al-Haditha.

——. (1966) *Al-Kamil fi'l-Ta'rikh*. Ed. C.J. Tornberg. 13 vols. Beirut: Dar Sadir.

——. (2006) *The Chronicle of Ibn al-Athir for the Crusading Period from al-Kamil fi'l-Ta'rikh: Part 1: The Years 491–541/1097–1146: The Coming of the Franks and the Muslim Response*. Trans. D.S. Richards. Crusade Texts in Translation 13. Aldershot, UK: Ashgate.

——. (2007) *The Chronicle of Ibn al-Athir for the Crusading Period from al-Kamil fi'l-Ta'rikh: Part 2: The Years 541–589/1146–1193: The Age of Nur al-Din and Saladin*. Trans. D.S. Richards. Crusade Texts in Translation 15. Aldershot, UK: Ashgate.

——. (2008) *The Chronicle of Ibn al-Athir for the Crusading Period from al-Kamil fi'l-Ta'rikh: Part 3: The Years 589–629/1193–1231: The Ayyubids after Saladin and the Mongol Menace*. Trans. D.S. Richards. Crusade Texts in Translation 17. Aldershot, UK: Ashgate.

Ibn al-Dawadari, Abu Bakr ibn 'Abd Allah. (1971) *Kanz al-Durar wa-Jami' al-Ghurar*. Vol. 8. Ed. Ulrich Haarmann. Cairo: al-Ma'had al-Almani li-l-Athar.

Ibn al-Jawzi, 'Abd al-Rahman ibn 'Ali. (1992) *Al-Muntazam fi Ta'rikh al-Muluk wa-l-Umam*. Ed. Muhammad 'A. al-Q. 'Ata and Mustafa 'A. al-Q. 'Ata. 19 vols. Beirut: Dar al-Kutub al-'Ilmiyya.

Ibn Jubayr, Muhammad ibn Ahmad. (1907) *The Travels of Ibn Jubayr*. Ed. William Wright and M.J. de Goeje. E.J.W. Gibb Memorial Series, Vol. 5. 2nd Ed. Leiden, Netherlands: E.J. Brill.

——. (2001) *The Travels of Ibn Jubayr*. Trans. R.J.C. Broadhurst. New Delhi: Goodword Books.

Ibn Khallikan, Ahmad ibn Muhammad. (1961) *Ibn Khallikan's Biographical Dictionary*. Trans. William Mac Guckin de Slane. 4 vols. New York: Johnson Reprint Corporation.

——. (1968–94) *Wafayat al-A'yan wa-Anba' Abna' al-Zaman*. Ed. Ihsan 'Abbas. 8 vols. Beirut: Dar Sadir.

Ibn al-Khayyat, Ahmad ibn Muhammad. (1994) *Diwan ibn al-Khayyat*. Ed. Kh. Mardam Bey. Beirut: Dar Sadir.

Ibn al-Qalanisi, Hamza ibn Asad. (1932) *The Damascus Chronicle of the Crusades*. Trans. H.A.R. Gibb. London: Luzac and Co.

——. (1983) *Ta'rikh Dimashq*. Ed. Suhayl Zakkar. Damascus: Dar Hassan li-l-Tiba'a wa-l-Nashr.

Ibn al-Qaysarani, Muhammad ibn Nasr. (1991) *Shi'r Ibn al-Qaysarani*. Ed. 'Adil J.S. Muhammad. Al-Zarqa', Jordan: al-Wakalat al-'Arabiyya li-l-Nashr wa-l-Tawzi'.

Ibn Shaddad, Baha' al-Din. (1964) *Al-Nawadir al-Sultaniyya wa-l-Mahasin al-Yusufiyya: Sirat Salah al-Din*. Ed. Jamal al-Din al-Shayyal. Cairo: al-Dar al-Misriyya li-l-Ta'lif wa-l-Tarjama.

——. (2001) *The Rare and Excellent History of Saladin*. Trans. D.S. Richards. Crusade Texts in Translation 7. Aldershot, UK: Ashgate.

Ibn Taghri Birdi, Jamal al-Din. (1963) *Al-Nujum al-Zahira fi Muluk Misr wa-l-Qahira*. Ed. M.'A. al-Q. Hatim. 12 vols. Cairo: Dar al-Kutub al-Misriyya.

Ibn Wasil, Jamal al-Din Muhammad. (1953–75) *Mufarrij al-Kurub fi Akhbar Bani Ayyub*. Ed. Jamal al-Din al-Shayyal, Hasanayn M. Rabi' and Sa'id 'A. al-F. 'Ashur. 5 vols. Cairo: Al-Matba'a al-Amiriyya.

'Interview with Usama bin Laden by His Followers, 1998'. (2004) Trans. Akram Fouad Khater, in Akram Fouad Khater (ed.), *Sources in the History of the Modern Middle East*. Boston, MA: Houghton Mifflin Company, pp. 360–3.

Al-Isfahani, 'Imad al-Din. (1965) *Al-Fath al-Qussi fi'l-Fath al-Qudsi*. Ed. Muhammad M. Subh. Cairo: al-Dar al-Qawmiyya li-l-Tiba'a wa-l-Nashr.

——. (1972) *Conquête de la Syrie et de la Palestine par Saladin (al-Fath al-Qussi fi l-Fath al-Qudsi)*. Trans. Henri Massé. Paris: Librairie Orientaliste Paul Geuthner.

'Jihad against Jews and Crusaders: World Islamic Front Statement'. (2004) Trans. Akram Fouad Khater, in Akram Fouad Khater (ed.), *Sources in the History of the Modern Middle East*. Boston, MA: Houghton Mifflin Company, pp. 363–5.

Al-Maqrizi, Ahmad ibn 'Ali. (1967–73) *Itti'az al-Hunafa' bi-Akhbar al-A'imma al-Fatimiyyin al-Khulafa'*. Ed. Jamal al-Din al-Shayyal and Muhammad H.M. Ahmad. 3 vols. Cairo: Lajnat Ihya' al-Turath al-Islami.

Al-Mas'udi, 'Ali ibn al-Husayn. (1894) *Kitâb at-Tanbîh wa'l-Ischrâf*. Ed. M.J. de Goeje. Bibliotheca Geographorum Arabicorum, Vol. 8. Leiden, Netherlands: E.J. Brill.

——. (1965–79) *Muruj al-Dhahab wa-Ma'adin al-Jawhar*. Ed. Charles Pellat. 7 vols. Beirut: Manshurat al-Jami'a al-Lubnaniyya.

Matériaux pour un Corpus Inscriptionum Arabicarum: Deuxième Partie, Tome Deuxième: Syrie du Sud – Jérusalem 'Haram'. (1925) Ed. Max van Berchem. Mémoires Publiés par les Membres de l'Institut Français d'Archéologie Orientale du Caire, Vol. 44. Cairo: Institut Français d'Archéologie Orientale.

The Meaning of the Holy Qur'an. (2004) Ed. and trans. 'Abdullah Y. 'Ali. 11th Ed. Beltsville, MD: Amana Publications.

The Sea of Precious Virtues (Bahr al-Fava'id): A Medieval Islamic Mirror for Princes. (1991) Trans. Julie Scott Meisami. Salt Lake City, UT: University of Utah Press.

Semeonis, Symon. (1960) *Itinerarium Symonis Semeonis ab Hybernia ad Terram Sanctam*. Ed. and trans. Mario Esposito. Scriptores Latini Hiberniae 4. Dublin: Dublin Institute for Advanced Studies.

Sibt ibn al-Jawzi, Yusuf ibn Qizughli. (1951–2) *Mir'at al-Zaman fi Ta'rikh al-A'yan*. 2 vols. Hyderabad-Deccan, India: Dairatu'l-Maarifil-Osmania.

Al-Sulami, 'Ali ibn Tahir. (in press) *The Book of the Jihad of 'Ali ibn Tahir al-Sulami (d. 1106): Text, Translation and Commentary*. Ed. and trans. Niall Christie. Crusade Texts in Translation. Aldershot, UK: Ashgate.

Usama ibn Munqidh. (1930) *Usamah's Memoirs entitled* Kitab al-I'tibar. Ed. Philip K. Hitti. Princeton, NJ: Princeton University Press.

———. (1987) *Lubab al-Adab*. Ed. Ahmad M. Shakir. Cairo: Dar al-Kutub al-Salafiyya.

———. (2000) *An Arab-Syrian Gentleman and Warrior in the Period of the Crusades: Memoirs of Usamah ibn-Munqidh (Kitab al-I'tibar)*. Trans. Philip K. Hitti. Records of Western Civilization. New York: Columbia University Press.

———. (2008) *The Book of Contemplation: Islam and the Crusades*. Trans. Paul M. Cobb. Penguin Classics. London: Penguin Books.

Al-Wasiti, Muhammad ibn Ahmad. (1979) *Fada'il al-Bayt al-Muqaddas*. Ed. Isaac Hasson. Max Schloessinger Memorial Series 3. Jerusalem: The Hebrew University.

SECONDARY SOURCES

Note that this is a list of scholarly works cited in this book, rather than a comprehensive list of secondary sources about the subject. Interested readers are encouraged to consult the bibliographies and notes of the works listed below for further reading on the topic.

Abouali, Diana. (2011) 'Saladin's Legacy in the Middle East before the Nineteenth Century', *Crusades* 10, pp. 175–89.

Abulafia, David. (1994) 'The Role of Trade in Muslim–Christian Contact during the Middle Ages', in Dionisius A. Agius and Richard Hitchcock (eds), *The Arab Influence in Medieval Europe*. Middle East Cultures Series 18. Reading, UK: Ithaca Press, pp. 1–24.

———. (1995) 'Trade and Crusade 1050–1250', in Michael Goodich, Sophia Menache and Sylvia Schein (eds), *Cross Cultural Convergences in the Crusader Period: Essays Presented to Aryeh Grabois on his Sixty-Fifth Birthday*. New York: Peter Lang, pp. 1–20.

Ali-Karamili, Sumbul. (2008) *The Muslim Next Door: The Qur'an, the Media and That Veil Thing*. Ashland, OR: White Cloud Press.

Amitai-Preiss, Reuven. (1995) *Mongols and Mamluks: The Mamluk–Ilkhanid War, 1260–1281*. Cambridge Studies in Islamic Civilization. Cambridge: Cambridge University Press.

Atiya, Aziz S. (1962) *Crusade, Commerce and Culture*. Bloomington, IN: Indiana University Press.

Atrache, Laila. (1996) *Die Politik der Ayyubiden: Die Fränkisch–Islamischen Beziehungen in der Ersten Hälfte des 7./13. Jahrhunderts unter Besonderer Berücksichtigung des Feindbildes*. Arabica Rhema 1. Münster, Germany: Rhema.

Ayalon, David. (1977) *Studies on the Mamluks of Egypt (1250–1517)*. London: Variorum Reprints.

———. (1994) *Islam and the Abode of War: Military Slaves and Islamic Adversaries.* Variorum Collected Studies Series. Aldershot, UK: Variorum.

Bachrach, Jere L. (1984) *A Middle East Studies Handbook*. Seattle, WA: University of Washington Press.

Bengio, Ofra. (1998) *Saddam's Word: Political Discourse in Iraq*. Studies in Middle Eastern History. New York: Oxford University Press.

Bonner, Michael. (1996) *Aristocratic Violence and Holy War: Studies in the Jihad and the Arab–Byzantine Frontier*. American Oriental Series 81. New Haven, CT: American Oriental Society.

———. (2006) *Jihad in Islamic History: Doctrines and Practice*. Princeton, NJ: Princeton University Press.

Bonney, Richard. (2004) *Jihad: From Qur'an to bin Laden*. London: Palgrave Macmillan.

Bosworth, Clifford E. (1996) *The New Islamic Dynasties: A Chronological and Genealogical Manual*. New York: Columbia University Press.

Bush, George W. (2001) 'Remarks by the President upon Arrival'. *The White House: President George W. Bush*. Posted 16 September 2001. Available online at <http://georgewbush-whitehouse.archives.gov/news/releases/2001/09/20010916-2.html> (accessed 24 June 2013).

Chamberlin, John M. (2007) *Imagining Defeat: An Arabic Historiography of the Crusades*. MA Thesis, Naval Postgraduate School, Monterey, CA. Posted 1 March 2007. Available online at <http://handle.dtic.mil/100.2/ADA467268> (accessed 13 September 2013).

Chevedden, Paul E. (2008) 'The Islamic View and the Christian View of the Crusades: A New Synthesis', *History: The Journal of the Historical Association* 93(310), pp. 181–200.

Christie, Niall. (1999) *Levantine Attitudes towards the Franks during the Early Crusades (490/1096–564/1169)*. PhD Thesis, University of St Andrews. Posted 12 June 2012. Available online at <http://hdl.handle.net/10023/2741> (accessed 24 June 2013).

———. (2004) 'Just a Bunch of Dirty Stories? Women in the "Memoirs" of Usamah Ibn Munqidh', in Rosamund Allen (ed.), *Eastward Bound: Travel and Travellers, 1050–1550*. Manchester: Manchester University Press, pp. 71–87.

———. (2006) 'Religious Campaign or War of Conquest? Muslim Views of the Motives of the First Crusade', in Niall Christie and Maya Yazigi (eds), *Noble Ideals and Bloody Realities: Warfare in the Middle Ages*. History of Warfare 37. Leiden, Netherlands: E.J. Brill, pp. 57–72.

———. (2007 a) 'Jerusalem in the *Kitab al-Jihad* of 'Ali ibn Tahir al-Sulami', *Medieval Encounters* 13(2), pp. 209–21.

———. (2007 b) 'Motivating Listeners in the *Kitab al-Jihad* of 'Ali ibn Tahir al-Sulami (d. 1106)', *Crusades* 6, pp. 1–14.

—— and Deborah Gerish. (2003) 'Parallel Preachings: Urban II and al-Sulami', *Al-Masaq: Islam and the Medieval Mediterranean* 15(2), pp. 139–48.

Clermont-Ganneau, Charles. (1896). *Archaeological Researches in Palestine during the Years 1873–1874*, vol. 2. Trans. John MacFarlane. London: Palestine Exploration Fund.

Cobb, Paul M. (2005) *Usama ibn Munqidh: Warrior Poet of the Age of the Crusades*. Makers of the Muslim World. Oxford: Oneworld.

———. (2014) *The Race for Paradise: An Islamic History of the Crusades*. Oxford: Oxford University Press.

Constable, Olivia Remie. (2003) *Housing the Stranger in the Mediterranean World: Lodging, Trade, and Travel in Late Antiquity and the Middle Ages*. Cambridge: Cambridge University Press.

Cook, David. (2005) *Understanding Jihad*. Berkeley, CA: University of California Press.

Daftary, Farhad. (1990) *The Isma'ilis: Their History and Doctrines*. Cambridge: Cambridge University Press.

———. (1994) *The Assassin Legends: Myths of the Isma'ilis*. London: I.B. Tauris.

Dahlmanns, Franz-Josef. (1975) *Al-Malik al-'Adil: Ägypten und der Vordere Orient in den Jahren 589/1193 bis 615/1218*. PhD Thesis. Gießen, Germany: Universität Gießen.

Dajani-Shakeel, Hadia. (1976) 'Jihad in Twelfth-Century Arabic Poetry: A Moral and Religious Force to Counter the Crusades', *The Muslim World* 66(2), pp. 96–113.

———. (1986) 'Al-Quds: Jerusalem in the Consciousness of the Counter-Crusader', in Vladimir P. Goss and Christine Verzár Bornstein (eds), *The Meeting of Two Worlds: Cultural Exchange between East and West during the Period of the Crusades*. Studies in Medieval Culture 21. Kalamazoo, MI: Medieval Institute Publications, pp. 201–21.

———. (1993) 'Diplomatic Relations between Muslim and Frankish Rulers 1097–1153 A.D.', in Maya Shatzmiller (ed.), *Crusaders and Muslims in Twelfth-Century Syria*. The Medieval Mediterranean: Peoples, Economies and Cultures, 400–1453 1. Leiden, Netherlands: E.J. Brill, pp. 190–215.

———. (1995) 'Some Aspects of Muslim–Frankish Christian Relations in the Sham Region in the Twelfth Century', in Yvonne Y. Haddad and Wadi Z. Haddad (eds), *Christian–Muslim Encounters*. Gainesville, FL: University Press of Florida, pp. 193–209.

Drory, Joseph. (1988) 'Hanbalis of the Nablus Region in the Eleventh and Twelfth Centuries', *Asian and African Studies* 22, pp. 93–112.

———. (2003) 'Al-Nasir Dawud: A Much Frustrated Ayyubid Prince', *Al-Masaq: Islam and the Medieval Mediterranean* 15, pp. 161–87.

Eddé, Anne-Marie. (1996) 'Saint Louis et la Septième Croisade Vus par les Auteurs Arabes', *Cahiers de Recherches Médiévales (XIIIe–XVe s.)* 1 (*Croisades et Idée de Croisade à la Fin du Moyen Âge*), pp. 65–92.

——. (1999) *La Principauté Ayyoubide d'Alep (579/1183–658/1260)*. Freiburger Islamstudien 21. Stuttgart, Germany: Franz Steiner Verlag.

——. (2011) *Saladin*. Trans. Jane Marie Todd. Cambridge, MA: Belknap Press of Harvard University Press.

Egger, Vernon O. (2004) *A History of the Muslim World to 1405*. Upper Saddle River, NJ: Pearson Prentice Hall.

Ehrenkreutz, Andrew S. (1972) *Saladin*. Albany, NY: State University of New York Press.

El-Azhari, Taef K. (1997) *The Saljuqs of Syria during the Crusades, 463–549 A.H./1070–1154 A.D.* Islamkundliche Untersuchungen 211. Berlin: Klaus Schwarz Verlag.

Elisséeff, Nikita. (1967) *Nur ad-Din: Un Grand Prince Musulman de Syrie au Temps des Croisades (511–569 H./1118–1174)*. 3 vols. Damascus: Institut Français de Damas.

Esposito, John L. (2003) *Unholy War: Terror in the Name of Islam*. New York: Oxford University Press.

Ettinghausen, Richard and Oleg Grabar. (1994) *The Art and Architecture of Islam, 650–1250*. New Haven, NJ: Yale University Press.

France, John. (1997) 'Technology and the Success of the First Crusade', in Yaacov Lev (ed.), *War and Society in the Eastern Mediterranean, 7th–15th Centuries*. The Medieval Mediterranean: Peoples, Economies and Cultures, 400–1453 9. Leiden, E.J. Brill, pp. 163–76.

Frenkel, Yehoshua. (1997) 'The Impact of the Crusades on Rural Society and Religious Endowments: The Case of Medieval Syria (*Bilad al-Sham*)', in Yaacov Lev (ed.), *War and Society in the Eastern Mediterranean, 7th–15th Centuries*. The Medieval Mediterranean: Peoples, Economies and Cultures, 400–1453 9. Leiden, E.J. Brill, pp. 237–48.

——. (2011) 'Muslim Responses to the Frankish Dominion in the Near East, 1098–1291', in Conor Kostick (ed.), *The Crusades and the Near East: Cultural Histories*. London: Routledge, pp. 27–54.

Friedman, Yvonne. (1995) 'Women in Captivity and their Ransom during the Crusader Period', in Michael Goodich, Sophia Menache and Sylvia Schein (eds), *Cross Cultural Convergences in the Crusader Period: Essays Presented to Aryeh Grabois on his Sixty-Fifth Birthday*. New York: Peter Lang, pp. 75–87.

——. (2011) 'Peacemaking: Perceptions and Practices in the Medieval Latin East' in Conor Kostick (ed.), *The Crusades and the Near East: Cultural Histories*. London: Routledge, pp. 229–57.

Gibb, H.A.R. *et al.* (ed.) (1960–2004) *The Encyclopaedia of Islam*. 2nd Ed. 11 vols plus supplements. Leiden, Netherlands: E.J. Brill.

Gibb, H.A.R. (1973) *The Life of Saladin*. Oxford: Clarendon Press.

Gottschalk, Hans L. (1958) *Al-Malik al-Kamil von Egypten und seine Zeit: Eine Studie zur Geschichte Vorderasiens und Egyptens in der Ersten Hälfte des 7./13. Jahrhunderts*. Wiesbaden, Germany: Otto Harrassowitz.

Halm, Heinz. (1992) *Shiism*. Edinburgh: Edinburgh University Press.

Hillenbrand, Carole. (1994) 'Jihad Propaganda in Syria from the Time of the First Crusade until the Death of Zengi: The Evidence of Monumental Inscriptions', in Khalil Athaminah and Roger Heacock (eds), *The Frankish Wars and their Influence on Palestine: Selected Papers Presented at Birzeit University's International Academic Conference Held in Jerusalem, March 13–15, 1992*. Birzeit, Palestine: Birzeit University Publications, pp. 60–9.

——. (1999 a) *The Crusades: Islamic Perspectives*. Edinburgh: Edinburgh University Press.

——. (2001) '"Abominable Acts": The Career of Zengi', in Jonathan Phillips and Martin Hoch (eds), *The Second Crusade: Scope and Consequences*. Manchester: Manchester University Press, pp. 111–32.

——. (2010) 'Jihad Poetry in the Age of the Crusades', in Thomas F. Madden, James L. Naus and Vincent Ryan (eds), *Crusades: Medieval Worlds in Conflict*. Farnham, UK: Ashgate, pp. 9–23.

Hillenbrand, Robert. (1999 b) *Islamic Art and Architecture*. World of Art. London: Thames and Hudson.

Holt, P.M. (1986) *The Age of the Crusades: The Near East from the Eleventh Century to 1517*. London: Longman.

——. (1995) *Early Mamluk Diplomacy (1260–1290): Treaties of Baybars and Qalawun with Christian Rulers*. Islamic History and Civilization: Studies and Texts 12. Leiden, Netherlands: E.J. Brill.

Housley, Norman. (2006) *Contesting the Crusades*. Contesting the Past. Malden, MA: Blackwell Publishing.

Humphreys, R. Stephen. (1977) *From Saladin to the Mongols: The Ayyubids of Damascus, 1193–1260*. Albany, NY: State University of New York Press.

——. (1998) 'Ayyubids, Mamluks and the Latin East in the Thirteenth Century', *Mamluk Studies Review* 2, pp. 1–17.

Irwin, Robert. (1986) *The Middle East in the Middle Ages: The Early Mamluk Sultanate 1250–1382*. Carbondale, IL: Southern Illinois University Press.

——. (1995) 'Islam and the Crusades, 1096–1699', in Jonathan Riley-Smith (ed.), *The Oxford Illustrated History of the Crusades*. Oxford: Oxford University Press, pp. 217–59.

——. (1998) 'Usamah ibn Munqidh, an Arab-Syrian Gentleman at the Time of the Crusades Reconsidered', in J. France and William G. Zajac (eds), *The Crusades and Their Sources: Essays Presented to Bernard Hamilton*. Aldershot, UK: Ashgate, pp. 71–87.

Kedar, Benjamin Z. (1990) 'The Subjected Muslims of the Frankish Levant', in James M. Powell (ed.), *Muslims under Latin Rule, 1100–1300*. Princeton, NJ: Princeton University Press, pp. 135–74.

———. (1992) 'The Battle of Hattin Revisited', in B.Z. Kedar (ed.), *The Horns of Hattin: Proceedings of the Second Conference of the Society of the Crusades and the Latin East*. Jerusalem: Yad Izhak Ben-Zvi, pp. 190–207.

———. (1996) 'Croisade et *Jihad* Vus par l'Ennemi', in Michel Balard (ed.), *Autour de la Première Croisade: Actes du Colloque de la Society for the Study of the Crusades and the Latin East (Clermont-Ferrand, 22–25 Juin 1995)*. Byzantina Sorbonensia 14. Paris: Publications de la Sorbonne, pp. 345–55.

———. (1997 a) 'Multidirectional Conversion in the Frankish Levant', in J. Muldoon (ed.), *Varieties of Religious Conversion in the Middle Ages*. Gainesville, FL: University Press of Florida, pp. 190–9.

———. (1997 b) 'Some New Sources on Palestinian Muslims before and during the Crusades', in H.E. Mayer (ed.), *Die Kreuzfahrerstaaten als Multikulturelle Gesellschaft*. Schriften des Historischen Kollegs, Kolloquien 37. Munich: Oldenbourg, pp. 129–40.

Kennedy, Hugh. (2004) *The Prophet and the Age of the Caliphates: The Islamic Near East from the Sixth to the Eleventh Century*. 2nd Ed. Harlow, UK: Pearson.

Khadduri, Majid. (1955) *War and Peace in the Law of Islam*. Baltimore, MD: Johns Hopkins Press.

Khowaiter, Abdul-Aziz. (1978) *Baibars the First: His Endeavours and Achievements*. London: Green Mountain Press.

Köhler, Michael A. (1991) *Allianzen und Verträge zwischen Fränkischen und Islamischen Herrschern im Vorderen Orient: Eine Studie über das Zwischenstaatliche Zusammenleben vom 12. bis ins 13. Jahrhundert*. Studien zur Sprache, Geschichte und Kultur des Islamischen Orients 12. Berlin: Walter de Gruyter.

———. (2013) *Alliances and Treaties between Frankish and Muslim Rulers in the Middle East*. Trans. Peter M. Holt. Ed. Konrad Hirschler. The Muslim World in the Age of the Crusades: Studies and Texts 1. Leiden, Netherlands: E.J. Brill.

Lev, Yaacov. (1991) *State and Society in Fatimid Egypt*. Arab History and Civilization 1. Leiden, Netherlands: E.J. Brill.

———. (1999) *Saladin in Egypt*. The Medieval Mediterranean 21. Leiden, Netherlands: E.J. Brill.

———. (2007) 'Saladin's Economic Policies and the Economy of Ayyubid Egypt', in U. Vermeulen and K. D'Hulster (eds), *Egypt and Syria in the Fatimid, Ayyubid and Mamluk Eras V*. Orientalia Lovaniensia Analecta 169. Leuven, Belgium: Uitgeverij Peeters, pp. 307–48.

——. (2008) 'The *Jihad* of Sultan Nur al-Din of Syria (1146–74): History and Discourse', *Jerusalem Studies in Arabic and Islam* 35, pp. 227–84.

Levanoni, Amalia. (1995) *A Turning Point in Mamluk History: The Third Reign of al-Nasir Muhammad Ibn Qalawun (1310–1341)*. Islamic History and Civilization: Studies and Texts 10. Leiden, Netherlands: E.J. Brill.

Lindsay, James E. (ed.) (2001) *Ibn 'Asakir and Early Islamic History*. Studies in Late Antiquity and Early Islam 20. Princeton, NJ: Darwin Press.

Little, Donald P. (1983) 'Religion under the Mamluks', *The Muslim World* 73, pp. 165–81.

——. (1997) 'Jerusalem under the Ayyubids and Mamluks 1187–1516 ad', in Kamil J. Asali (ed.), *Jerusalem in History: 3000 BC to the Present Day*. Revised Ed. London: Kegan Paul International, pp. 177–99.

Lyons, Malcolm Cameron and David E.P. Jackson. (1984) *Saladin: The Politics of the Holy War*. University of Cambridge Oriental Publications 30. Cambridge: Cambridge University Press.

Maalouf, Amin. (1984) *The Crusades through Arab Eyes*. Trans. Jon Rothschild. London: Al Saqi Books.

Mallett, Alex (ed.) (2014 a) *Medieval Muslim Historians and the Franks in the Levant, 1097–1291*. Leiden, Netherlands: E.J. Brill.

Mallett, Alex. (2014 b) *Popular Muslim Reactions to the Frankish Presence in the Levant, 1097–1291*. Aldershot, UK: Ashgate.

Möhring, Hannes. (1980) *Saladin und der Dritte Kreuzzug: Aiyubidische Strategie und Diplomatie im Vergleich Vornehmlich der Arabischen mit den Lateinischen Quellen*. Frankfurter Historische Abhandlungen 21. Wiesbaden, Germany: Franz Steiner Verlag.

Momen, Moojan. (1985) *An Introduction to Shi'i Islam: The History and Doctrines of Twelver Shi'ism*. New Haven, CT: Yale University Press.

Morabia, Alfred. (1993) *Le Gihâd dans l'Islam Médiéval: Le 'Combat Sacré' des Origines au XIIe Siècle*. Paris: Albin Michel.

Morgan, David. (1988) *Medieval Persia, 1040–1797*. London: Longman.

Mourad, Suleiman A. and James E. Lindsay. (2007) 'Rescuing Syria from the Infidels: The Contribution of Ibn 'Asakir of Damascus to the *Jihad* Campaign of Sultan Nur al-Din', *Crusades* 6, pp. 37–55.

——. (2013) *The Intensification and Reorientation of Sunni Jihad Ideology in the Crusader Period: Ibn 'Asakir of Damascus (1105–1176) and His Age, with an Edition and Translation of Ibn 'Asakir's The Forty Hadiths for Inciting Jihad*. Islamic History and Civilization: Studies and Texts 99. Leiden, Netherlands: E.J. Brill.

Munir, Fareed Z. (2008) 'Sultan al-Malik Muhammad al-Kamil and Saint Francis: Interreligious Dialogue and the Meeting at Damietta', *Journal of Islamic Law and Culture* 10, pp. 305–14.

Murray, Alan V. (ed.) (2006) *The Crusades: An Encyclopedia*. 4 vols. Santa Barbara, CA: ABC-Clio.

Nicholson, Helen J. (ed.) (2005) *Palgrave Advances in the Crusades*. Palgrave Advances. Houndmills, UK: Palgrave Macmillan.

Nicolle, David. (1994) *Saracen Faris, AD 1050–1250*. Warrior 10. Oxford: Osprey Publishing.

——. (1999) *Arms and Armour of the Crusading Era, 1050–1350: Islam, Eastern Europe and Asia*. London: Greenhill Books.

——. (2007) *Crusader Warfare*. 2 vols. London: Hambledon Continuum.

Northrup, Linda S. (1998) *From Slave to Sultan: The Career of al-Mansur Qalawun and the Consolidation of Mamluk Rule in Egypt and Syria (678–689 A.H./1279–1290 A.D.)*. Freiburger Islamstudien 18. Stuttgart, Germany: Franz Steiner Verlag.

Phillips, Jonathan. (2002) *The Crusades, 1095–1197*. Harlow, UK: Pearson.

Prawer, Joshua. (1964) 'La Bataille de Hattin', *Israel Exploration Journal* 14, pp. 160–79.

——. (2001) *The Crusaders' Kingdom: European Colonialism in the Middle Ages*. London: Phoenix Press.

Rabie, Hassanein. (1975) 'The Training of the Mamluk Faris', in V.J. Parry and M.E. Yapp (eds), *War, Technology and Society in the Middle East*. London: Oxford University Press, pp. 153–63.

Raphael, Kate. (2011) *Muslim Fortresses in the Levant: Between Crusaders and Mongols*. Culture and Civilization in the Middle East. London: Routledge.

Richards, Donald S. (1998) 'Mamluk Amirs and Their Families and Households', in Thomas Philipp and Ulrich Haarmann (eds), *The Mamluks in Egyptian Politics and Society*. Cambridge: Cambridge University Press, pp. 32–54.

Riley-Smith, Jonathan. (1987) *The Crusades: A Short History*. New Haven, CT: Yale University Press.

Riley-Smith, Jonathan (ed.) (1991) *The Atlas of the Crusades*. New York: Facts on File.

Rippin, Andrew. (2011) *Muslims: Their Religious Beliefs and Practices*. 4th Ed. London: Routledge.

Runciman, Steven. (1965) *A History of the Crusades*. 3 vols. New York: Harper & Row.

Al-Sarraf, Shihab. (2004) 'Mamluk *Furusiyah* Literature and Its Antecedents', *Mamluk Studies Review* 8(1), pp. 141–200.

Sivan, Emmanuel. (1968) *L'Islam et la Croisade: Idéologie et Propagande dans les Réactions Musulmanes aux Croisades*. Paris: Librairie d'Amérique et d'Orient.

——. (1973) *Modern Arab Historiography of the Crusades*. Occasional Papers (Mekhon Shiloah le-Heker ha-Mizrah ha-Tikhon ve-Afrikah). Tel Aviv: Tel Aviv University, Shiloah Center for Middle Eastern and African Studies.

Smail, R.C. (1995) *Crusading Warfare, 1097–1193*. 2nd Ed. Cambridge: Cambridge University Press.

Tabbaa, Yasser. (1986) 'Monuments with a Message: Propagation of *Jihad* under Nur al-Din (1146–74)', in Vladimir P. Goss and Christine Verzár Bornstein (eds), *The Meeting of Two Worlds: Cultural Exchange between East and West during the Period of the Crusades*. Studies in Medieval Culture 21. Kalamazoo, MI: Medieval Institute Publications, pp. 223–40.

———. (2001) *The Transformation of Islamic Art during the Sunni Revival*. Seattle, WA: University of Washington Press.

Talmon-Heller, Daniella (2007 a) *Islamic Piety in Medieval Syria: Mosques, Cemeteries and Sermons under the Zangids and Ayyubids (1146–1260)*. Jerusalem Studies in Religion and Culture 7. Leiden, Netherlands: E.J. Brill.

———. (2007 b) 'Islamic Preaching in Syria during the Counter-Crusade (Twelfth–Thirteenth Centuries)', in Iris Shagrir, Ronnie Ellenblum and Jonathan Riley-Smith (eds), *In Laudem Hierosolymitani: Studies in Crusades and Medieval Culture in Honour of Benjamin Z. Kedar*. Crusades – Subsidia 1. Aldershot, UK: Ashgate, pp. 61–75.

Thorau, Peter. (1992) *The Lion of Egypt: Sultan Baybars I and the Near East in the Thirteenth Century*. Trans. P.M. Holt. London: Longman.

Tolan, John. (2009) *Saint Francis and the Sultan: The Curious History of a Christian–Muslim Encounter*. Oxford: Oxford University Press.

Van Steenbergen, Jo. (2006) *Order out of Chaos: Patronage, Conflict and Mamluk Socio-Political Culture, 1341–1382*. Leiden, Netherlands: E.J. Brill.

Walker, Paul E. (2002) *Exploring an Islamic Empire: Fatimid History and its Sources*. Ismaili Heritage Series 7. London: I.B. Tauris/Institute of Ismaili Studies.

Weigert, Gideon. (1997) 'A Note on Hudna: Peace Making in Islam', in Yaacov Lev (ed.), *War and Society in the Eastern Mediterranean, 7th–15th Centuries*. The Medieval Mediterranean: Peoples, Economies and Cultures, 400–1453 9. Leiden: E.J. Brill, pp. 399–405.

White Jr, Lynn. (1975) 'The Crusades and the Technological Thrust of the West Faris', in V.J. Parry and M.E. Yapp (eds), *War, Technology and Society in the Middle East*. London: Oxford University Press, pp. 97–112.

Zouache, Abbès. (2008) *Armées et Combats en Syrie de 491/1098 à 569/1174: Analyse Comparée des Chroniques Médiévales Latines et Arabes*. Damascus: Institut Français du Proche-Orient.

Index